# THE ALMANAC
# OF INTERNATIONAL
# JOBS AND CAREERS

# Books and CD-ROM by Drs. Ron and Caryl Krannich

*The Almanac of American Government Jobs and Careers*
*The Almanac of International Jobs and Careers*
*Best Jobs for the 1990s and Into the 21st Century*
*Change Your Job, Change Your Life*
*The Complete Guide to International Jobs and Careers*
*The Complete Guide to Public Employment*
*Discover the Best Jobs for You!*
*Dynamite Answers to Interview Questions*
*Dynamite Cover Letters*
*Dynamite Resumes*
*Dynamite Salary Negotiations*
*Dynamite Tele-Search*
*The Educator's Guide to Alternative Jobs and Careers*
*Find a Federal Job Fast*
*From Army Green to Corporate Gray*
*High Impact Resumes and Letters*
*Interview for Success*
*Job Power Source* (CD-ROM)
*Job Search Letters That Get Results*
*Jobs and Careers With Nonprofit Organizations*
*Jobs for People Who Love Travel*
*Mayors and Managers*
*Moving Out of Education*
*Moving Out of Government*
*The New Network Your Way to Job and Career Success*
*The Politics of Family Planning Policy*
*Re-Careering in Turbulent Times*
*Shopping and Traveling in Exotic Asia*
*Shopping and Traveling in Exotic Hong Kong*
*Shopping and Traveling in Exotic India*
*Shopping and Traveling in Exotic Indonesia*
*Shopping and Traveling in Exotic Morocco*
*Shopping and Traveling in Exotic Singapore and Malaysia*
*Shopping and Traveling in Exotic Thailand*
*Shopping and Traveling the Exotic Philippines*
*Shopping in Exciting Australia and Papua New Guinea*
*Shopping in Exotic Places*
*Shopping the Exotic South Pacific*

# THE ALMANAC OF INTERNATIONAL JOBS AND CAREERS

## A Guide to Over 1001 Employers

Second Edition

Ronald L. Krannich, Ph.D.
Caryl Rae Krannich, Ph.D.

IMPACT PUBLICATIONS
Manassas Park, VA

# THE ALMANAC OF INTERNATIONAL JOBS AND CAREERS

Second Edition

Copyright © 1994 by Ronald L. Krannich and Caryl Rae Krannich

**Library of Congress Cataloging-in-Publication Data**

Krannich, Ronald L.
   Almanac of international jobs and careers : a guide to over
1001 employers / Ronald L. Krannich, Caryl Rae Krannich—2nd ed.
        p. cm.
   Includes bibliographical references and index.
   ISBN 0-942710-99-1 : $34.95. — ISBN 0-942710-95-9
   (pbk.) : $19.95
        1. Americans—Employment—Foreign countries—Handbooks,
manuals, etc. 2. Employment in foreign countries—
Handbooks, manuals, etc.
   I. Krannich, Caryl Rae. II. Title.
   HF5549.5.E45K72  1994
   650.14—dc20                                            94-9323
                                                            CIP

For information on distribution or quantity discount rates, Tel. 703/361-7300, Fax 703/335-9486, or write to: Sales Department, IMPACT PUBLICATIONS, 9104-N Manassas Drive, Manassas Park, VA 22111-5211. Distributed to the trade by National Book Network, 4720 Boston Way, Suite A, Lanham, MD 20706, Tel. 301/459-8696 or 800/462-6420.

# CONTENTS

# ACKNOWLEDGEMENTS

**W**e wish to acknowledge with special thanks several organizations and individuals who assisted with this project. The Peace Corps' Returned Volunteer Office and Library provided us with access to their excellent international career resource collection. The Office of Procurement, U.S. Agency for International Development, continues to produce one of the richest and most revealing databases on the "who", "what", "where", and "how much" of international contractors, private voluntary organizations, and educational institutions. We appreciate the fact that the U.S. Congress, in performing its oversight function, requires this agency to make this hard-to-find information available to the public. Without this database our so-called "Beltway Bandits" would be difficult to identify and profile as potential sources for international employment.

Special thanks goes to the staff at Impact Publications for assisting with this revised edition. Judy Hopkins spent numerous hours working the telephones, checking names and addresses, and entering esoteric information into a final, usable form. We appreciate her unfailing persistence and dedication to what is indeed a laborious task. Bob Peterson checked the accuracy of numerous entries, and Marissa Turner helped in meeting last minute deadlines.

# NOTE TO USERS

*W*hile we have attempted to provide accurate and up-to-date information in this book, please be advised that names, addresses, and phone and fax numbers do change and that organizations do move, go out of business, or change management. This is especially true for organizations located in the New York City and Washington, DC metropolitan areas. Application deadlines, fees, prices, and product and service orientations may also change. We regret any inconvenience such changes may cause to your international job search.

If you have difficulty contacting a particular organization included in this book, please do one or all of the following:

- Consult the latest edition of *The National Directory of Addresses and Telephone Numbers* (Omnigraphics: Detroit, MI).

- Contact the Information or Reference section of your local library. They may have online services or directories which include the latest contact information.

- Call Information for current phone numbers.

Inclusion of organizations in this book in no way implies endorsements by the authors or Impact Publications. The information and recommendations appearing in this book are provided solely for your reference. As indicated in the "Strategies" sections of various chapters, it is the reader's responsibility to take initiative in contacting and following-through with employers.

The names, addresses, phone and fax numbers, and services appearing in this book provide one important component for conducting a successful international job search. Placed within the larger context of an effective job search, this component should be carefully linked to your self-asseesment, research, networking, and resume writing and distribution activities.

# 1

# INTERNATIONAL EMPLOYMENT OPPORTUNITIES

$D$o we ever live in interesting times! This is especially true in the international arena where old ideas and territories seem to regularly get turned into new concepts and countries. Take, for example, the recently arrived small enterprise development Peace Corps Volunteer in Almaty, Kazakhstan (former Soviet Union) whose ostensible mission is to promote American-style capitalism in this former communist country. Writing home after a few weeks of in-country training (*Peace Corps Today,* Fall 1993), she tries to put her experience in perspective:

> Almaty, Kazakhstan is an amazing place to be! I had dinner with some Russian business people who were scientists under the Soviet regime, but now wish to buy American products to sell on the streets of Almaty. This is not so unusual as it is evidently about the only way to make money here because privatization has not gotten a foothold yet, and State owned companies are not paying "competitive" wages. The uniqueness of the meeting is that we were sharing a meal with a man who had been sent to

1

Cuba to spend three years teaching the Cubans about the evils of
American capitalism. Now he is requesting assistance from the Peace
Corps in finding a U.S. supplier to be his partner in a joint venture....My
experiences have been so rich that I cannot begin to paint in words
anything but an outline. I miss my good friends and associates, but I
would rather have them come to visit me than to return home!

Today's international arena offers numerous exciting job opportunities
for enterprising job seekers. International job opportunities are being
rapidly created in response to new economic and political developments.
The collapse of communism and the rise of newly independent states in
the former Soviet Union and Eastern Europe; the development of an
economically unified Western Europe; the emergence of dynamic regional
trade blocs; continuing poverty in numerous Third and Fourth World
countries; the realignment of the Japanese economy; the rapidly developing economies of China, India, and the Pacific Rim; the continuing
expansion of the U.S. economic activity abroad; and the growth of travel
and tourism have created unprecedented opportunities for individuals
interested in finding international jobs and pursuing international careers.

## THE NEW EMPLOYMENT ORDER

We live in more than just interesting times. These are rapidly changing
times in which the jobs of yesterday may be poor predictors of the jobs
of tomorrow. What course of international studies college students pursue
today may ill-prepare them for the international job opportunities of
tomorrow. In fact, in the 1960s and 1970s, international jobs for
Americans were most likely found with government, educational
institutions, nonprofit organizations, and consulting firms specializing in
problems of development in Third and Fourth World countries. These
institutions and organizations hired large numbers of international
specialists with backgrounds in agriculture, economics, anthropology,
linguistics, and political science. A government assistance-centered model
of development resulted in government-to-government transfer of
resources via such popular government organizations as the U.S. Agency
for International Development, the Peace Corps, and the United States
Information Agency and hundreds of contractors that helped carry out
their missions. Much of this concept of international development was
rooted in an overall Cold War foreign policy effort to combat the threat
of communism.

Whether wrapped in the development theories enunciated by the U.S.
Agency for International Development and its army of contractors or in

the grassroots efforts of Peace Corps Volunteers, U.S. international development efforts were primarily nonmilitary responses to communism; their ultimate goal was to transfer economic benefits to peoples who might otherwise find an alternative path to development—revolutionary communism. Those who found jobs in these development organizations were most likely motivated by altruism rather than by a political consciousness aimed at combating communism.

How times have changed within the space of only three years! Like it or not, we live in a new, yet ill-defined political and economic order. But a few things are certain. The old government-to-government transfer of resources approach to problems of development has fallen in disfavor with the collapse of the Cold War and all its ideological underpinnings. Such an approach resulted in few cases of success; it tended to enhance corruption, strengthen government bureaucracies, and create dependency rather than increase self-sustaining capacity. The Peace Corps has now moved into Russia, other former Soviet republics, and Eastern Europe where it demonstrates the virtues of small business development and entrepreneurism. The U.S. Agency for International Development (USAID)—under fire for achieving few measurable results—seeks to transform itself into a force for promoting American-style business and entrepreneurism abroad. In the midst of all these changes, millions of people throughout the world still live in grinding poverty, experience wars and natural disasters, suffer from famine and pestilence, and lack basic sanitation, education, nutrition, and health services. Environmental degradation, accompanied with a failure of governments and businesses to manage natural resources, continues on a massive scale throughout the world. Child care, family planning, social welfare, and vocational services remain in great demand in the developing world.

The name of the game today is business, but the needs of the international community go far beyond business. Never before have we witnessed such a major shift in international jobs from government and development to business and entrepreneurism. The evidence is everywhere. Take a quick survey of international airports or visit major hotels in New York, London, Amsterdam, Paris, Rome, Frankfurt, Prague, Moscow, Cairo, Rabat, New Delhi, Bangkok, Singapore, Jakarta, Manila, Hanoi, Hong Kong, Bejing, Shanghai, Tokyo, Sydney, Mexico City, and Rio and you will quickly discover a new breed of international employee —young business people who are sourcing for new products or seeking new markets and trading partners for their products. The airport and restaurant conversations are similar—expanding international operations. A San Francisco-based architectural firm designs a new condominium and resort complex in Thailand; they must meet with their Thai counterparts in Bangkok to finalize the plans and financial arrangements. Representatives of a leading fashion house in New York City meet in Manila to discuss their new fall line with their Philippine factory representatives. A computer software company representative based in Boston meets with its field staff in Hong Kong to discuss its failed marketing efforts in China. Representatives of Apple Computer and Mars Candy Company celebrate after opening their new offices in Vladivostok—until recently a city closed to outsiders. A Houston-based cellular phone company sends its representatives to New Delhi to survey the market potential for its products in South Asia. A Washington, DC-based contractor specializing in government finance spends three months in Hanoi installing the latest computer software for handling Vietnam's government financial system. They stay at the Metropole Hotel where they have breakfast with representatives of an international hotel chain who are finalizing plans with the Ministry of Finance to build a new 600-room, five-star hotel to accommodate the growing number of business travelers to Saigon.

## SOURCING AND SELLING

Few international workers we encounter today are in the business of transferring resources from one government to another. Rather, they are primarily in the business of international business—sourcing and selling products and services for a profit. New first-class hotels continue to spring up in major cities throughout the world. While some cater to tourists, most are responding to the tremendous growth in business travel that has evolved during the past five years. Eighty percent or more of their hotel clients are business travelers. We expect this trend will continue for at least the next ten years.

The best international job opportunities will be with companies of all sizes—large to small—engaged in sourcing and selling products for international trade. While ten or twenty years ago many large international companies sent managers abroad to oversee their international operations, today fewer and fewer companies export their managerial talent. Many countries now have a large pool of local managerial talent from which to staff their field operations. Businesses, in turn, find it is less expensive and more productive to hire local managers. After all, expatriate employees demand much higher compensation packages as well as require numerous perks attendant with an expatriate position. Local talent tends to be less expensive and more competent than expatriates. Indeed, the day of the expatriate landing positions of major responsibility abroad are quickly coming to an end as more and more locals have as much, if not more, international education, training, and experience. As a result, experienced expatriates are finding fewer job opportunities abroad as they must face greater competition from highly skilled and competent locals.

## A DEVELOPING, DEVELOPING WORLD

While business is today's newest and most fashionable international trend and job arena, the development work of hundreds of nonprofit organizations, educational institutions, international organizations, government agencies, and consulting firms continues unabated and on an ever grander scale than only four years ago. The collapse of communism in Eastern Europe and the former Soviet Union has opened new frontiers and challenges for these organizations. The work of these organizations, especially in the areas of child care, environmental and natural resource management, disaster relief, agricultural and water resource development, and communication, continues to expand into these newly developing countries. As these and other new nations emerge—possibly from the future disintegration of China and India—and undergo complex and chaotic economic, social, and political changes, the services of these international groups will be in even greater demand in the years ahead.

While many of these major international players have focused their field operations on Asia, Africa, Latin America, and the Caribbean during the past 50 years, several of these organizations have recently moved into a new frontier where they apply their development expertise. They have quickly extended their operations into Eastern Europe and the former Soviet republics—today's new developing world: Albania, Armenia, Belarus, Bosnia-Hercegovina, Bulgaria, Croatia, Czech Republic, Estonia, Georgia, Hungary, Kazakhstan, Kyrgystan, Latvia, Lithuania, Moldova, Poland, Romania, Russia, Serbia, Slovak Republic, Tajikistan, Turkmenistan, and the Ukraine. This new frontier reflects a new evolving, yet still unsettled, political geography of the 1990s.

## CHANGING EMPLOYMENT SETTINGS

Just three years ago opportunities looked plentiful in Europe, the Middle East, and many countries in the developing world. Today, opportunities in Europe appear disappointing given employment restrictions and the high costs of doing business in Europe. More and more opportunities are available in Russia and the Commonwealth of Independent States (CIS), Eastern Europe, Hong Kong, China, India, Indonesia, and Mexico. Given the emphasis on sourcing and selling, job opportunities in business will tend to be found in countries offering cheap labor and large consumer markets. Consequently, during the next ten years we expect the new frontiers for international business jobs will be found in China, India, Pakistan, Indonesia, Russia, Mexico, Vietnam, Burma, Egypt, South Africa, Brazil, and Argentina. The emphasis will continue to be on sourcing and selling in a highly competitive international trade market.

## SEEKING AN INTERNATIONAL JOB

Many highly motivated jobs seekers don't know how or where to look for opportunities in today's dynamic international job market. Lacking both information on and appropriate job search strategies for the international job market, they engage in a random and often frustrated exercise of using the wrong methods and targeting the wrong employers. After months of failed expectations, many of these people abandon their dreams of working in the international arena. Many believe in the often-heard lament of the failed job seeker—"There are no job opportunities available for me."

What most international job seekers lack is a clear understanding of how to find a job in this often difficult and frustrating employment arena. With the help of this book and other international employment resources, this should not happen to you. You should acquire the necessary knowledge and skills to be effective in this challenging job market.

## AN ALMANAC OF OPPORTUNITIES

*The Almanac of International Jobs and Careers* is the sequel and critical organization companion volume to our first international jobs and careers book—*The Complete Guide to International Jobs and Careers*. It outlined the structure of the international job market, addressed the key issues of individual motivations and skills, and proposed strategies for organizing and implementing an effective job search targeted toward particular organizations and industries. It is the first book anyone interested in international jobs and careers should read before putting this present book to use in attempting to connect with the many organizations that offer the majority of international job opportunities.

Indeed, this present book answers the critical "where" questions of the international job seeker: "Where are the international jobs?" *The Complete Guide to International Jobs and Careers* addressed the critical "what" and "how" questions: "What are the jobs and how can I best find one?" Consequently, we say very little about strategies for finding an international job in this volume, because the strategies are outlined in detail—including information on self-assessment, goal setting, research, resume writing, interviews, and salary negotiations—in *The Complete Guide to International Jobs and Careers*. Here we focus solely on identifying organizations that are involved in the international arena and are noted for hiring individuals for international positions.

Our focus on the "where" of finding an international job leads us into ten different sets of organizations that are invariably linked together in the international arena:

- Federal government agencies
- International organizations
- Associations and societies
- Research institutes
- Businesses
- Contracting and consulting firms
- Private voluntary organizations (PVOs)
- Nonprofit corporations
- Foundations
- Colleges and universities

These organizations largely define the "where" of international jobs.

We also include new chapters on internships and teaching abroad as well as an annotated bibliography of international employment resources. In addition, you may want to contact foreign chambers of commerce in the U.S. as well as world trade associations or clubs that operate in most major U.S. cities. Names, addresses, and phone numbers for these organizations are easily accessed through *The National Directory of Addresses and Telephone Numbers*, one of the most invaluable resources for international job seekers and one we highly recommend as part of your "essential" resource package for international job hunting. Such contact information is especially important for individuals interested in identifying firms operating in individual countries as well as those interested in starting or expanding their own businesses abroad. The embassy and consulate contact information will assist you in answering any questions concerning work permits in specific countries.

Our classification of international jobs and careers along these organizational lines should not be interpreted as the only way to organize this information nor should these organizations be viewed in isolation from one another. Indeed, as we observe in *The Complete Guide to*

*International Jobs and Careers* (Chapter 9), there is a tremendous amount of blurring between the public and private sectors in the international arena. You will quickly discover there is a great deal of overlap between categories as well as numerous linkages among organizations which, in turn, provide "opportunity structures" for enterprising international job seekers. Many firms appearing in Chapter 6 (Contracting and Consulting Firms), for example, should also appear in Chapter 5 (Businesses). However, since many of these private firms are primarily oriented toward working in developing countries, we put them into a separate chapter. The same is true for the associations appearing in Chapter 4. Many of the organizations appearing in Chapters 7, 8, and 9 could also be included in Chapter 4. But, again, since the organizations in Chapters 7, 8, and 9 are primarily oriented toward working in developing countries and depend on funding from government, international organizations, and foundations, they are best examined in these separate chapters.

While many of these organizations (government, nonprofits, PVOs) are primarily oriented toward achieving public goals, others pursue their own private agendas (businesses). However, many are linked together by the nature of their activities. International engineering and construction firms, for example, rely heavily on public infrastructure funding; contracting and consulting firms as well as many nonprofits, PVOs, and universities depend on public funding of "development projects" by government, the United Nations, the World Bank, regional financial institutions, and private foundations. In the end, there is a great deal more interaction and cooperation between the public and private-oriented organizations than what you might initially think.

## DO FIRST THINGS FIRST

How you use this book will largely determine whether or not you will be successful in finding an international job with the organizations outlined here. The insatiable quest amongst many job seekers to first know who the employers are and where they are located, leads to the temptation to immediately identify a few "interesting" organizations and then send off resumes and letters or make phone calls in the hopes someone will hire them. Such a random and mindless approach is naive and borders on being "job dumb". It demonstrates little understanding of both how the job market operates and what employers seek in potential employees. Most employers simply don't hire people who approach them in this manner. Such an approach will tend to make you a nuisance in the eyes of many employers who don't have time to be pestered by individuals who appear high on motivation but low on job search intelligence. Employers use their networks, job banks, and advertising expertise to locate qualified candidates. You especially need to know how to gain access to employers' networks.

You must do first things first. Using this book without first organizing your job search around the critical seven-step career development and job search process outlined in *The Complete Guide to International Jobs and Careers* is a sure way of creating new frustrations and dashing hopes of finding an international job. Doing first things first means using this book only after you have completed a self assessment, set goals, conducted research, and developed a powerful international targeted resume. Then, and only then, should you direct your other job search activities—prospecting, networking, informational interviews, and direct applications—toward the organizations identified in this book or elsewhere.

If you fail to do these first things first, you may quickly join thousands of other wishful thinkers who have yet to learn how to link effective international job search strategies to the specific names, addresses, and telephone numbers outlined in this and other directories of potential international employers. Please don't become one of them! The jobs are out there, but you must approach the market properly.

## THE WORLD OF WORK PERMITS

Work permits are one of the major obstacles to finding employment abroad. While you may be interested in working in Australia, Great Britain, or Norway, restrictive work permit, visa, and immigration policies may quickly dash your hopes of working in these countries. At the very least, they make living and working abroad a big hassle.

Work permits and resident visas go hand in hand. Most countries require foreign employees to acquire a resident visa that includes a work permit. The normal procedure is to require the foreigner to apply for the work permit and resident visa before entering the country, although some countries do allow you to apply after being in country and securing an employment contract. In other words, in most instances, you cannot just arrive in country, look for employment, and then apply for a resident visa. Instead, you must have an employment contract in hand before arriving in country. This procedure achieves what most countries intentionally design—discourage foreigners from seeking employment in their countries.

The easiest way to get a work permit is to have an employment contract with a company that routinely takes care of work permit requirements. They, rather than you, must deal with the complexities of the government bureaucracy.

Most countries follow a similar pattern in regards to work permits and resident visas. Except in the cases of the European Economic Community (EEC) countries where employment in member countries is relatively open (no work permits required) for EEC citizens, most countries protect local labor by placing similar restrictions on foreign workers:

1.  Foreigners are forbidden to acquire jobs that compete with local labor and skills. When applying for a work permit and resident visa, employers must provide evidence that the job in question cannot be filled by a local worker with similar skills.

2.  Work permits and resident visas are temporary and thus must be renewed periodically though a Ministry, Department, Bureau, or Office of Labor—every 6, 12, or 24 months. The bureaucracy takes its time in processing such applications. You will witness a great deal of bureaucratic inertia in the process of acting on your application.

3.  Foreigners must pay local taxes and special resident visa fees. Furthermore, they may be restricted on how much local currency they can take out of the country. Leaving the country even for a short holiday may require tax clearances —including a large cash deposit—and special permissions so you can re-enter without invalidating your work permit and resident visa.

4.  Work permit and resident visa requirements may restrict the number of times foreigners can exit and re-enter a country. In some countries the work permit and resident visas becomes invalid upon leaving the country. Consequently, the whole application process must be once again initiated upon re-entering the country.

While many of these restrictions seem illogical and the bureaucratic process can be slow, they are designed with one purpose in mind— discourage foreign workers from entering and staying in their countries. Not surprisingly, countries increasingly emphasize "locals only" employment/immigrant policies due to a combination of nationalism and high unemployment rates.

Such restrictions can complicate international jobs considerably and take the excitement out of what was once considered to be the glamorous world of working abroad. While it is difficult to get the work permit in the first place, other restrictions can make life difficult once you get the necessary permissions. Currency, mobility, and re-application restrictions constitute the major headaches in this foreign employment game. Bureaucracies tend to be slow and cumbersome in processing the initial application as well as renewing work permits and resident visas. Indeed, even with an employment contract in hand and having completed all necessary paperwork, you may still have to wait two to six months before getting the proper documentation for entering the country as a foreign worker. You may also have second thoughts about leaving a country that automatically invalidates your hard-to-get-in-the-first-place work permit as well as requires a tax clearance to depart.

Consequently, it is always best to negotiate your employment contract with an international company before arriving in country. Be sure to clarify your understanding of local rules and regulations governing your employment, tax, and mobility status prior to accepting a position. The company will know the local regulations and it should be organized for arranging all work permits and resident visas for you and your family. In other words, it should be the responsibility of the employer to acquire all necessary work permits and resident visas to ensure your employment stability. If you fail to do this, you may be unpleasantly surprised to learn that you are literally "stuck" in a country for the duration of your contract as you are subjected to numerous rules and regulations governing your "foreign worker" status.

Many foreign workers successfully avoid work permit and resident visa requirements by working illegally. They arrive in country on a 90-day to 6-month tourist visa, find employment, periodically leave the country in order to renew the visa, and return to their jobs—until the authorities catch them playing this game. This is a risky business and it often results in low-paying and menial jobs. In addition, you may not be eligible for health insurance and other employment benefits that automatically come with "legal" jobs. If you are a student looking for part-time or summer work abroad, you can usually find low-paying jobs in the tourism industry or agriculture without incurring the wrath of the local labor and immigration authorities. But in many countries, such as Denmark and Finland, authorities are even vigilant in enforcing foreign labor laws at this end of the labor spectrum.

It is always best to inquire about the local labor restrictions affecting foreign workers prior to seeking employment in a particular country. You can do this by contacting the foreign embassy or consulate in your

your country for information on work permits and resident visas. Again, keep in mind that in most cases it will be the responsibility of the employer to acquire the necessary work permits and visas. And in most cases this means receiving an employment contract prior to entering the country. While you may travel to the country on a tourist visa for a job interview, you may not be able to enter the country on a tourist visa to begin work while waiting for your work permit and resident visa applications to be processed. Since each country differs somewhat in how they structure this situation, check with the embassy or consulate nearest you for clarifying the rules and regulations.

## KEY RESOURCES

While this book identifies a few thousand of the largest international employers, numerous other organizations operate in the international arena. As you begin narrowing your choices, you may want to supplement this book with a few others that provide access to additional organizations. We strongly recommend consulting the following directories which are available in most major libraries; several can be ordered directly from Impact Publications (see order form at the end of this book):

**Guide to Careers in World Affairs** (Manassas Park, VA: Impact Publications, VA, 1993, $14.95). One of the best international careers books available today. An annotated directory to hundreds of major international employers appropriate for professionals.

**National Directory of Addresses and Telephone Numbers** (Detroit: Omnigraphics, 1994, $99.95). An invaluable resource with nearly 1,000 pages packed with names, addresses, and phone numbers of corporations, associations, and universities. Includes a special international section with information on foreign chambers of commerce in the U.S., foreign corporations, and trade contacts and well as a section on the travel industry.

**Directory of Executive Recruiters** (Fitzwilliam, NH: Kennedy Publications, 1994, $39.95). This annual directory of executive recruiters includes numerous firms operating in the international arena. These firms work for employers in recruiting individuals with the right mix of skills and experience for specific international positions.

**Encyclopedia of Associations** (Detroit, MI: Gale Research, 1994, $910.00). This essential four-volume reference work is updated annually. It is the single most authoritative resource for identifying nearly 22,000 national and international associations headquartered in the U.S., from trade to public affairs associations. The two-volume companion directory, **Encyclopedia of Associations: International Organizations** ($455.00) identifies nearly 10,000 international associations headquartered abroad.

**Research Centers Directory** (Detroit, MI: Gale Research, 1994). Another essential reference work produced by Gale Research Inc. Includes over 10,000 university and nonprofit research organizations in the United States. Many specialize in area studies, international trade, and foreign relations.

**Internet Profiles, 1989-1990** (Network for International Technical Assistance, P.O. Box 3245, Chapel Hill, NC 27515, 1989, $500). This used to be the "bible" for locating all types of organizations involved in development assistance, from engineering and construction firms operating in the Middle East and Asia to consulting firms, nonprofit organizations, and PVOs involved in delivering technical assistance in the areas of health care, population planning, and rural development in Africa and Latin America. Provides detailed information on all development-oriented organizations. Not widely available in public libraries and is now out of print. Contact the publisher (919/968-8324) for details.

**Directory of American Firms Operating in Foreign Countries** (World Trade Academy Press, 50 E. 42nd St., Suite 509, New York, NY 10017, 1994, $195.00). This three-volume, 2,500+ page directory is invaluable for locating the more than 3,200 U.S. companies operating in more than 120 countries. Provides information on the products/service lines of each company as well as identifies the countries in which they operate. Includes employment statistics and contact information.

We identify and annotate numerous other useful resources in the final chapter of this book. These include directories, job search books, job listings and subscriptions, electronic databases, computer software, audiocassette programs, and CD-ROM. These resources will help you develop the necessary job search skills—from self-assessment to writing resumes and conducting job interviews—and contact potential international employers. Taken together, these resources constitute a rich information base from which you should be able to conduct a successful international job search.

We wish you well as you take this journey into the exciting and sometimes confusing world of international jobs and careers. While this book identifies the key organizations that hire in the international area, other books will take you through the most important stages of the job search. These stages are outlined in our other books: *Discover the Best Jobs For You!, Change Your Job Change Your Life, High Impact Resumes and Letters, Dynamite Resumes, Dynamite Cover Letters, Interview for Success, The New Network Your Way to Job and Career Success,* and *Dynamite Salary Negotiations.* We also address particular job and career fields in the following books: *The Complete Guide to Public Employment, Find a Federal Job Fast, The Complete Guide to International Jobs and Careers, The Almanac of American Government Jobs and Careers, Jobs and Careers With Nonprofit Organizations, Jobs for People Who Love Travel,* and *The Educator's Guide to Alternative Jobs and Careers.* These and many other job search books are available directly from Impact Publications. For your convenience, you can order them by completing the order form at the end of this book or by acquiring a copy of the publisher's catalog.

Indeed, as a user of this book, you may request a free copy of the most comprehensive career catalog available today—*"Jobs and Careers for the 1990s".* To receive the latest edition of this catalog of annotated job and career resources, write to:

IMPACT PUBLICATIONS
ATTN: Job/Career Catalog
9104-N Manassas Drive
Manassas Park, VA 22111-5211

They will send you a copy upon request. This catalog contains almost every important career and job finding resource available today, including many titles that are difficult if not impossible to find in bookstores and libraries. You will find everything from self-assessment books to books on resume writing, interviewing, government and international jobs, military, women, minorities, students, entrepreneurs as well as videos and computer software programs. This is an excellent resource for keeping in touch with the major resources that can assist you with every stage of your job search as well as with your future international career development plans.

# 2

# THE U.S. FEDERAL GOVERNMENT

*I*nternational positions with the Federal government are numerous. They encompass many more agencies than the most popular and visible "big six" Federal agencies specializing in international affairs:

- Department of State
- Department of Defense
- U.S. Agency for International Development (USAID)
- United States Information Agency (USIA)
- Peace Corps
- Central Intelligence Agency (CIA)

Thousands of additional international positions are found in the Executive Office of President, within other executive departments and agencies, and throughout congressional agencies, committees, and personal staffs.

# THE FEDERAL GOVERNMENT

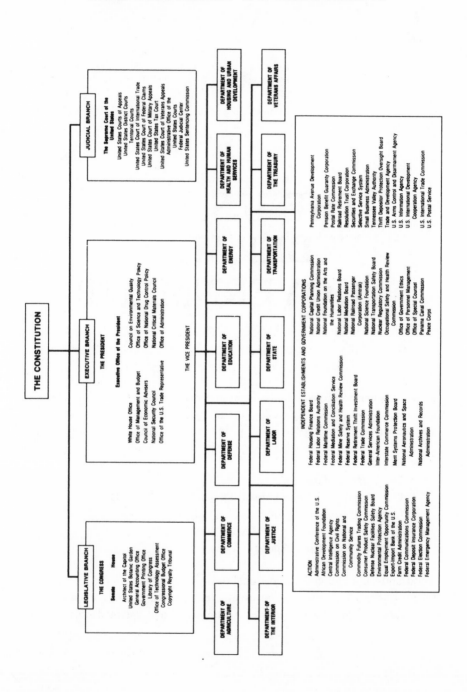

THE CONSTITUTION

**LEGISLATIVE BRANCH**

THE CONGRESS
Senate    House

Architect of the Capitol
United States Botanic Garden
General Accounting Office
Government Printing Office
Library of Congress
Office of Technology Assessment
Congressional Budget Office
Copyright Royalty Tribunal

**EXECUTIVE BRANCH**

THE PRESIDENT

Executive Office of the President

White House Office
Office of Management and Budget
Council of Economic Advisers
National Security Council
Office of the U.S. Trade Representative

Council on Environmental Quality
Office of Science and Technology Policy
Office of National Drug Control Policy
National Critical Materials Council
Office of Administration

THE VICE PRESIDENT

**JUDICIAL BRANCH**

The Supreme Court of the United States
United States Courts of Appeals
United States District Courts
Territorial Courts
United States Court of International Trade
United States Court of Federal Claims
United States Court of Military Appeals
United States Tax Court
United States Court of Veterans Appeals
Administrative Office of the United States Courts
Federal Judicial Center
United States Sentencing Commission

DEPARTMENT OF AGRICULTURE
DEPARTMENT OF THE INTERIOR
DEPARTMENT OF COMMERCE
DEPARTMENT OF JUSTICE
DEPARTMENT OF DEFENSE
DEPARTMENT OF LABOR
DEPARTMENT OF EDUCATION
DEPARTMENT OF STATE
DEPARTMENT OF ENERGY
DEPARTMENT OF TRANSPORTATION
DEPARTMENT OF HOUSING AND URBAN DEVELOPMENT
DEPARTMENT OF HEALTH AND HUMAN SERVICES
DEPARTMENT OF THE TREASURY
DEPARTMENT OF VETERANS AFFAIRS

INDEPENDENT ESTABLISHMENTS AND GOVERNMENT CORPORATIONS

ACTION
Administrative Conference of the U.S.
African Development Foundation
Central Intelligence Agency
Commission on Civil Rights
Commission on National and Community Service
Commodity Futures Trading Commission
Consumer Product Safety Commission
Defense Nuclear Facilities Safety Board
Environmental Protection Agency
Equal Employment Opportunity Commission
Export-Import Bank of the U.S.
Farm Credit Administration
Federal Communications Commission
Federal Deposit Insurance Corporation
Federal Election Commission
Federal Emergency Management Agency

Federal Housing Finance Board
Federal Labor Relations Authority
Federal Maritime Commission
Federal Mediation and Conciliation Service
Federal Mine Safety and Health Review Commission
Federal Reserve System
Federal Retirement Thrift Investment Board
Federal Trade Commission
General Services Administration
Inter-American Foundation
Interstate Commerce Commission
Merit Systems Protection Board
National Aeronautics and Space Administration
National Archives and Records Administration

National Capital Planning Commission
National Credit Union Administration
National Foundation on the Arts and the Humanities
National Labor Relations Board
National Mediation Board
National Railroad Passenger Corporation (Amtrak)
National Science Foundation
National Transportation Safety Board
Nuclear Regulatory Commission
Occupational Safety and Health Review Commission
Office of Government Ethics
Office of Personnel Management
Office of Special Counsel
Panama Canal Commission
Peace Corps

Pennsylvania Avenue Development Corporation
Pension Benefit Guaranty Corporation
Postal Rate Commission
Railroad Retirement Board
Resolution Trust Corporation
Securities and Exchange Commission
Selective Service System
Small Business Administration
Tennessee Valley Authority
Thrift Depositor Protection Oversight Board
Trade and Development Agency
U.S. Arms Control and Disarmament Agency
U.S. Information Agency
U.S. International Development Cooperation Agency
U.S. International Trade Commission
U.S. Postal Service

# INTERNATIONAL AGENCIES AND POSITIONS

The "big six" agencies offer the largest number of international positions. In addition, these agencies constitute an important international "network" for job seekers. Many former Peace Corps Volunteers, for example, move into positions in the U.S. Agency for International Development, Department of State, and the United States Information Agency. Within the intelligence community, individuals who work for the Defense Intelligence Agency (DIA) or Federal Bureau of Investigation also find international job opportunities with the Central Intelligence Agency and the Drug Enforcement Agency (DEA). Many other Federal agencies have international interests, offices, and positions. Some of them, such as international agencies within the Department of Agriculture and Department of Commerce, hire a large number of international specialists. Other agencies only have a small number of international positions.

# JOB FINDING STRATEGIES

Finding an international job with the Federal government requires carefully observing the formal hiring procedures as well as making personal contacts within targeted agencies. In most cases, hiring takes place at the agency level. Once a vacancy is announced, individuals should submit an application package. In most cases the requested application package is a completed Standard Form 171 (SF 171), the Federal government's version of a lengthy resume. How well you complete the SF 171 in reference to the position specifications outlined in the vacancy announcement will largely determine your rating in reference to other competing applications. Consequently, the more you know about the agency and position and tailor your application to the position, the better your chances of getting the job.

Some agencies have their own hiring procedures and personnel systems. For example, entry into many positions in the Department of State, U.S. Agency for International Development, and the United States Information Agency is via the Foreign Service. Applicants must pass the Foreign Service Exam which is given each year in early December. For more information on this recruitment procedure, telephone 703/875-7490 or 1-800/JOB-OVERSEAS or write to: United States Department of State, Recruitment Division, Box 9317, Arlington, VA 22209. Other agencies, such as the Central Intelligence Agency, Defense Intelligence Agency, Smithsonian Institution, and the Library of Congress also have their own application procedures and personnel systems.

The following Federal agencies and congressional organizations are the major sources for international employment within the Federal government. We recommend that you use the addresses and telephone numbers for gathering information on the various agencies. When vacancies occur, they will be announced through the agency personnel office in the form of a position vacancy announcement. The position may also be listed through the Office of Personnel Management or published in such job listing publications as the *Federal Career Opportunities* or the *Federal Jobs Digest* (see the end of this chapter for order information). However, coverage of vacancies is not always complete nor timely through these published sources. It is always best to keep in close contact with the hiring agency in order to learn about impending vacancies. You can do this by calling the agency personnel office for information on current vacancies. Better still, make contact with the hiring officials within the agency to learn if and when a vacancy will become available.

# EXECUTIVE OFFICE OF THE PRESIDENT

### Council of Economic Advisors
Old Executive Office Building
Washington, DC 20500
Tel. 202/395-3000

Analyzes the economy and makes policy recommendations to the President for economic growth and stability.

### National Security Council (NSC)
Old Executive Office Building
Washington, DC 20506
Tel. 202/395-4974

Advises the President on all policy matters (domestic, foreign, and military) relating to national security. Includes area (Asia, Africa, Europe, Russia, the former Soviet republics, Near East, and South Asia) and policy (arms control, intelligence, economic affairs, and legislative affairs) divisions.

### Office of Management and Budget (OMB)
Executive Office Building
Washington, DC 20503
Tel. 202/395-3080

Assists the President in preparing and formulating the federal budget as well as controlling the administration of the budget. Informs the President on the progress of government agencies. Includes a **National Security and International Affairs** office (Tel. 202/395-4657)

## Office of National Drug Control Policy
Executive Office of the President
Washington, DC 20500
Tel. 202/395-6377

Coordinates Federal, state, and local efforts to control illegal drug abuse as well as devises national strategies relating to anti-drug activities.

## Office of Science and Technology Policy
New Executive Office Building
Washington, DC 20506
Tel. 202/395-7347

Advises the President on all matters relating to science, engineering, and technology relevant to the economy, national security, health, foreign relations, and the environment.

## Office of the United States Trade Representative
600 - 17th Street, NW
Washington, DC 20506
Tel. 202/395-3204

Responsible for formulating and coordinating all trade policy for the United States. Functions as the country's chief trade representative and negotiator for all multinational (GATT, UN) and bilateral trade matters. Many former employees who worked in this office as U.S. trade negotiators are noted for playing the "revolving door" game by becoming high paid consultants to foreign governments on U.S. trade matters after working in this office.

## White House Office
1600 Pennsylvania Avenue, NW
Washington, DC 20500
Tel. 202/456-1414

Provides the President with staff assistance necessary for the orderly day-to-day administration of the Office of President. Includes such divisions as Chief of Staff, Counsel to the President, Press Secretary, Presidential Personnel, Communications, Presidential Advance, Presidential Scheduling, Legislative Affairs, Economic and Domestic Policy, Public Liaison, Administration, National Service, Military, Office of the First Lady, Cabinet Affairs, Domestic Policy Council, Economic Policy Council, and Agriculture, Trade, Food Assistance.

# THE DEPARTMENTS

## Department of Agriculture
14th Street and Independence Ave., SW
Washington, DC 20250
Tel. 202/720-8732

The Department of Agriculture is one of the largest employers of international specialists who are involved with foreign agricultural issues affecting U.S. agricultural and trade policies. The **Foreign Agricultural Service**, for example, posts nearly 100 agricultural specialists in more than 60 American embassies and consulates worldwide. It monitors foreign agriculture policies and commercial trade relations and promotes U.S. agricultural products. Other offices and divisions within the department deal with specific policy matters (conservation, forestry, inspection, transportation) or provide policy support services (research, marketing, information). The major international-related agencies within the department include:

- **Foreign Agricultural Service:** Tel. 202/720-3935
- **Office of International Cooperation and Development:** Tel. 202/690-2796 or 202/690-0709
- **International Affairs and Commodity Programs:** Tel. 202/720-3111
- **Economic Research Service:** 1301 New York Ave., NW, Washington, DC 20005-4788, Tel. 202/219-0515
- **Economics Management Staff:** Tel. 202/720-3535
- **Agricultural Marketing Service:** Tel. 202/720-3115
- **Agricultural Research Service:** Tel. 301/720-3656
- **Animal and Plant Health Inspection Service:** 6505 Belcrest Road, Hyattsville, MD 20782, Tel. 301/436-7550
- **Food Safety and Inspection Service:** International Programs, Tel. 202/720-3473
- **Forest Service:** International Forestry Staff, 202/205-1650
- **Soil Conservation Service:** International Conservation Division, Tel. 202/720-2218
- **World Agricultural Outlook Board:** Tel. 202/720-6030

## Department of Commerce
14th and Constitution Avenue, NW
Washington, DC 20230
Tel. 202/482-2000

The mission of this department is to promote the Nation's international trade, economic growth, and technological advancement. Its international interests and activities are extensive, from promoting competitive foreign trade, standardization, and telecommunications and protecting trademarks and copyrights to encouraging foreign travel to the U.S. The major international employers within the Department of Commerce include:

- **International Trade Administration:** Tel. 202/482-3301

- **United States and Foreign Commercial Service:** Tel. 202/482-3133
- **Bureau of Census:** Tel. 301/763-5190
- **Import Administration:** 14th and Constitution Ave., NW, Washington, DC 20230, Tel. 202/482-1780
- **Export Administration:** 14th and Constitution Ave., NW, Washington, DC 20230, Tel. 202/482-1455
- **Trade Development:** Tel. 202/482-1461
- **National Oceanic and Atmospheric Administration:** Tel. 202/482-6076
- **National Environmental Satellite Data and Information Service:** Federal Building #4, Washington, DC 20233, Tel. 301/763-4586
- **Bureau of Economic Analysis:** International Economics Office, 1401 K Street, NW, Washington, DC 20230, Tel. 202/606-9602
- **United States Travel and Tourism Administration:** Tel. 202/492-0136
- **Tourism Marketing:** Tel. 202/482-4752
- **National Marine Fisheries Service:** 1335 East-West Highway, Silver Spring, MD 20917, Tel. 301/713-2239
- **National Institute of Standards and Technology:** Building 101, Room 123, Gaithersburg, MD 20899, Tel. 301/975-3000
- **National Technical Information Service:** International Office of Acquisition, 5385 Port Royal Road, Springfield, VA 22161, Tel. 703/487-4822
- **National Telecommunications and Information Administration:** Tel. 202/482-1304
- **Oceanic and Atmospheric Research:** 1335 East-West Hwy., Silver Spring, MD 20910, Tel. 301/713-2458
- **United States Patent and Trademark Office:** International Patent Documentation Office, 2231 Crystal Drive, Arlington, VA 22202, Tel. 703/308-4357 and the Scientific and Technical Information Center, 2021 Jefferson Davis Hwy., Arlington, VA 22202, Tel. 703/308-0808.

## Department of Defense and Related Agencies

The Pentagon
Washington, DC 20310
Tel. 703/545-6700

The Department of Defense is by definition extensively involved in international affairs. Its activities involve everything from defense and security matters to educating the children of U.S. military personnel assigned abroad. International-related jobs in this department range from high-level policy, information, and security positions based in Washington, DC to blue-collar positions at U.S. military bases abroad. The major offices that hire international specialists include:

- **Deputy Undersecretary for Security Policy:** Tel. 703/697-0286
- **Defense Security Assistance Agency:** Tel. 703/695-3291
- **Advanced Research Projects Agency (ARPA):** 3701 North Fairfax Drive, Arlington, VA 22203-1714, 703/694-3077
- **Defense Intelligence Agency:** 703/695-7353

- **Department of Defense Dependents Schools:** 4040 North Fairfax Drive, Arlington, VA 22203, Tel. 703/696-4413
- **National Security Agency:** 9800 Savage Rd., Fort George G. Meade, MD 20755-6000, Tel. 301/688-6311

Many civilian government positions are available with U.S. military bases in Europe, Asia, and the Pacific.

## Department of Education
400 Maryland Avenue, SW
Washington, DC 20202
Tel. 202/732-6061

The Department of Education is involved in providing training and research services related to international education through its **Center for International Education** (7th & D Streets, SW, Washington, DC 20202, Tel. 202/732-6061).

## Department of Energy
1000 Independence Ave., SW
Washington, DC 20585
Tel. 202/586-5000

The Department of Energy is responsible for developing a comprehensive national energy plan, promoting energy technology, marketing federal power, conserving energy, operating the nuclear weapons program, and collecting and analyzing data on energy. This is a unique department in which over 80 percent of its personnel are private contractors. Since energy policy has important international dimensions, the department has important international interests. The major agencies and offices within the department hiring international specialists include:

- **Office of International Affairs:** Tel. 202/586-5493
- **Nuclear Energy:** International Programs Division, Route 270, Germantown, MD 20545, Tel. 301/353-3218
- **Intelligence:** Foreign Intelligence Division, Tel. 202/586-5174
- **Energy Information Administration:** Energy Markets and End Use, International and Contingency Information Division, Tel. 202/586-6555
- **Office of Energy Research:** Fusion Energy, International Programs Staff, 19901 Germantown Rd., Germantown, MD 20874, Tel. 301/903-3068

## Department of Health and Human Services
200 Independence Ave., SW
Washington, DC 20201
Tel. 202/619-0257

The Department of Health and Human Services is responsible for promoting the Nation's health and welfare. Extensively involved in international health matters, its international activities primarily center on conducting research and promoting international health policy. The major agencies and offices within the department with international interests and which tend to hire international specialists include:

- **Office of International Health:** 5600 Fishers Lane, Room 1875, Rockville, MD 20857, Tel. 301/443-1774
- **Social Security Administration:** Division of International Operations and Office of International Policy, 6401 Security Blvd. Room 142 Altmayer Bldg., Baltimore, MD 21235, Tel. 410/965-7389
- **National Institutes of Health:** Fogarty International Center Bldg. 31, Room B2C02, 9000 Rockville Pike, Bethesda, MD 20892, Tel. 301/496-1415; National Library of Medicine, Bldg. 38, 8600 Rockville Pike, Bethesda, MD 20894, Tel. 301/496-6481
- **National Center for Health Statistics:** 6525 Belcrest Road, Hyattsville, MD 20782, Tel. 301/436-7039
- **National Institute of Mental Health:** 5600 Fishers Lane, Rockville, MD 20857, Tel. 301/443-1828
- **Food and Drug Administration:** Health Affairs, 5600 Fishers Lane, Rockville, MD 20857, Tel. 301/443-4480
- **Centers for Disease Control:** International Health Program Office, 1600 Clifton Road, NE, Atlanta, GA 30333, Tel. 404/639-3311; Center for Prevention Services, Tel. 404/639-8262
- **Health Resources and Services Administration:** 5600 Fishers Lane, Rockville, MD 20857, Tel. 301/443-6152
- **National Cancer Institute:** Bldg. 31, Room 4B47, 9000 Rockville Pike, Bethesda, MD 20892, Tel. 301/496-4761
- **National Institute of Environmental Health Sciences:** Research Triangle Park, NC 27709, Tel. 919/541-3406

## Department of Housing and Urban Development
451 Seventh St., SW
Washington, DC 20410
Tel. 202/708-1422

While the Department of Housing and Urban Development is primarily responsible for administering Federal housing programs and for improving and developing communities within the United States, it also has some international interests. While in 1989 the department abolished the Office of International Affairs—which used to be the center for international housing and urban development specialists—it still pursues international interests. However, it remains unclear where these interests are centered. The best bet for now is the Office of Policy Development and Research (Tel. 202/708-1600).

## Department of Interior
1849 C Street, NW
Washington, DC 20240
Tel. 202/208-6761

The Department of Interior is responsible for protecting and managing federally owned lands and natural resources. It is also responsible for American Indian reservation communities and for the peoples populating island territories under U.S. jurisdiction. The major agencies and offices within the department with international interests include:

- **Office of Territorial and International Affairs:** Tel. 202/208-4822
- **National Park Service:** International Affairs, 1100 L St., NW, Washington, DC 20013-7127, Tel. 202/343-7063
- **Bureau of Mines:** International Minerals, 810 7th St., NW, Washington, DC 20241, Tel. 202/501-9446; Statistics and Information Services, 810 7th St., NW, Washington, DC 20241, Tel. 202/501-9545
- **U.S. Geological Survey:** International Geological Office, 12201 Sunrise Valley Drive, Reston, VA 22092, 703/648-7442
- **Bureau of Land Management:** 202/208-3431
- **Bureau of Reclamation:** External Affairs, Tel. 202/208-4291
- **U.S. Fish and Wildlife Service:** External Affairs, International Affairs, Arlington Square, 4401 N. Fairfax Dr., Arlington, VA 22203, Tel. 703/358-1754

## Department of Justice and Related Agencies
Constitution Avenue and 10th St., NW
Washington, DC 20530
Tel. 202/514-2000

One of the fastest growing Federal departments, the Department of Justice is responsible for enforcing federal laws. Its thousands of lawyers, investigators, and agents are involved in protecting citizens from criminals and subversion, ensuring business competition, safeguarding consumers, and enforcing drug, immigration, and naturalization laws. Its international interests are especially pronounced in the areas of drug enforcement and immigration matters. The major offices and agencies within the **Department of Justice** with international interests include:

- **Antitrust Division:** Foreign Commerce Section, Tel. 202/514-2464
- **Civil Division:** International Trade Field Office, Tel. 212/264-9232
- **Criminal Division:** International Affairs Office, Tel. 202/514-0000
- **Drug Enforcement Administration:** International Programs, 700 Army-Navy Drive, Arlington, VA 22202, Tel. 703/307-4000
- **U.S. Marshals Service:** 600 Army-Navy Drive, Arlington, VA 22202, Tel. 703/307-9630
- **Interpol-U.S. National Central Bureau:** Tel. 202/272-8383
- **Foreign Claims Settlement Commission of the United States:** Tel. 202/653-5883

Other Department of Justice related agencies with international interests include:

- **Federal Bureau of Investigation:** 9th & Pennsylvania Ave., NW, Washington, DC 20535, Tel. 202/324-5555

- **Immigration and Naturalization Service:** Foreign Operations, 425 Eye Street, NW, Washington, DC 20536, Tel. 202/514-4660

## Department of Labor
200 Constitution Ave., NW
Washington, DC 20210
Tel. 202/219-8271

The Department of Labor is responsible for the welfare of wage earners in the U.S. It administers federal labor laws relating to the safety, welfare, and compensation of workers, including unemployment insurance and workers' compensation. The major agencies and offices with international interests include:

- **International Labor Affairs:** Tel. 202/219-6043
- **Prices and Living Conditions:** International Price Indexes, 441 G Street, NW, Washington, DC 20212, Tel. 202/272-5025; International Training, Tel. 202/606-7101
- **Solicitor:** International Affairs Counsel, 202/219-8633

## Department of State
2201 C Street, NW
Washington, DC 20520
Tel. 202/647-4000

The Department of State is responsible for advising the President on foreign policy matters and for implementing U.S. foreign policy. It represents the U.S. abroad through its network of embassies and consulates and participates in the United Nations and over 50 major international organizations. It is the Federal government's major employer of international specialists with a total personnel level of over 25,000. Entry into many positions within this department involves taking the Foreign Service examination (Recruitment Division, Department of State, Box 9317, Arlington, Virginia 22209 or Tel. 703/875-7490 or 1-800/JOB-OVER) which is given each year in December. The examination also is used for several Foreign Service Officer (FSO) positions with the Agency for International Development (USAID), the U.S. Information Agency (USIA), and the U.S. Department of Commerce. The Foreign Service constitutes a separate personnel system within the federal government with its own rules, regulations, and procedures. Other positions within the Department of State fall under the personnel system administered by the Office of Personnel Management (OPM) and its General System (GS) salary schedule. Some of the most interesting agencies and offices in this department include:

- **Economic and Business Affairs Bureau**
- **International Communication and Information Policy Bureau**
- **International Security Affairs**
- **African Affairs Bureau**
- **East Asian and Pacific Affairs Bureau**

- **European and Canadian Affairs Bureau**
- **Intelligence and Research Bureau**
- **Bureau of Inter American Affairs**
- **International Organization Affairs Bureau**
- **International Narcotics Matters**
- **Near Eastern and South Asian Affairs Bureau**
- **Oceans and International Environmental and Scientific Affairs Bureau**
- **Bureau of Politico Military Affairs**
- **Bureau of Refugee Programs**
- **Bureau of Consular Affairs**

## Department of Transportation
400 Seventh St., SW
Washington, DC 20590
Tel. 202/366-4000

The Department of Transportation is responsible for the Nation's overall transportation policy in the areas of highways, mass transit, railways, aviation, waterways, and ports. It is also responsible for the safety of oil and gas pipelines. Its international transportation interests center on aviation, maritime, and trade issues. These are centered in the following agencies and offices:

- **Policy and International Affairs:** International Aviation, Tel. 202/366-2423; International Transportation and Trade, Tel. 202/366-4368
- **Policy, Planning, and International Aviation:** 800 Independence Ave., SW, Washington, DC 20591, Tel. 202/267-3033
- **Maritime Administration:** External Affairs Office, Tel. 202/366-1707
- **Federal Aviation Administration:** Office of International Aviation Affairs. Tel. 202/267-3111
- **Aviation Standards:** 800 Independence Ave., SW, Washington, DC 20591, Tel. 202/267-3133
- **Federal Highway Administration:** International Programs Office, Tel. 202/366-0111
- **Saint Lawrence Seaway Development Corporation:** Tel. 202/366-0118
- **United States Coast Guard:** Tel. 202/267-2390

## Department of Treasury
1500 Pennsylvania Ave., NW
Washington, DC 20220
Tel. 202/622-2000

The Department of Treasury is responsible for formulating and recommending economic, financial, tax, and fiscal policies. It is the Federal government's chief financial agent enforcing tax laws and manufacturing coins and currency. Its international interests focus on international tax and revenue, monetary, finance, trade, investment, and banking issues as well as the U.S. Custom Service. The major offices and agencies involved with international issues include:

- **Under Secretary for International Affairs:** 15th & Pennsylvania Ave., NW, Washington, DC 20220, Tel. 202/622-1080; Developing Nations Office, International Development and Debt Policy Office, Trade and Investment Office, International Monetary and Financial Policy Affairs, Eastern Europe and the former Soviet Union, and Middle East and Energy Policy located at 1500 Pennsylvania Ave., NW, Washington, DC 20005
- **United States Custom Service:** 1301 Constitution Avenue, NW, Washington, DC 20229, Tel. 202/927-0400
- **Assistant Secretary for Tax Policy:** 15th & Pennsylvania Ave., NW, Washington, DC 20220, Tel. 202/622-0050—International Tax Counsel; International Taxation Division
- **Bureau of Alcohol, Tobacco, and Firearms**: Tel. 202/927-8600
- **Internal Revenue Service:** 15th & Pennsylvania Ave., NW, Washington, DC 2022, Tel. 202/622-0455—International Taxation Division
- **Office of the Comptroller of the Currency:** International Banking and Finance, Independence Square, 250 E Street, SW, Washington, DC 20219, Tel. 202/847-4730
- **United States Secret Service:** 1800 G Street, NW, Washington, DC 20223, Tel. 202/435-5708

# INDEPENDENT AGENCIES AND GOVERNMENT CORPORATIONS

The following independent agencies and government corporations offer numerous international job opportunities. Inquiries and applications should be addressed directly to each organization.

## African Development Foundation
1400 Eye Street, NW, 10th Floor
Washington, DC 20005
Tel. 202/673-3916

This nonprofit, government corporation supports self-help efforts of grassroots organizations in Africa to solve development problems. It provides grants, loans, and loan guarantees to private African groups, associations, and other organizations engaged in such self-help activities.

## Central Intelligence Agency (CIA)
Washington, DC 20505
Tel. 703/482-1100

The Central Intelligence Agency is one of three major Federal intelligence agencies involved in collecting, evaluating, and disseminating information on political, military, economic, and scientific developments relevant to national security. It hires numerous international specialists with area and foreign language skills who become intelligence officers and analysts.

## Consumer Product Safety Commission
5401 Westbard Avenue
Bethesda, MD 20816
Tel. 301/504-0500

The Consumer Product Safety Commission is responsible for maintaining the safety of consumer products. It does this by setting uniform product safety standards and by conducting research and investigating the causes and prevention of product-related deaths, illnesses, and injuries. Its international activities are centered in the Office of International Affairs (Tel. 301/492-6554).

## Board for International Broadcasting
1201 Connecticut Ave., NW
Washington, DC 20036
Tel. 202/254-8040

Provides television and radio broadcast services for international interests.

## Environmental Protection Agency
401 M Street, SW
Washington, DC 20460
Tel. 202/260-4700

The Environmental Protection Agency is responsible for controlling and abating pollution in the areas of air, water, solid waste, pesticides, radiation, and toxic substances. While most of its activities center on coordinating federal, state, and local government efforts, it has become increasingly involved in international environmental issues. Its international interests are centered in the **Office of International Activities** (Tel. 202/260-4870).

## Export-Import Bank of the United States
811 Vermont Avenue, NW
Washington, DC 20571
Tel. 202/566-8990

The Export-Import Bank is responsible for promoting the export of U.S. products. It does this by assisting private firms with commercial export financing involving loans, guarantees, and insurance. Most offices and positions within this organization involve international activities. For example, the **Export Finance Group** is organized by regions (Asia, Europe, Latin America, Africa, and Middle East) with loan officers attached to each region.

## Federal Communications Commission
1919 M Street, NW
Washington, DC 20554
Tel. 202/632-7000

The Federal Communications Commission is responsible for regulating interstate and foreign communications (radio, television, wire, satellite, and cable) as well as developing and operating broadcast services and providing for rapid, efficient nationwide and worldwide telephone and telegraph services at reasonable rates. Its international interests are centered in:

- **Mass Media:** Policy and Rules Division, International Branch, Tel. 202/254-3394
- **Common Carrier Bureau:** The International Facilities Division, Tel. 202/632-7834
- **Federal Operations Bureau:** Tel. 202/632-7592
- **Private Radio Bureau:** Tel. 202/632-7197

## Federal Emergency Management Agency (FEMA)
500 C St., SW
Washington, DC 20472
Tel. 202/646-3923

The Federal Emergency Management Agency is responsible for coordinating the nation's emergency preparedness, mitigation, and response activities. Its international interests center on the **International Affairs Office** (Tel. 202/646-4200).

## Federal Maritime Commission
800 N. Capitol St., NW
Washington, DC 20573
Tel. 202/523-5773

The Federal Maritime Commission is responsible for regulating waterborne foreign and domestic offshore commerce of the U.S. It ensures that waterborne commercial activities are conducted on a fair and equitable basis. Works with the Department of State in eliminating discriminatory practices against U.S.-flag shipping.

## Federal National Mortgage Association
3900 Wisconsin Ave., NW
Washington, DC 20016
Tel. 202/752-7000

The Federal National Mortgage Association is responsible for promoting the health of the mortgage insurance industry. Its international interests are centered in the office of **International Housing Finance** (Tel. 202/752-6661).

## Federal Reserve System
20th and C Streets, NW
Washington, DC 20551
Tel. 202/452-3000

As the central bank of the United States, the Federal Reserve System is responsible for administering and making policy for the nation's credit and monetary affairs. It is responsible for promoting a sound banking system that is responsive to both domestic and international needs of the nation. Its international interests are centered on the **International Finance Staff** (Tel. 202/452-3614).

## General Services Administration
18th and F Streets, NW
Washington, DC 20405
Tel. 202/501-0398

The General Services Administration establishes policy for and provides economical and efficient management of Government property and records, including construction and operation of buildings, procurement and distribution of supplies, utilization and disposal of property; transportation, traffic, and communications management; and management of the government-wide automatic data processing resources program.

## Inter-American Foundation
901 North Stuart, 10th Floor
Arlington, VA 22203-1821
Tel 703/841-3800

This independent government corporation is responsible for supporting social and economic activities in Latin American and the Caribbean by providing grants to private, indigenous organizations that operate self-help projects benefiting poor people.

## National Aeronautics and Space Administration
400 Maryland Avenue, SW
Washington, DC 20546
Tel. 202/453-1000

The National Aeronautics and Space Administration (NASA) conducts research and operates programs relating to flight within and outside the Earth's atmosphere, including the Nation's major space programs and centers. Its international interests center on the office of **Policy, Coordination and International Relations** (International Relations Division, Tel. 202/358-0900, International Programs Policy, Tel. 202/358-1651, and International Planning and Programs, Tel. 202/358-1665).

## National Science Foundation
1800 G Street, NW
Washington, DC 20550
Tel. 202/357-5000

The National Science Foundation is responsible for promoting research and education programs in science and engineering. It does this through grants, contracts, and cooperative agreements with universities, university consortia, and nonprofit and other research organizations. Its international interests center on several offices and divisions within the office of **Science and Technology Infrastructure** (Tel. 202/357-9808).

## Nuclear Regulatory Commission
11555 Rockville Pike
Rockville, MD 20852
Tel. 301/492-7000

The Nuclear Regulatory Commission is responsible for licensing and regulating civilian use of nuclear energy to protect public health and safety and the environment. Makes rules, sets standards, and inspects those licensed to build and operate nuclear reactors and other facilities as well as to own and use nuclear materials. Its international interests center on the **International Programs Office**, Tel. 301/492-0347).

## Panama Canal Commission
1825 I Street, NW, Suite 1050
Washington, DC 20006
Tel. 202/634-6441

The Panama Canal Commission operates the Panama Canal to ensure efficient, safe, and economical transit service for the benefit of world commerce.

## Peace Corps
1990 K Street, NW
Washington, DC 20526
Tel. 202/606-3387 or 1-800/424-8580

The Peace Corps promotes world peace, friendship, and understanding by providing over 6,500 volunteers to work in nearly 100 developing countries for periods of two to three years. Volunteers work in a variety of programs, from teaching English to community development, health care, and small enterprise development. For many individuals interested in international jobs and careers, the Peace Corps offers excellent "entry-level" opportunities to get international experience that will become invaluable for later finding jobs with the U.S. State Department, U.S. Agency for International Development, private contractors and consultants, nonprofit organizations, and PVOs. All positions within the Peace

Corps, either Volunteer or Staff, should be considered "international" positions because they involve international operations.

## Securities and Exchange Commission
450 5th Street, NW
Washington, DC 20549
Tel. 202/272-3100

The Securities and Exchange Commission is responsible for administering federal securities laws that protect investors and ensure that the securities markets are operated fairly and honestly. Its international interests center on the following offices and divisions:

- **Corporation Finance:** International Corporate Finance Office, Tel. 202/272-3246
- **General Counsel:** International Litigation and Administrative Practices, 202/272-2454
- **Enforcement:** International Affairs, Tel. 202/272-2306

## Smithsonian Institution
1000 Jefferson Drive, SW
Washington, DC 20560
Tel. 202/357-1300

The Smithsonian Institution is responsible for promoting historical, technological, scientific, and artistic knowledge of the Nation. It does this by presenting exhibits, conducting research, publishing studies, and participating in cooperative international programs of scholarly exchange. Its international-related activities are found in numerous positions throughout the organization, including the museums and galleries. However, the largest concentration of international specialists are found in:

- **International Center:** Tel. 202/357-4795
- **Woodrow Wilson International Center for Scholars:**
  Tel. 202/357-2429

## U.S. Institute of Peace
1550 M Street, NW
Washington, DC 20001-1708
Tel. 202/457-1700

The U.S. Institute of Peace is responsible for strengthening the Nation's ability to promote international peace and the peaceful resolution of conflicts throughout the world. It does this by providing grants and fellowships to individual scholars, conducting in-house research, and sponsoring educational activities.

## U.S. Arms Control and Disarmament Agency
320 21st Street, NW
Washington, DC 20451
Tel. 202/647-8677

The U.S. Arms Control and Disarmament Agency is responsible for formulating and implementing arms control and disarmament policies for promoting U.S. national security. It participates in discussions and negotiations with the Soviet Union and other countries on issues dealing with strategic arms limitations, conventional force reductions in Europe, limiting the spread of nuclear weapons capabilities, prohibiting chemical weapons, and reducing the international arms trade. Most positions within this organization deal with international matters.

## U.S. Information Agency (USIA)
301 Fourth Street, SW
Washington, DC 20547
Tel. 202/619-4700

USIA, known abroad as the United States Information Service or USIS, is responsible for U.S. overseas information and cultural programs, including the Voice of America. It is involved in a wide range of overseas communication activities—from academic and cultural exchanges to press, radio, television, film, seminar, library, and cultural centered programs. It maintains a full-time staff abroad which is primarily recruited and promoted through the Foreign Service.

## U.S. International Development Cooperation Agency
320 21st St., NW
Washington, DC 20523-0001
Tel. 202/663-1449

This is the Nation's major international development organization which consists of three organizations: U.S. Agency for International Development (USAID), U.S. Trade and Development Program, and the Overseas Private Investment Corporation.

### U.S. Agency for International Development
320 21st St, NW
Washington, DC 20523
Tel. 202/647-1770

The Agency for International Development is responsible for developing and implementing U.S. economic assistance programs aimed at developing countries. This is the single most important U.S. government agency involved in the developing world which encompasses nearly 75 percent of the world's population. It defines the focus and provides the funding for a great deal of public and private sector development efforts in Third and Fourth World countries. AID missions abroad are staffed with project officers and specialists in agriculture, rural development, health, nutrition, population planning, education, human resource development, private sector development, environment, and energy. It provides billions of dollars in funds for projects that are implemented by the many private contractors, nonprofit organizations, and PVOs outlined in subsequent chapters. Although not a part of the Department of State, entry into most AID positions is via the Foreign Service. AID is primarily organized by both area (Africa Bureau; Asia, Near East, and Europe Bureau; Latin America and the Caribbean Bureau) and program offices (Trade and Development Programs; Private Enterprise Bureau; U.S. Foreign Disaster Assistance; Food for Peace and Voluntary Assistance Bureau; and Program and Policy Coordination Bureau).

## U.S. Trade and Development Program
1621 North Kent Street
Rosslyn, VA 22209
Tel. 703/875-4357

Established in 1988 as an independent agency within the International Development Cooperation Agency, the Trade and Development Program promotes economic development in Third World and middle-income development countries through the export of U.S. goods and services. It sponsors feasibility studies conducted by U.S. firms for high-priority development projects to be funded by the World Bank, other international lending institutions, or through host country resources.

## Overseas Private Investment Corporation
1615 M Street, NW
Washington, DC 20527
Tel. 202/336-8530

The Overseas Private Investment Corporation assists U.S. companies in making profitable investments in over 100 developing countries. While helping companies minimize investment risks abroad, the Corporation also encourages investment projects that will assist countries with social and economic development. It provides U.S. investors with assistance in finding investment opportunities, insurance to protect investments, and loans and loan guaranties to help finance their projects.

## U.S. International Trade Commission
500 E Street, SW
Washington, DC 20436
Tel. 202/205-2651

The International Trade Commission is responsible for providing the President, Congress, and other Government agencies with studies, reports, and recommendations relating to international trade and tariffs. Its major activities involve conducting investigations, public hearings, and research projects concerning the international policies of the U.S. as well as the trade and tariff policies of other countries that affect U.S. trade and trade negotiations. For example, the Commission's work plays an important role in selecting items included in the Generalized System of Preferences (GSP), identifying unfair import practices, and interference with U.S. agricultural programs. Since much of its work involves laws, rules, and regulations, this organization is heavily staffed with lawyers.

### U.S. Postal Service
475 L'Enfant Plaza West, SW
Washington, DC 20260
Tel. 202/268-4800

The U.S. Postal Service is responsible for the orderly processing and delivery of mail. Since its work involves international mail—individuals, businesses, and military—the U.S. Postal Service is increasingly involved in international matters. Its major international interests are centered in the **International and Military Mail Operations Division** (Tel. 202/268-4365). The U.S. Postal Service operates its own personnel system separate from other government agencies.

## U.S. CONGRESS

The U.S. Congress is very much involved in the international arena. International job opportunities are found on "Capitol Hill" (Senate and House personal and committee staffs) as well as amongst congressional agencies. While not as numerous as executive departments and agencies, nonetheless, many international positions are available in this branch of government. These positions often become "stepping stones" to other international positions in the executive departments and with private firms.

## Agencies

Congressional agencies are the bureaucratic equivalent to executive agencies. They are responsible to and under the control of Congress rather than the Executive branch. Reflecting the international interests and work of Congress, these agencies offer several international opportunities for enterprising job seekers. Congressional agencies with the largest number of international activities include the Library of Congress, Congressional Budget Office, and the General Accounting Office.

## The Library of Congress
101 Independence Avenue, SE
Washington, DC 20540
Tel. 202/707-5000

The Library of Congress is the national library. It maintains an extensive collection of documents, provides important publishing and library services, and serves as a critical information base for Congress. Its international activities are found in several offices but especially in the **Congressional Research Service** which provides congressional committees and members of Congress with information on questions relating to their day-to-day work, including foreign policy matters. Other offices involved in international matters include:

- **Collections Services:** Acquisitions Office, Overseas Operations, Tel. 202/707-5273
- **Constituent Services:** Public Service and Collection Management— African-Middle Eastern Division (Tel. 202/707-7937) and Asian Division (Tel. 202/707-5420), both located at 2nd and Independence Ave., SE, Washington, DC 20540; European Division (Tel. 202/707-5414) and Hispanic Division (Tel. 202/707-5400)

## Congressional Budget Office
Ford House Office Building
2nd and D Streets, SW
Washington, DC 20515
Tel. 202/226-2626

The Congressional Budget Office is Congress' counterpart to the Executive's Office of Management and Budget. It provides Congress with basic budget data and well as analyzes alternative fiscal, budgetary, and programmatic policy issues. Its international activities are centered in the **International Affairs Unit** of the office of Fiscal Analysis (Tel. 202/226-2761).

## General Accounting Office (GAO)
441 G Street, NW
Washington, DC 20548
Tel. 202/275-5067

The General Accounting Office is the investigative arm of Congress which is responsible for examining all matters relating to the receipt and disbursement of public funds. As such, it closely monitors and audits all executive agencies involved in international matters, especially the Department of State, Department of Defense, and the U.S. Agency for International Development. Its major international activities are centered in the office of **National Security and International Affairs**. However, other offices within GAO also have international responsibilities (General Counsel, Tel. 202/275-5205, Accounting and Financial Management, Tel. 202/275-9459).

# Congress

International positions within Congress are found in two different areas:

- on personal staffs of members of the House and Senate
- on committee staffs within both the House and Senate

Both the House and Senate have their own administrative staffs, but these have little to do with international matters other than foreign travel.

## Senate

International jobs opportunities in the Senate center on the staffs of the following committees and subcommittees:

- **Appropriations:** Foreign Operations, Tel. 202/224-7284
- **Banking, House, and Urban Affairs:** International Finance and Monetary Policy, Tel. 202/224-7391
- **Budget:** Tel. 202/224-0642
- **Commerce, Science, and Transportation:** Foreign Commerce and Tourism, Tel. 202/224-9325.
- **Finance:** International Trade; International Debt; Tel. 202/224-4515
- **Foreign Relations:** Tel. 202/224-4651
- **Judiciary:** Immigration and Refugee Affairs, Tel. 202/224-7878
- **Intelligence Select Committee:** Tel. 202/224-1700

Senators who chair or are members of these committees and subcommittees also hire staff members who are responsible for international-related issues. Each Senator hires one to four Legislative Assistants and other staffers who are responsible for foreign affairs, foreign relations, foreign trade, military, arms control, intelligence, human rights, immigration, refugee, and international drug and terrorism issues.

## House of Representatives

International positions in the House of Representatives follow the same pattern as in the Senate—committee and subcommittee staffs and personal staffs. House committees and subcommittees with international specialists include the following:

- **Agriculture:** Department of Operations and Nutrition, Research, and Foreign Agriculture and Hunger, Tel. 202/225-1867
- **Appropriations:** Defense, Tel. 202/225-2847; Foreign Operations, Export Financing, and Related Programs, Tel. 202/225-2041

- **Armed Services:** Tel. 202/225-4151
- **Banking, Finance, and Urban Affairs:** International Development, Finance, Trade, and Monetary Policy, Tel. 202/226-7515
- **Budget:** 202/226-7234
- **Foreign Affairs:** 202/225-5021
- **Judiciary:** Immigration, Refugees, and International Law, Tel. 202/225-5727
- **Science, Space, and Technology:** International Advisor, Tel. 202/226-6375
- **Ways and Means:** Trade, Tel. 202/225-3625
- **Intelligence Select Committee:** Tel. 202/225-4121

Several members of the House of Representatives also designate one to three Legislative Assistants or other staff members to handle international-related issues. Like their Senate counterparts, these individuals are also responsible for other policy areas which may or may not be related to international concerns.

## KEY RESOURCES

If you are interested in pursuing international jobs with the Federal government, we recommend the following books and computer software programs:

**How to Find an Overseas Job With the U.S. Government**, Will Cantrell and Francine Modderno (Oakton, VA: WorldWise Books, 1992, $28.95). The only book to focus exclusively on international positions within the federal government. Includes an extensive section on the State Department and profiles many other agencies. Describes agencies, qualifications required, and application procedures.

**Guide to Careers in World Affairs**, Foreign Policy Association, eds. (New York: Foreign Policy Association, 1993, $14.95). Includes an extensive chapter on international job opportunities with federal agencies as well as state and local governments. Complete with program information and application details.

**Find a Federal Job Fast: How to Cut the Red Tape and Get Hired**, Ron and Caryl Krannich (Manassas Park, VA: Impact Publications, 1994, $14.95). A basic primer on how to find a federal job. Dispels myths and covers everything from application procedures and the SF 171 to networking and interviewing.

**The Right SF 171 Writer: The Complete Guide to Communicating Your Qualifications to Employers**, Russ Smith (Manassas Park, VA: Impact Publications, 1994, $19.95). The definitive guide to completing the all-important Standard Form 171. Outlines what federal employers look for on the SF 171, major writing principles, the best language to use, and how to customize the form. Includes examples of completed SF 171s.

**Quick and Easy 171s** (Harrisburg, PA: DataTech, 1994). This easy-to-use computerized program produces SF 171's on blank paper. Uses most printers on the market. Direct support provided for over 50 dot matrix printers, the DeskJet 500, and laser printers that are compatible with the Hewlett Parkard LaserJet II. Prints the form which is approved by OPM. Available in 4 versions: Personal (single user only, $49.95); Family (2 users only, $59.95); Office (8 users only, $129.95); and Professional/ Organization (unlimited users, $399.95).

**FOCIS—Federal Occupational and Career Information System** (Washington, DC: Office of Personnel Management, $59.95). This interactive program helps federal employees and job seekers obtain information about Federal careers, occupations, agencies, current job openings, and training. Contains database on nearly 600 Federal occupations and 300 Federal organizations. Users with modems can dial into an OPM bulletin board, electronically transfer current job vacancy listings to their computer, and search for job openings using FOCIS. Federal employees can access information on more than 1,000 nationwide training courses. Software: three 3½ diskettes, 1.44 M high density. Documentation included. System: IBM-PC or compatible, PC-DOS 3.0 or higher operating system, 400K. Hard disk requires 2.5 to 12.7 Mb depending on the combination of modules installed. Language: dBase III plus compiled in Clipper. Drive should be a 286 or higher processor.

**Federal Career Opportunities** (Vienna, VA: Federal Research Service). This comprehensive listing of current federal job vacancies includes 3,400 positions from grades GS5 thru SES in each issue. Organized by GS series within each agency. Published biweekly as a 64-90 page directory. Subscriptions: 6 issues, $39; 26 issues (1 year), $186. APO/FPO subscribers should add $1 per issue for first-class shipping.

**Federal Jobs Digest** (Ossining, NY: Breakthrough Publications). Largest source of current job openings listing over 15,000 immediate civil service vacancies in the US and overseas in each issue. Published biweekly: 6 issues, $29; 25 issues (1 year), $110.

All of these resources are available directly through the individual publishers or they can be purchased through Impact Publications (see the order form at the end of this book).

# 3

# INTERNATIONAL ORGANIZATIONS

*I*nternational organizations provide numerous job opportunities for international specialists who are interested in a variety of issues relating to economic and social development as well as regional security. The largest employer of international specialists is the United Nations bureaucracy and its complex of affiliated organizations. While headquartered in New York City, many of its specialized agencies are headquartered in Geneva, Vienna, Rome, Montreal, and Washington, DC. Additional UN organizations operate from other major cities around the world.

Many other international organizations employ international specialists. The World Bank, for example, offers excellent job opportunities for individuals with expertise in international economics and finance. Like many jobs with the United Nations, positions with the World Bank tend to be well paid and come with numerous benefits. Compensation, benefits, and perks with these organizations are much better than with the U.S. government.

Each international organization has its own hiring procedures. Indeed, even within the United Nations, hiring is decentralized to the individual agencies. Therefore, it's important to understand the structure and function of each organization in order to properly approach its hiring process and procedures.

International organizations tend to hire professionals with a great deal of international experience and higher educational degrees. Many positions within the United Nations and the World Bank, for example, involve research, writing, consulting, and meeting skills as well as procurement—obligating funds for projects. Indeed, if you are interested in getting involved in the nitty-gritty of development—working with people at the local level on development projects—becoming employed by one of these international organizations may frustrate you. Few of these organizations are involved in implementing projects. At best, they fund the implementation activities of government agencies, contractors, and nonprofit organizations and host frequent meetings where they function as a forum for "exchanging ideas". The United Nations, for example, is well noted for its culture of meetings, reports, and consultation. If you are interested in working for one of these organizations, you may quickly discover that you are competing with many other individuals who have lengthy resumes that demonstrate their extensive international-relevant education, research, writing, consulting, and meeting skills.

The international organizations outlined in this chapter represent the major ones employing U.S. citizens. Numerous other international organizations also provide job opportunities for enterprising job seekers. If you are interested in exploring additional international organizations, we recommend consulting the following directories:

- **Encyclopedia of Associations: International Organizations**
- **Europa Year Book**
- **Yearbook of International Organizations**
- **Yearbook of the United Nations**

Current volumes of these four directories are available in most major libraries.

# UNITED NATIONS AND ITS SPECIALIZED AGENCIES

The United Nations offers numerous international job opportunities within the Secretariat and specialized agencies. It is the largest employer of international specialists with a bureaucracy of nearly 67,000 individuals working in over 600 duty stations throughout the world. Fewer than 10 percent of the UN civil servants are U.S. citizens.

# The Organization

A mammoth organization, the United Nations consists of six major organizational units and numerous specialized and autonomous agencies, standing committees, commissions, and other subsidiary bodies. Given the decentralized nature of the United Nations, all specialized agencies and related organizations recruit their own personnel. The six principal United Nations organs are:

- General Assembly
- Security Council
- Economic and Social Council
- Trusteeship Council
- International Court of Justice
- Secretariat

While job opportunities are available with all of these organs, the most numerous jobs are found with the Economic and Social Council and the UN Secretariat.

The **Economic and Social Council** is under the General Assembly. It coordinates the economic and social work of the United Nations and numerous specialized agencies, standing committees, commissions, and related organizations. The work of the Council involves international development, world trade, industrialization, natural resources, human rights, status of women, population, social welfare, science and technology, crime prevention, and other social and economic issues.

The Economic and Social Council is divided into a headquarters staff in New York City and five regional economic commissions:

- Economic Commission for Africa (Addis Ababa)
- Economic and Social Commission for Asia and the Pacific (Bangkok)
- Economic Commission for Europe (Geneva)
- Economic Commission for Latin America (Santiago)
- Economic Commission for Western Asia (Beirut)

Each Commission maintains a large staff of specialists. Furthermore, they promote the work of several standing committees and commissions which also have their own staffs.

Specialized or intergovernmental agencies are autonomous organizations linked to the United Nations by special intergovernmental agreements. In addition, they have their own membership, budgets, personnel systems, legislative and executive bodies, and secretariats. The Food and Agriculture Organization (FAO), for example, consists of a staff drawn from 160 member nations. It is administered by a professional staff of nearly 3,200 which is headquartered in Rome; some employees work in FAO regional offices located in Ghana, Thailand, Chile, New York City, and Washington, DC. Each year the FAO hires nearly 500 staff members; 60 to 65 of these new hirees are U.S. citizens.

The Economic and Social Council coordinates the work of these organizations with the United Nations as well as with each other. Altogether, there are 12 specialized agencies:

- Food and Agriculture Organization (FAO)
- International Civil Aviation Organization (ICAO)
- International Fund for Agricultural Development (IFAD)
- International Labour Organization (ILO)
- International Maritime Organization (IMO)
- International Monetary Fund (IMF)
- International Telecommunication Union (ITU)
- United Nations Educational, Scientific, and Cultural Organization (UNESCO)
- United Nations Industrial Development Organization (UNIDO)
- Universal Postal Union (UPU)
- World Health Organization (WHO)
- World Intellectual Property Organization (WIPO)
- World Meteorological Organization (WMO)

Several other major organizations also are attached to the Economic and Social Council as well as the Secretariat. These consist of:

- General Agreement on Tariffs and Trade (GATT)
- International Sea-Bed Authority
- International Atomic Energy Agency (IAEA)
- International Bank for Reconstruction and Development (IBRD or World Bank)
- Office of the United Nations Disaster Relief Co-ordinator (UNDRO)

- United Nations Centre for Human Settlements (HABITAT)
- United Nations Children's Fund (UNICEF)
- United Nations Development Program (UNDP)
- United Nations Environment Programme (UNEP)
- United Nations Fund for Population Activities (UNFPA)
- United Nations High Commission for Refugees (UNHCR)
- United Nations Industrial Development Organization (UNIDO)
- United Nations Institute for Training and Research (UNITAR)
- United Nations Observer Mission and Peacekeeping Forces in the Middle East
- United Nations Relief and Works Agency for Palestine Refugees in the Near East (UNRWA)
- World Food Council (WFC)
- World Food Programme (WFP)

The UN Secretariat employs nearly 14,000 international civil servants from 160 countries. Most are stationed at the United Nations headquarters in New York City. The Secretariat is the central "bureaucracy" in charge of carrying out the day-to-day work of the United Nations.

The largest UN agencies—those employing at least 1,500 individuals—consist of the following:

- Food and Agriculture Organization
- World Health Organization
- United Nations Development Programme
- World Bank
- UNESCO
- International Labor Organization
- UNICEF
- International Monetary Fund

The United States is especially involved in the following United Nations organizations which are headquartered in various cities throughout the world:

- Food and Agricultural Organization (Rome)
- International Atomic Energy Agency (Vienna)
- International Bank for Reconstruction and Development or World Bank (Washington, DC)
- International Civil Aviation Organization (Montreal)
- International Finance Corporation (Washington, DC)
- International Monetary Fund (Washington, DC)

- International Telecommunication Union (Geneva)
- Universal Postal Union (Bern, Switzerland)
- World Health Organization (Geneva)

Consequently, U.S. citizens may have a higher probability of landing jobs with these UN agencies than with other agencies.

## Hiring Process

Since the hiring process is largely decentralized within the United Nations and among the specialized agencies and related organizations, you should directly contact each agency for job vacancy information. If, for example, you are interested in working for the UN Secretariat in New York City, contact the following offices for information on job vacancies:

United Nations
Recruitment Programs Section
Office of Personnel Services
New York, NY 10017

Most agencies and organizations have personnel offices which issue job vacancy announcements. Bulletin boards outside personnel offices or cafeterias often include the latest vacancy announcements.

For technical assistance positions, you should contact the following office for information:

Technical Assistance Recruitment Service
Department of Technical Cooperation
United Nations
New York, NY 10017

The U.S. Department of State provides recruitment and job referral services for U.S. citizens interested in working for the United Nations. The Office of UN Employment Information and Assistance identifies qualified U.S. citizens who are then referred for UN assignments. Most candidates should have specialized and advanced academic degrees and several years of recent international experience. The categories of positions covered include: public information personnel; computer programmers; military personnel; administrative posts; legal posts; translators; interpreters; summer employment; clerical personnel; UN guides; intern programs; political affairs posts; telecommunication posts;

economists; and UN volunteers. The Bureau maintains a computerized roster of qualified professional candidates whose backgrounds are matched against the qualifications specified in UN vacancy announcements. It also maintains a mailing list of individuals who wish to receive vacancy announcements. To get on this roster, be referred, and receive vacancy announcements, send a detailed resume to:

> Staffing Management Officer
> Office of UN Employment Information and Assistance
> Bureau of International Organization Affairs
> IO/EA—Room 3536, NW
> Department of State
> Washington, DC 20520-6319
> Tel. 202/647-3396

If you need more information on the UN and this referral system, write or call the above office for the following materials:

- *Fact Sheet*
- *United Nations People*

The Fact Sheet gives the names and addresses of various UN agencies to which you can apply directly for vacancies. It also includes a useful list of U.S. counterpart agencies that work with the United Nations. These include:

| UN agency | U.S. counterpart agency |
|---|---|
| Food and Agriculture Organization (FAO) | Foreign Agriculture Service, Department of Agriculture |
| International Atomic Energy Agency (IAEA) | Office of International Affairs, Department of Energy |
| International Civil Aviation Organization (ICAO) | Office of International Organization Aviation Affairs, Federal Aviation Administration |
| Universal Postal Union | International Postal Affairs, U.S. Postal Service |

| World Health | Office of International Health, |
| Organization (WHO) | Public Health Service, Department |
| | of Health and Human Services |

| World Meteorological | Office of International Affairs, |
| Organization (WMO) | National Oceanic and Atmospheric |
| | Administration |

## Secretariat and Special Programs

### United Nations High Commissioner for Refugees
Office of Recruitment, Career Development and Placement
154, rue de Lausanne
CH-1202 Geneva
Switzerland

Responsible for protecting refugees throughout the world. Coordinates international relief efforts for refugees. Maintains a professional staff of 2,500 in 80 countries. Its New York and Washington offices have 10 staff members. For U.S.-based positions, contact: Washington Liaison Office, UNHCR, 1718 Connecticut Avenue, NW, Suite 200, Washington, DC 20009.

### United Nations Childrens' Fund (UNICEF)
Chief, Recruitment and Staff Development Section
3 United Nations Plaza, Room H-5F
New York, NY 10017
Tel. 212/326-7000

Conducts programs to protect children and enhance their development. Involved in maternal health, child nutrition, sanitation, and training programs. Helps equip health centers, schools, and day-care and community centers. Has a professional staff of nearly 1,700 (150 U.S. citizens) operating from 100 field offices. Main offices are located in New York, Tokyo, Geneva, and Copenhagen. The New York office alone employs nearly 300.

### United Nations Development Programme (UNDP)
Chief, Recruitment Section
Division of Personnel
1 United Nations Plaza
New York, NY 10017
Tel. 212/906-5279

The official development agency of the United Nations, UNDP provides financial and technical assistance to developing countries in numerous fields, from agriculture to education and housing. Has a professional staff of nearly

1000 operating through a network of 115 field offices. Also supports nearly 20,000 technical experts and consultants who work on projects funded and monitored by UNDP but implemented by the specialized UN agencies.

## United Nations Environment Program (UNEP)
Chief, Recruitment Union
P.O. Box 30552
Nairobi, Kenya

A small coordinating body that monitors environmental issues and initiatives for the United Nations. Employs nearly 300 professionals who are stationed in 15 countries.

## United Nations Population Fund
220 East 42nd St.
New York, NY 10017-5880
Tel. 212/297-5000

Supports population and family planning by coordinating information and providing financial and technical assistance to both developing and developed countries. Functions as the focal point for strengthening government population and family planning programs.

## United Nations Industrial Development Organization (UNIDO)
Vienna International Centre
P.O. Box 300
A-1400 Vienna, Austria
Tel. (43-1) 21131 or Fax (43-1) 232156

Promotes industrial development in developing countries by providing information and financial assistance for industrial projects. Has a staff of nearly 1,400. Operates offices in New York and Washington, DC. Hires nearly 2,000 experts and consultants for special projects.

## United Nations Institute for Training and Research (UNITAR)
Chief, Program Support Service
801 United Nations Plaza
New York, NY 10017
Tel. 212/370-1122

Conducts research on problems facing the international community as well as provides training for UN officials and officials of members' governments. Has a professional staff of 50 based in Geneva, Rome, Nairobi, and New York.

## United Nations Relief and Works Agency for Palestine Refugees in the Near East (UNRWA)

Chief, Personnel Services Division
Vienna International Centre, P.O. Box 700
A-1400 Vienna, Austria

Provides refugee relief services in the areas of health, education, and welfare for Palestinian refugees living in Lebanon, Syria, East Jordan, and the West Bank. Operates more than nearly 600 schools staffed with more than 8,000 Palestinian teachers. Has a staff of 150 based in Vienna, Lebanon, Syria, Jordan, and Israel.

## United Nations University

Toho Sheimei Building
15-1 Shibuya 2-Chome, Shibuya-ku
Tokyo, 150, Japan

Offers educational programs focusing on the problems of developing countries, such as hunger, water resources, human rights, international trade, and law.

## United Nations Volunteers

Palais des Nations
CH-1211 Geneva 10
Switzerland

Similar in concept and operation to the U.S. Peace Corps, United Nations Volunteers provide technical assistance in the fields of health, education, engineering, and community development at the local level. Has a professional staff of 200 in Geneva and 400 support staff for volunteers in other countries throughout the world. U.S. citizens interested in applying for Volunteer positions must do so through the U.S. Peace Corps: UN Volunteers, 1990 K Street, NW, Washington, DC 20526, Tel. 800/424-8580, ext. 2243.

# Specialized Agencies

## Food and Agricultural Organization (FAO)

Via delle Terme di Caracalla
00100 Rome, Italy

U.S. Liaison Office:  1001 22nd St., NW
                      Washington, DC 20437
                      Tel. 202/653-2498

Promotes better nutrition and the improved production and distribution of food and agricultural products amongst rural populations by collecting and disseminating information on food production and providing technical assistance to governments. Has a professional staff of 3,200 operating from Rome, Ghana, Thailand, Chile, and New York.

## International Atomic Energy Agency
Wagramerstrasse 5
Vienna, Austria

    U.S. address:        1 UN Plaza, Suite DC1-1155
                        New York, NY 10017
                        Tel. 212/963-6011

Monitors compliance to the 1970 Non-Proliferation Treaty, promotes the peaceful uses of atomic energy, coordinates research, and promotes scientific exchanges relevant to atomic energy.

## International Civil Aviation Organization
1000 Sherbrooke Street West
Montreal, PQ, Canada H3A 2R2
Tel. 514/285-8219

Promotes international cooperation in air transportation. Establishes international aviation standards relevant to licensing personnel, safety, aeronautical charts, rules of the air, and the development of adequate ground facilities. Has a professional staff of nearly 100 operating from Montreal, Bangkok, Cairo, Dakar, Lima, Mexico City, Nairobi, and Paris.

## International Fund for Agricultural Development
Via del Serafico 107
EUR 00142 Rome, Italy

Promotes increased agricultural production in developing countries by promoting low-cost loans and providing technical assistance.

## International Labor Organization (ILO)
Personnel Development Branch
4, route des Morillons
CH-1211 Geneva 22
Switzerland

Formulates international policies and programs for improving labor conditions, promoting employment opportunities, and creating international labor standards. Provides technical assistance as well as conducts training and research. Has a professional staff of 900 stationed in 41 countries.

### International Maritime Organization (IMO)
4 Albert Embankment
London, SE1 7SR
United Kingdom

Promotes the safety of international shipping and serves as a mechanism for cooperation in establishing international standards for ship building, navigation, pollution control, and maritime trade.

### International Telecommunications Union
Place des Nations
CH 1211 Geneva 20, Switzerland

Promotes the international cooperation among its 157 members in the field of telecommunications. Provides technical assistance to member countries for developing and improving their telecommunications systems.

### International Trade Center (ITC)
54-56 Rue de Montbrillant
CH-1202 Geneva, Switzerland

Promotes trade among member nations by developing national trade promotion strategies, training government trade officials and businesspeople in export marketing, and providing information and advice on marketing opportunities for export products.

### United Nations Educational, Scientific, and Cultural Organization (UNESCO)
2 UN Plaza, Rm. 900
New York, NY 10017
Tel. 212/963-5995

Promotes cooperation among member states in the fields of education, science, and culture. Conducts research, provides training services, and hosts international conferences.

### Universal Postal Union (UPU)
International Bureau
Weltpostrasse 4
3000 Bern 15, Switzerland

Promotes improving the organization and efficiency of the international postal system through education, training, and technical assistance.

## World Food Council (WFC)
Via della Fermedi Caracalla
00100 Rome, Italy

Promotes the increased food production and more effective distribution of food. Monitors the world food situation and attempts to coordinate government efforts to resolve food problems.

## World Health Organization (WHO)
Head, Manpower Resources
Personnel Division
20 Avenue Appia
CH-1211, Geneva 27
Switzerland

Serves as a coordinating body for international health work. Supports national health programs in developing countries, gathers and disseminates information on diseases, and establishes standards for drugs and vaccines. Has a staff of over 1,500 operating from Geneva (600) and numerous regional and field offices (900).

## World Intellectual Property Organization (WIPO)
Personnel Recruitment Section
34, chemin des Colombettes
1211-Geneva 20
Switzerland

Promotes the protection of intellectual property by encouraging member states to cooperate in matters concerning patent and trademark laws. Conducts studies and publishes newsletters, reports, and books. Has a staff of 125 stationed primarily in Geneva and Vienna.

## World Meteorological Organization (WMO)
Case postale No. 5
CH-1211
Geneva 20, Switzerland

Promotes the coordination, standardization, and improvement of meteorological activities throughout the world. Provides technical assistance for strengthen member states' meteorological and hydrological services.

# INTERNATIONAL FINANCIAL INSTITUTIONS

## Africa Development Bank
B.P. No. 1387
Abidjan, Ivory Coast

Promotes the economic and social development of its regional members by providing loans for high priority development projects.

## Asian Development Bank
2330 Roxas Boulevard
Metro Manila, Philippines

Promotes regional economic growth by providing financial assistance for development projects in Asia and the South Pacific. Provides low-cost loans for high priority projects.

## Inter-American Development Bank
1300 New York Ave., NW
Washington, DC 20577
Tel. 202/623-1000

Promotes regional economic and social development by providing financial assistance for development projects in Latin America and the Caribbean. Helps mobilize private capital from the international financial markets.

## International Monetary Fund
Recruitment Division, Room 6-525
700 19th St., NW
Washington, DC 20431
Tel. 202/623-7000

Promotes international monetary cooperation, balanced international trade, and exchange stability. It does this by monitoring the economic problems of countries and providing financial assistance when necessary for improving the balance-of-payments problems of member nations. Has a Washington-based professional staff of 2,000 and an overseas staff of 40.

## The World Bank Group

### International Bank for Reconstruction and Development (The World Bank)
1818 H Street, NW
Washington, DC 20433
Tel. 202/477-1234

The largest international lending institution primarily concerned with promoting economic development in the developing countries of Asia, Africa, and Latin America. Provides direct loans, technical assistance, and policy advice. Has a professional staff of 3,500.

### International Development Association (IDA)

Operated by the World Bank staff, IDA operates a special loan program that provides funds for the very poorest countries on concessionary terms.

### International Finance Corporation
1818 H Street, NW
Washington, DC 20433
Tel. 202/477-1234

Provides loans to and makes equity investments in private growth enterprises of developing countries. In contrast to the IBRD and IDA loans, IFC loans are not backed by government guarantees.

# REGIONAL ORGANIZATIONS

### Inter-American Defense Board
2600 16th St., NW
Washington, DC 20441
Tel. 202/939-6600

Studies and recommends to the governments of the American Republics measures necessary for close military collaboration in preparation for the collective self-defense of the American continents.

### Inter-American Institute for Cooperation on Agriculture
Apartado 55, 2200 Coronado
San Jose, Costa Rica

| U.S. address: | 1889 F St., NW, Suite 840 |
| | Washington, DC 20006 |
| | Tel. 202/458-3767 |

Promotes the agricultural development efforts of member states of the Organization of American States (OAS). Conducts research and provides technical assistance.

## International Organization for Migration
17 Route des Morillons, Grand-Saconnex
Geneva, Switzerland

| U.S. office: | 1750 K St., NW, Suite 1110 |
| | Washington, DC 20006 |
| | Tel. 202/862-1826 |

Formerly known as the Intergovernmental Committee for Migration as will as the Intergovernmental Committee for European Migration, this organization promotes the resettlement of refugees and the orderly migration of peoples to other countries for employment and educational purposes.

## North American Treaty Organization (NATO)
110 Brussels, Belgium

An intergovernmental defense alliance with 15-member nations of Europe and the North Atlantic. Promotes the peace and stability of the North Atlantic region through collective defense mechanisms and actions.

## Organization of American States (OAS)
17th St. and Constitution Ave., NW
Washington, DC 20006
Tel. 202/458-3000

Promotes the political, social, economic, and cultural cooperation of member states. Functions as a forum for resolving political disputes, enhancing regional security, and promoting trade, investment, and the transfer of technology.

## Organization for Economic Cooperation and Development (OECD)
2 rue Andre-Pascal 75775
Paris CE DEX 16, France
Tel. 4524-8200

Promotes economic growth, employment, and stability among member European countries.

## Pan American Health Organization
Chief, Manpower Planning and Staffing Unit
Department of Personnel
525 23rd St., NW
Washington, DC 20037
Tel. 202/861-3200

Promotes and coordinates the efforts of the countries of the Western Hemisphere to combat disease, lengthen life, and promote the physical and mental health of the people.

## South Pacific Commission
B.P. D-5
Noumea, New Caldeonia

Advises participating governments and administrations on matters affecting the economic and social development of the territories within SPC's area for the welfare and advancement of their people: American Samoa, Australia, the Cook Islands, the Federated States of Micronesia, Fiji, France, French Polynesia, Guam, Kiribati, the Marshall Islands, Nauru, New Caledonia, New Zealand, Niue, the Northern Mariana Islands, Palau, Papua New Guinea, Pitcairn Island, the Solomon Islands, Tokelau, Tonga, Tuvalu, the United Kingdom the United States, Vanuatu, Wallis and Futuna, and Western Samoa.

# 4

# ASSOCIATIONS, SOCIETIES, & RESEARCH INSTITUTES

*T*he United States is truly an organizational society. Every industry and interest appears to be represented by some type of organization. The organizations engage in many different types of activities: education, training, research, publishing, lobbying, and extending insurance and travel benefits to their members. While many organizations are very small and loosely structured, others are very large and are operated by full-time staffs. The largest association, the American Association of Retired Persons (AARP), has over 30 million members and is operated by a full-time staff of nearly 1,000. These organizations are disproportionately headquartered in three metropolitan areas: Washington, DC, New York City, and Chicago.

## STRATEGIES

Unknown to many job seekers, associations, societies, and research institutes offer numerous international job opportunities. Some of these organizations, such as Amnesty International and the Center for Strategic and International Studies, focus solely on the international arena. Others, such as the Chamber of Commerce of the United States and American Bar Association, have international sections within what is primarily a U.S.-oriented organization. Many of these organizations also maintain placement services or provide job assistance to their members.

If you are interested in exploring employment opportunities with associations, societies, and research institutes, you should begin examining three directories which are available in most libraries:

- **Encyclopedia of Associations** (4 volumes)
- **National Trade and Professional Associations in the U.S.**
- **Research Center Directory**

These directories also can be ordered directly from Impact Publications (see order form at the end of this book).

While all of the organizations included in this chapter are based in the United States, several thousands of similar organizations are headquartered in other countries. If you are interested in identifying these organizations, we recommend consulting the following directories:

- **Encyclopedia of Associations: International Organizations** (2 volumes)
- **Europa Year Book**
- **Yearbook of International Organizations**

These directories also are available in major libraries.

If you plan to investigate employment opportunities with these organizations in depth, we recommend contacting three organizations that maintain extensive libraries on associations as well as operate either referral or placement services for job seekers:

**American Society of Association Executives**
1575 Eye St., NW
Washington, DC 20005
Tel. 202/626-2750 (Newsletter)
    202/626-2742 (Information)

**Greater Washington Society of Association Executives**
1426 21st St., NW, Suite 200
Washington, DC 20036-5901
Tel. 202/429-9370

**U.S. Chamber of Commerce**
1615 H St., NW
Washington, DC 20062
Tel. 202/463-5560

# THE ORGANIZATIONS

The following associations, societies, and research institutes have
international interests as well as offer international job opportunities.
Several additional associations and research institutes are identified in
Chapters 6, 7, 8, and 9 as major recipients of government and foundation
funding; they provide technical assistance to developing countries while
also performing functions normally associated with associations and
research institutes. Therefore, you may want to include those organizations with the ones found in this chapter when you examine international
job opportunities with associations and research institutes.

## Aerospace Industries
## Association of America
1250 I St,. NW, Suite 1100
Washington, DC 20005-3924
Tel. 202/371-8400

This 54-member association represents the interests of manufacturers of aerospace
products—aircraft, spacecraft, guided missiles, navigation and guidance systems,
parts, accessories, and materials.

## Agribusiness Council
2550 M St., NW, Suite 275
Washington, DC 20037
Tel. 202/296-4563

The 50 members of this organization represent businesses, universities,
foundations, and others interested in promoting agribusiness for solving world
food problems. Operated by a staff of 5.

## Air Line Pilots Association, International, PAC
1625 Massachusetts Ave., NW
Washington, DC 20036-2283
Tel. 202/797-4033

This 42,000-member association is operated by a staff of 360. It serves as the collective bargaining agent for airline pilots.

## American Bar Association
750 N. Lake Shore Dr.
Chicago, IL 60611-4497
Tel. 312/988-5000

This 378,000-member association is operated by a staff of 650. Considered one of the most powerful and active interest groups in the United States. Promotes the interests of attorneys through research, education, and lobbying activities at the national, state, and local levels. Publishes the quarterly *International Lawyer* as well as operates a membership International Law and Practice Section within the association.

## American Chemical Society
1155 16th Street, NW
Washington, DC 20036-4899
Tel. 202/872-4600

One of the oldest (since 1876) and largest scientific and educational societies with a membership of nearly 145,000 and a staff of over 2,100. Conducts studies, provides special programs, monitors legislation, offers courses, publishes newsletters and journals, and offers employment assistance.

## American Concrete Institute
P.O. Box 19150
22400 W. Seven Mile Road
Detroit, MI 48219-0000
Tel. 313/532-2600

A 20,000-member technical society of engineers, architects, contractors, and educators operated by a staff of 50. Promotes improved techniques of design construction and maintenance relating to concrete products and structures. Publishes the monthly magazine *Concrete International*.

## American Enterprise Institute
1150 17th St., NW, Suite 1100
Washington, DC 20036-0000
Tel. 202/862-5800

A conservative public policy research institute operated by a staff of 100. Conducts research on a variety of domestic and foreign policy issues.

## American Geophysical Union
2000 Florida Ave., NW
Washington, DC 20009-1275
Tel. 202/462-6903

This 30,000-member organization is operated by a staff of 110. It promotes the study of geophysics through research, education, and publication programs. Involved with many international activities including publications on the Soviet Union and the Antarctic.

## American Institute for Foreign Study
102 Greenwich Avenue
Greenwich, CT 06830-5577
Tel. 203/869-9090

Has 650,000 participants and a staff of 495. Sponsors international courses, homestays, and cultural exchanges for students and teachers at all levels.

## American Institute of Chemical Engineers
345 E. 47th Street, 12th Floor
New York, NY 10017-2395
Tel. 212/705-7338

This 56,000-member professional society of chemical engineers is operated by a staff of 90. Promotes the interests of members through educational programs. Maintains a career guidance and job placement service.

## American Institute of Merchant Shipping
1000 16th St., NW, Suite 511
Washington, DC 20036
Tel. 202/775-4399

A 23-member institute operated by a staff of 6. Promotes the interests of the U.S. Merchant Marine industry (owners and operators of ocean-going vessels) through research, publication, and lobbying activities.

## American Institute of Physics
One Physics Ellipse
College Park, MD 20740
Tel. 516/576-2478

This corporation of 10 national society representing 110,000 members has a staff of 476. Promotes the development and application of physics through research, education, and publications programs. Translates and publishes several Soviet journals.

## American Insurance Association
1130 Connecticut Ave., NW, Suite 1000
Washington, DC 20036
Tel. 202/828-7100

This association of 195 members with a staff of 150 represents the interests of companies offering property and liability insurance and suretyship.

## American International
## Automobile Dealers Association
99 Canal Center Plaza, Suite 500
Alexandria, VA 22314
Tel. 703/519-7800

Represents the interests of 9,200 members who are import automobile dealers. Conducts research and issues reports on the import automobile industry.

## American Management Association International
135 W. 50th Street, 15th Floor
New York, NY 10020-1201
Tel. 202/586-8100

Includes a membership of 10,000 and a staff of 149. This is the international division of the 75,000 member American Management Association. Represents the professional interests of managers in industry, commerce, and government as well as educators and administrators abroad. Conducts training programs.

## American Forest and Paper Institute
1250 Connecticut Avenue, NW
Washington, DC 20036
Tel. 202/463-2700

This 166 member organization is operated by a staff of 140. It represents the interests of U.S. manufacturers of pulp, paper, and paperboard. Includes an International Department which focuses on the international aspects of the American paper industry.

## American Petroleum Institute
1220 L St., NW
Washington, DC 20005-4070
Tel. 202/682-8000

This association is comprised of 200 members with a staff of over 400. It represents the interests of petroleum industries, including producers, marketers, and transporters of crude oil, gasoline, natural gas, lubricating oil, and oil refiners.

## American Plywood Association
P.O. Box 11700
Tacoma, WA 98411-0700
Tel. 206/565-6600

A 136-member association operated by a staff of 180. Represents the interests of plywood manufacturers. Includes an International Markets committee.

## American Society of International Law
2223 Massachusetts Ave., NW
Washington, DC 20008-2864
Tel. 202/265-4313

A 4,200-member study group with a staff of 16. Focuses on the study and application of international law relevant to maintaining an orderly system of international relations. Members consist of lawyers, educators, government officials, students, businessmen, clergy, and others.

## Amnesty International of the USA
322 Eighth Avenue
New York, NY 10001-4808
Tel. 212/807-8400

A 300,000-member organization operated by a staff of 60. A human rights organization dedicated to freeing political detainees throughout the world.

## Automotive Parts and Accessories Association
4600 East-West Highway, Suite 300
Bethesda, MD 20814-3415
Tel. 301/654-6664

Includes a membership of over 2,000 and a staff of 30. Furthers the interests of automotive parts and accessories manufacturers, retailers, and distributors. Includes an International Trade division, a *Foreign Buyers Directory,* and a bimonthly *International Report.*

## Bank Administration Institute
1 North Franklin
Chicago, IL 60606
Tel. 312/553-4600

This 8,000-member group is operated by a staff of 160. Organized as a resource for the banking industry—conducts studies, provides information, and publishes reports. International interests center around the bimonthly international banking journal, *World of Banking: The International Magazine of Bank Management.*

## Bread for the World
802 Rhode Island Ave., NE
Washington, DC 20018-1763
Tel. 202/269-0200

A 45,000-member organization with a staff of 70. A Christian organization dedicated to fighting world hunger and poverty. Lobbies members of congress and conducts the Bread for the World program.

## Brookings Institution
1775 Massachusetts Ave., NW
Washington, DC 20036-2188
Tel. 202/797-6000

A public policy research organization and think tank operated by a staff of 241. Conducts economic, government, and foreign policy studies as well as sponsors conferences and publishes journals, reports, and books.

## CATO Institute
224 Second St., SE
Washington, DC 20003-0000
Tel. 202/546-0200

A conservative public policy research institute and think tank operated by a staff of 25. Conducts research on numerous domestic and international related issues.

## Center for Applied Linguistics
1118 22nd St., NW
Washington DC 20037
Tel. 202/429-9292

Operates with a staff of 80. Conducts research, provides technical assistance, and serves as a clearinghouse for applied linguistics. Emphasizes adult language education, literacy testing, and cross-cultural communications.

## Center for Global Education

Augsburg College
2211 Riverside Ave.
Minneapolis, MN 55454
Tel. 612/330-1159

Operated by a staff of 34. Promotes experiential education on international development. Conducts international education programs and travel seminars.

## Center for International Private Enterprise

1615 H St., NW
Washington, DC 20062
Tel. 202/463-5901

Promotes the development of voluntary business organizations and private enterprise abroad. Conducts training programs, promotes exchange programs with local U.S. Chambers of Commerce, and serves as a clearinghouse for research on international businesses.

## Center for Strategic and International Studies

1800 K Street, NW, Suite 400
Washington, DC 20006-0000
Tel. 202/887-0200

Operated with a staff of over 150, this public policy research institute and think tank conducts studies on numerous international issues. Affiliated with Georgetown University. Publishes monographs and books.

## Chamber of Commerce of the United States

1615 H St., NW
Washington, DC 20062-0001
Tel. 202/659-6000

This nationwide network of business organizations maintains important linkages to affiliated Chambers of Commerce abroad. Represents the interests of businesses. Conducts research, publishes newsletters and magazines, operates own television and radio programs, and has its own placement program for professionals. Operated by a staff of 1,100.

## Chicago Mercantile Exchange

30 S. Wacker Drive
Chicago, IL 60606-7499
Tel. 312/930-1000

This 2,724-member commodity futures exchange organization is operated by a staff of 880. Deals with live hogs, cattle, lumber, gold, foreign currencies, government securities, and options on equity futures.

## Citizen Exchange Council
12 W. 31st St., 4th Fl.
New York, NY 10001
Tel. 212/643-1985

This 750-member organization is operated by a staff of 12. Promotes mutual learning, understanding, and cooperative between Americans and citizens of the USSR by sponsoring intercultural programs involving citizens of both countries. Organizes travel groups to the USSR and coordinates conferences.

## Council for International Exchange of Scholars
3007 Tilden Street, NW
Washington, DC 20036
Tel. 202/686-4000

Operated by a staff of 75. Works with the U.S. Information Agency and the Board of Foreign Scholarships in administering the Fulbright-Hays program. Arranges for visiting scholars and awards grants and scholarships.

## Council of the Americas
680 Park Avenue
New York, NY 10021
Tel. 212/628-3200

An association of 200 members operated by a staff of 20. Represents the interests of U.S. corporations operating in Latin America. Aims to promote understanding and cooperation between U.S. corporations and the peoples and countries doing business with each other.

## Council on Foreign Relations
58 E. 68th St.
New York, NY 10021-5984
Tel. 212/734-0400

This organization of 2,500 members is operated by a staff of 95. Conducts research on international affairs. Awards grants to international specialists and publishes the popular *Foreign Affairs* journal.

## Council on International Educational Exchange
205 E. 42nd St.
New York, NY 10017-5776
Tel. 212/661-1414

Operated by a staff of 350. Promotes international education exchanges among member institutions. Administers many study programs abroad, sponsors international work camps and educational exchange programs, hosts international conferences, arranges inexpensive travel programs, issues international student identification cards, and assists U.S. students in finding summer employment abroad. Publishes several useful international education, travel, and work guides for students.

## Earthwatch
680 Mt. Auburn St., Box 403
Watertown, MA 02272
Tel. 617/926-8200

A 40,000-member research and education organization operated with a staff of 44. Places individuals who are interested in the sciences and humanities on two to three-week field research projects. Many archaeology, marine, and earth science projects are conducted abroad.

## Electronic Industries Association
2001 Pennsylvania Ave., NW
Washington, DC 20006-1807
Tel. 202/457-4900

This trade association of 1,200 members is operated by a staff of 150. It represents the interests of manufacturers of electronics. Includes a placement service and an international business council.

## Ethics and Public Policy Center
1015 15th St., NW, Suite 900
Washington, DC 20005
Tel. 202/682-1200

Operated by a staff of 165. Conducts research, publishes, and sponsors conferences on major domestic and foreign policy issues.

## Foreign Affairs Recreation Association
Department of State Building, Rm. 2928
320 21st St., NW
Washington, DC 20520
Tel. 202/647-3574

## Institute of European and Asian Studies
223 W. Ohio Street
Chicago, IL 60610
Tel. 312/944-1750

Has a staff of 36. Operates undergraduate study programs for U.S. students who attend European and Asian universities

## International Association of Drilling Contractors
15810 Park Ten Place., Suite 242
Houston, TX 77084-5139
Tel. 713/578-7171

This 2,170 member organization is operated by a staff of 30. It represents the interests of oil well contract drilling firms. Conducts research and education and training programs.

## International Association of Fire Chiefs
4025 Fair Ridge Drive
Fairfax, VA 22033
Tel. 703/273-0911

This 9,000-member association is operated by a staff of 25. Promotes the interests of fire chiefs in government, industry, and the military through research and education. Publishes the bimonthly *International Connections.*

## International Center for Development Policy
731 Eighth St., SE
Washington, DC 20003
Tel. 202/547-3800

Operated by a staff of 23. Focuses on analyzing U.S. foreign policy in developing countries of Asia, Africa, and Latin America. A public interest group that develops policy options.

## International Communications Industries Association
3150 Spring St.
Fairfax, VA 22031
Tel. 703/273-7200

A 1,500 member association managed by a staff of 15. Members are manufacturers, suppliers, and dealers of audiovisual, video, and microcomputer products. Includes international members and an international trade council.

## International Fashion Group
597 Fifth Ave., 8th Floor
New York, NY 10017
Tel. 212/593-1715

This 6,400-member organization is operated by a staff of 10. Includes 29 state groups and 10 international groups. Members are women executives in fashion and allied fields who meet on numerous topics relevant to the American and European fashion industry.

## International Federation of Accountants
114 West 47th St., Suite 2410
New York, NY 10036
Tel. 212/302-5952

This 100-member international organization with a staff of 5 represents accounting firms in 75 countries with over 1 million members. Promotes international standards for accountants.

## International Food Policy Research Institute
1776 Massachusetts Ave., NW
Washington, DC 20036-1998
Tel. 202/862-5600

Operated by a staff of 100, this research center analyzes and develops alternative public policy strategies for solving world hunger and malnutrition.

## International Foundation of Employee Benefit Plans
18700 W. Bluemound Rd.
P.O. Box 69
Brookfield, WI 53045-2922
Tel. 414/786-6700

This 31,000-member organization is operated by a staff of 110. Promotes employee benefit plans in the United States and Canada through consultation, educational programs, research, and publications.

## International Freedom Foundation
200 G St., NE, Suite 300
Washington, DC 20002
Tel. 202/546-5788

Operated by a staff of 5, this conservative organization promotes free and open societies following the principles of free enterprise. Engages in research and education programs and sponsors fellowships and international exchanges.

## International Law Institute
1615 New Hampshire Ave., NW
Washington, DC 20009
Tel. 202/483-3036

Operated by a staff of 15, the institute conducts research and training relating to the legal aspects of international business and trade. Sponsors an international exchange program and conferences.

## International Narcotics Association
112 State St., Suite 1200
Albany, NY 12207
Tel. 518/463-6232

This 7,500-member association is operated by a staff of 8. Promotes the interests of narcotic enforcement officers through education and training programs and lobbies for the improvement of international, national, state, and local laws and law enforcement pertaining to drugs. Publishes the monthly *International Drug Report*.

## International Research and Exchange Board
1616 H Street, NW
Washington, DC 20006
Tel. 202/628-8188

Sponsored by the American Council of Learned Societies and the Social Science Research council and operated with a staff of 29. Responsible for the academic exchange programs with the USSR, Bulgaria, Czechoslovakia, Germany, Hungary, Poland, Romania, and Yugoslavia.

## International Road Federation
525 School St., SW
Washington, DC 20024
Tel. 202/554-2106

Operated by a staff of 7, this 500-member organization promotes the development of highways and highway transportation throughout the world. Members are drawn from over 70 countries.

## International Schools Services
15 Roszel Road
P.O. Box 5910
Princeton, NJ 08543
Tel. 609/452-0990

Has a staff of 275. Serves as the key organization in providing educational services—personnel, procurement, facility planning, curriculum and administrative guidance—for American and international schools. Operates some schools for U.S. industry abroad. Conducts research and publishes newsletters and reports.

## International Trade Council
3114 Circle Hill Road
Alexandria, VA 22305
Tel. 703/548-1234

Consists of 850 members and a staff of 50. Promotes the free trade interests of importers and exporters in over 300 major industries. Conducts research, sponsors educational programs, and publishes reports.

## Meridian House International
1630 Crescent Pl., NW
Washington, DC 20009-4099
Tel. 202/667-6800

Operated by a staff of 100, Meridian House International promotes international understanding through intercultural exchange programs. Provides visitor service program for international visitors and diplomats as well as sponsors meetings and exhibits.

## National Association for Foreign Student Affairs
1875 Connecticut, NW, Suite 1000
Washington, DC 20009-5737
Tel. 202/462-4811

A 6,200-member organization operated by a staff of 35. Promotes international educational by working with foreign student advisers, teachers of English as a second language, U.S. students abroad, overseas education advisors, and embassy personnel involved with educational matters.

## National Association of Credit Management
8815 Centre Park Dr., Suite 2000
Columbia, MD 21045
Tel. 410/740-5560

The 1000 members of this organization are managed by a staff of 12. Promotes the interests of exporters through international credit workshops and studies.

## National Association of Broadcasters
1771 N St., NW
Washington, DC 20036-2805
Tel. 202/429-5300

This 7,500-member association is managed by a staff of 150. It represents the interests of radio and television stations and networks. Includes an International committee.

## National Association of Manufacturers (NAM)
1331 Pennsylvania Ave., NW, Suite 1500N
Washington, DC 20004-1703
Tel. 202/637-3000

This 13,500-member association is operated by a staff of 180. Represents the interests of major U.S. manufacturers relating to national and international problems. Lobbies government, maintains public relations program, and publishes information on issues and activities. Includes an International Economic Affairs policy group.

## National Association of Wheat Growers
415 Second St., NE, Suite 300
Washington, DC 20002-4900
Tel. 202/547-7800

This 60,000-member association has a staff of 15. Promotes the interests of American wheat growers through education and research. Includes an International Market Development committee.

## National Foreign Trade Council
1270 Avenue of the Americas, Suite 206
New York, NY 10020-0000
Tel. 212/399-7128

Includes 550 members and a staff of 15. Promotes the foreign trade and investment interests of its members which include manufacturers, insurance companies, law firms, exporters, importers, and foreign investors.

## National Geographic Society
1145 17th St., NW
Washington, DC 20036-4688
Tel. 202/857-7588

This 10,500,000-member organization is operated by a staff of 2,400. Promotes knowledge on geography, natural history, archaeology, astronomy, ethnology, and oceanography through research and study programs. Operates exhibits, education programs, and a large library as well as produces radio and television shows.

## National Institute for Public Policy
3031 Javier, Suite 300
Fairfax, VA 22031-4662
Tel. 703/698-0563

Operated by a staff of 20. Conducts public policy studies relating to national and international security. Sponsors seminars and publishes research findings.

## Near East Foundation
342 Madison Ave., Suite 1030
New York, NY 10173-0020
Tel. 212/867-0064

Operated by a staff of 25, the foundation promotes food production and rural and community development in the Middle East and Africa by funding start-up projects and assigning specialists to provide technical assistance abroad.

## New Orleans Board of Trade
316 Board of Trade Place
New Orleans, LA 70130
Tel. 504/525-3271

A 250-member organization consisting of representatives from banking, insurance, transportation, export-import, warehouse, and commodity industries and operated by a staff of 8. Promotes trade and commerce interests in New Orleans. Operates the Mayor's Council on International Trade and Economic Development.

## New York Board of Trade
1328 Broadway, Suite 1033
New York, NY 10001-2121
Tel. 212/661-6300

This 580 member organization is operated by a staff of 30. Promotes trade and commerce in New York through educational and cultural programs. Includes an international division.

## New York Mercantile Exchange
Four World Trade Center, 8th Floor
New York, NY 10048-0896
Tel. 212/938-2222

This 816-member commodity trade organization is operated by a staff of 227. Deals in commodity futures and trade options.

## Overseas Development Council
1717 Massachusetts Ave., NW, Suite 501
Washington, DC 20036-2058
Tel. 202/234-8701

Operates with a staff of 30. Conducts research, sponsors conferences, and publishes information for better understanding the economic and social problems facing developing countries.

## Pharmaceutical Manufacturers Association
1100 15th St., NW, Suite 900
Washington, DC 20005-1797
Tel. 202/835-3400

This association consists of 105 members and a staff of 90. It represents the interests of pharmaceutical manufacturers through research, information, and public relations activities. Includes an international section.

## Professional Secretaries International
10502 NW Ambassador Drive
Kansas City, MO 64153-1289
Tel. 816/891-6600

This 45,000 member organization of professional secretaries is operated by a staff of 30. It certifies secretaries (Certified Professional Secretary), sponsors programs, and provides insurance and retirement benefits for members.

## Rand Corporation
P.O. Box 2138
Santa Monica, CA 90407-2138
Tel. 213/393-0411

Operates with a staff of over 1000. Conducts public policy research on numerous domestic and foreign policy issues. Noted for its involvement in classified national security research. Publishes a newsletter, reports, and books.

## Rodale Institute
222 Main St.
Emmaus, PA 18098-0155
Tel. 215/967-8405

This 75,000 member association is operated by a staff of 13 and associated with the Rodale Institute. Promotes the use of regenerative agricultural techniques in preserving farms, soil, and food quality.

## Rodale Press, Inc.
33 E. Minor St.
Emmaus, PA 18098-0001
Tel. 215/967-5171

Operated by a staff of 8, Rodale International (a division of Rodale Institute) promotes the use of regenerative agriculture, gardening, preventive health, and community development techniques among small-scale producers and entrepreneurs in Africa, Asia, and Latin America. Conducts research and publishes newsletters and reports.

## Sierra Club
730 Polk Street
San Francisco, CA 94109-7897
Tel. 415/776-2211
Fax 415/776-0350

This 420,000-member organization of environmentalists is operated by a staff of 250. Seeks to stop the abuse of wilderness lands, save endangered species, and protect the global environment through grassroots conservation efforts and an extensive publication and information dissemination program. Operates programs in education, environment and natural resource management, and public policy and advocacy. Operates with a $52 million annual budget.

## Society of Petroleum Engineers
222 Palisades Creek Drive
Richardson, TX 75080-20403
Tel. 214/952-9435

This 51,000-member organization of petroleum engineers promotes the interests of petroleum engineers through research and education programs. Publishes newsletters and journals.

## South Africa Foundation
1001 Connecticut Ave., NW, Suite 822
Washington, DC 20036
Tel. 202/223-5486

A 5,000-member organization operated by a staff of 44. Represents the interests of private firms in South Africa. Promotes peaceful change in South Africa through private efforts. Provides information on South Africa.

## Trilateral Commission
345 E. 46th St.
New York, NY 10017
Tel. 212/661-1180

Operated by a staff of 16, the 300 international members of the commission are drawn from business, labor, higher education, and the media in North America, Western Europe, and Japan. Promotes cooperation among the three industrialized regions of the world through research and publications.

## US-China Business Council
1818 N. St., NW, Suite 500
Washington, DC 20036
Tel. 202/429-0340

Includes 325 members with a staff of 30. Represents the trading interests of American companies doing business in the People's Republic of China. Provides information, assistance, and business advisory services as well as sponsors conferences and briefings on trade with China.

## United States Council for International Business
1212 Avenue of the Americas
New York, NY 10036
Tel. 212/354-4480

Consisting of 300 members and operated by a staff of 27, this council is part of the International Chamber of Commerce. Represents the interests of multinational enterprises to governments and maintains communication among members through publications and meetings.

## United States Olympic Committee
1750 E. Boulder St.
Colorado Springs, CO 80909-5760
Tel. 719/632-5551

This 58-member organization is operated by a staff of 60. Consisting of a federation of amateur sports governing bodies, it is responsible for supporting the U.S. Olympic Team. Operates three Olympic Training Centers.

## World Future Society
7910 Woodmont Ave., Suite 450
Bethesda, MD 20814-0000
Tel. 301/656-8274

This 30,000-member association is operated by a staff of 13. It promotes the study of the future through research, education, and publication programs.

## World Learning
Kipling Road
P.O. Box 676
Brattleboro, VT 05302-06676
Tel. 802/257-7751

Operates with a staff of 250. Previously known as the Experiment in International Living School for International Training, World Learning provides extensive international educational, training, travel, and development services. Conducts language classes, sponsors homestay and travel programs, and offers a four-year college degree program in world studies.

## World Neighbors
4127 NW 122nd.
Oklahoma City, OK 73120-8869
Tel. 405/752-9700

A 10,000-member organization operated by a staff of 28. Promotes world understanding by sponsoring community development and self-help efforts in 17 countries of Asia, Africa, and Latin America.

## World Trade Center of New Orleans
Two Canal St., Suite 2900
New Orleans, LA 70130
Tel. 504/529-1601

This 3,300 member organization is operated by a staff of 140. Organized to promote international trade, friendship, and understanding by sponsoring visits of foreign VIPs and sending U.S. business and civic leaders abroad. Sponsors language programs and produces television programs on international affairs.

## Youth for Understanding International Exchange
3501 Newark St., NW
Washington, DC 20016-3167
Tel. 202/966-6800

Operates with a staff of 250. Sponsors international student exchange programs for teenagers as well as administers scholarship programs.

# 5

# BUSINESSES

***B***usinesses employ the largest number of individuals in the international arena. Indeed, as the world economy continues to expand and nations become more interdependent, so too does international trade and the role of international businesses.

While businesses may employ many people internationally, don't expect to find many entry-level international business positions except in sales. In contrast to other types of organizations which may hire individuals for entry-level international positions, many businesses promote employees to positions that involve international operations only *after* several years of progressive experience within the organization.

The businesses identified in this chapter represent only a few, albeit some of the largest firms, with international operations. For a more complete listing, including U.S. firms operating in specific countries, consult the following directories which are available at most major libraries:

- **World Business Directory**
- **Directory of American Firms Operating in Foreign Countries**
- **Directory of Foreign Firms Operating in the U.S.**

- The International Corporate 1,000
- The Multinational Marketing and Employment Directory
- American Register of Exporters and Importers
- Dun and Bradstreet Exporter's Encyclopedia
- Hoover's Handbook of World Business
- Jane's Major Companies of Europe
- Principal International Business
- Directory of U.S. Firms Operating in Latin America
- Major Companies of Europe

In addition, many of the contracting and consulting firms identified in Chapter 6 could be incorporated with those found in this chapter. Large firms, such as the M. W. Kellogg Company, Ralph M. Parson Company, Metcalf & Eddy International, and Lummus Crest, operate throughout the world in developing and implementing major engineering and construction projects, especially roads, bridges, dams, airports, tunnels, sewerage systems, nuclear power facilities, petrochemical factories, and pharmaceutical plants. Chapter 6 also includes numerous businesses involved in providing financial and technical assistance services to developing countries in the areas of accounting, agricultural development, health care, education, and energy. Major firms such as Ernst & Young and Coopers & Lybrand are identified there too. You may also want to get a copy of *The National Directory of Addresses and Phone Numbers* which includes the names, addresses, and phone numbers of thousands of businesses involved in the international arena.

# MAJOR CORPORATIONS

**Allied Signal Corporation**
*aerospace, chemical, oil, gas*
Columbia Road & Park Ave.
Morristown, NJ 07962-4658
Tel. 201/455-2000

**Amerada Hess**—*petroleum exploration and production*
1185 Ave. of the Americas
New York, NY 10036-2665
Tel. 212/997-8500

**American Cyanimid**
*pharmaceuticals, chemicals, toiletries*
One Cyanimid Plaza
Wayne, NJ 07470-8428
Tel. 201/831-2000

**American Home Products**
*prescription drugs and home products*
685 Third Avenue
New York, NY 10017-4085
Tel. 212/878-5000

**American International Group**—*insurance*
70 Pine St.
New York, NY 10270-0002
Tel. 212/770-7000

**AT&T**—*communications*
550 Madison Ave.
New York, NY 10022-3297
Tel. 212/605-5500

**Avon Products, Inc.**
*cosmetics*
9 West 57th Street
New York, NY 10019-2683
Tel. 212/546-6015

**Bell & Howell Co.**
*business equipment*
6800 N. McCormack Blvd.
Chicago, IL 60645-2775
Tel. 708/675-7600

**BellSouth Corporation**
*communications*
1155 W. Peachtree St., NE
Atlanta, GA 30367-6000
Tel. 404/249-2000

**Black & Decker**—*electrical tools and machines*
701 East Joppa Road
Baltimore, MD 21204-5559
Tel. 410/583-3900

**Boeing Company**—*aircraft and aerospace manufacturer*
P.O. Box 3707
Seattle, WA 98124-2207
Tel. 206/655-2121

**Borg-Warner Corporation**
*automotive parts, chemicals*
200 S. Michigan
Chicago, IL 60604-2488
Tel. 312/322-8500

**Carnation Company**
*food manufacturer*
800 Brand Blvd.
Glendale, CA 90036-0000
Tel. 818/549-6000

**Caterpillar Tractor Company**
*earthmoving equipment*
100 N.E. Adams St.
Peoria, IL 61629-0001
Tel. 309/675-1000

**Chevron USA, Inc.**—*oil*
575 Market St.
San Francisco, CA 94103-2894
Tel. 415/894-7700

**The Coca-Cola Company**
*beverage manufacturer*
P.O. Drawer 1734
Atlanta, GA 30301-1734
Tel. 404/676-2121

**CPC International**
*food manufacturer*
International Plaza
700 Sylvan Ave.
Englewood Cliffs, NJ 07632
Tel. 201/894-4000

**Chubb & Son, Inc.**
*insurance*
15 Mountain View Road
P.O. Box 1615
Warren, NJ 07061-1615
Tel. 908/580-2063

**Coopers & Lybrand**
*financial services*
1251 Avenue of the Americas
New York, NY 10020
Tel. 212/536-2000

**Dow Chemical Company**
*chemical manufacturer*
Willard H. Dow Center
Suite 2030
Midland, MI 48674-0001
Tel. 517/636-1000

**Du Pont El de Nemours
& Co., Inc.**—*chemicals*
1007 Market Street
Wilmington, DE 19898
Tel. 302/774-1000

**Eastman Kodak**—*photographic
supplies and equipment*
343 State Street
Rochester, NY 14650-0001
Tel. 716/724-4000

**Eli Lilly & Co.**
*pharmaceutics and cosmetics*
Lilly Corporate Center
Indianapolis, IN 46285-0001
Tel. 317/276-2000

**Emerson Electric Company**
*electronics manufacturer*
8000 West Florissant Avenue
St. Louis, MO 63136-1415
Tel. 314/553-2000

**Exxon Corporation**—*oil*
225 E. John W. Carpenter Fwy
Irving, TX 75062-2298
Tel. 214/444-1000

**Firestone Tire & Rubber Co.**
*tire producer*
2500 N. 22nd St.
Decatur, IL 62526-4744
Tel. 217/428-2141

**Ford Motor Company**
*auto manufacturer*
The American Road
Dearborn, MI 48121-0000
Tel. 313/322-3000

**General Dynamics Corp.**
*aerospace, chemical, oil, gas*
300 Wall St.
Abilene, TX 79603
Tel. 915/691-2000

**General Electric**—*electronics,
consumer products*
3135 Easton Turnpike
Fairfield, CT 06431-0001
Tel. 203/373-2211

**General Motors Corporation**
*auto manufacturer*
3-251 GM Building
3044 West Grand Blvd.
Detroit, MI 48202
Tel. 313/556-5000

**Goodyear Tire & Rubber Co.**
*tire manufacturer*
1144 East Market St.
Akron, OH 44316-0001
Tel. 216/796-2121

**Grumman International**
*aircraft and aerospace*
1111 Stewart Avenue
Bethpage, NY 11714-3533
Tel. 516/575-0574

**Hewlett-Packard Co.**
*computers and electronics*
3000 Hanover St.
Palo Alto, CA 94304-1185
Tel. 415/857-1501

**Honeywell**—*computers and
automated systems*
Honeywell Plaza
2701 4th Ave., South
Minneapolis, MN 55408-1746
Tel. 612/951-1000

**IBM**—*computers, electronics*
Old Orchard Road
Armonk, NY 10504-1783
Tel. 914/765-1900

**ITT**—*communications, hotels,
electronics, finance, wood*
1330 Avenue of the Americas
New York, NY 10019
Tel. 212/258-1000

**Johnson & Johnson**
*health care products*
One Johnson & Johnson Plaza
New Brunswick, NJ 08933
Tel. 908/524-0400

**Johnson Controls, Inc.**
*plastic containers, auto seats
and batteries, commercial
facility control systems*
P.O. Box 591
Milwaukee, WI 53201-0591
Tel. 414/228-2339

**Lockheed Corporation**
*aircraft and aerospace*
4500 Park Granada Blvd.
Calabasas, CA 91399
Tel. 818/876-2000

**Minnesota Mining and Man-
ufacturing Co. (DBA 3M)**
*3M product line*
3M Center Staffing Dept.
Building 224-1W-01
St. Paul, MN 55144-0001
Tel. 612/733-1110

**Monsanto Chemical Co.**
*chemicals*
800 North Lindbergh Blvd.
St. Louis, MO 63167-0001
Tel. 314/694-1000

**Motorola, Inc.**
*electronics manufacturer*
1303 E. Algonquin Rd.
Schaumburg, IL 60196-1079
Tel. 708/576-5000

**Nike, Inc.**—*footwear,
apparel and accessories*
One Bowerman Drive
Beaverton, OR 97005
Tel. 503/671-6495

**PepsiCo Food Services
International**
*beverage manufacturer*
700 Anderson Hill Road
Building 2/3
Purchase, NY 10057-0000
Tel. 914/253-2000

**Pfizer International**
*pharmaceuticals
and health care*
235 East 42nd St.
New York, NY 10017
Tel. 212/573-2323

**Philip Morris, Inc.**
*tobacco and beverages*
120 Park Avenue
New York, NY 10017-5592
Tel. 212/880-5000

**Phillips Petroleum Co.**
*oil and gas producer*
4th & Keeler St.
5 D4 Phillips Building
Bartlesville, OK 74004-0001
Tel. 918/661-6600

**Procter & Gamble
International (SY-4)**
*consumer products*
P.O. Box 599
Cincinnati, OH 45201-0599
Tel. 513/983-1100

**Raytheon Company**—*high-tech
electronics producer*
141 Spring St.
Lexington, MA 02173-7899
Tel. 617/862-6600

**Revlon Group**—*cosmetics*
49th Floor
New York, NY 10153-0000
Tel. 212/572-5190

**R. J. Reynolds Tobacco**
*tobacco products*
401 N. Main St.
Winston-Salem, NC 27105
Tel. 919/741-5000

**Rockwell International Corp.**
*aviation and electronics*
625 Liberty Ave.
Pittsburgh, PA 15222-3123
Tel. 412/565-2000

**Sperry Univac**
*computers and data
processing equipment*
P.O. Box 500
Blue Bell, PA 19424
Tel. 215/542-4011

**Sprint International**
*telecommunications*
12490 Sunrise Valley Drive
Reston, VA 22096
Tel. 703/689-5469

**Texaco, Inc.**—*oil producer*
2000 Westchester Avenue
White Plains, NY 10650-0001
Tel. 914/253-4000

**Texas Instruments, Inc.**
*computers and electronics*
13500 N. Central Expressway
Dallas, TX 75243
Tel. 214/995-3333

**TRW, Inc.**—*electronics and
equipment producer*
1900 Richmond Road
Cleveland, OH 44124-3760
Tel. 216/291-7000

**Union Carbide**—*chemical and
plastics manufacturer*
39 Old Ridgebury Road
Danbury, CT 06817-0001
Tel. 203/794-2000

**Unisys Corp.**—*computers*
P.O. Box 500
Blue Bell, PA 19424
Tel. 215/986-3527

**Weyerhaeuser Company**
*wood producer*
33663 Weyerhaeuser Way S.
Tacoma, WA 98603
Tel. 206/924-2345

**Xerox Corporation**
*computers, data processing,
office products*
800 Long Ridge Road
Stamford, CT 06902-1288
Tel. 203/968-3000

# BANKING
# AND FINANCE

**Advent International**
101 Federal Street
Boston, MA 02110
Tel. 617/951-9400

**Alliance Capital Management**
1345 Avenue of the Americas
New York, NY 10105
Tel. 212/969-1000

**Allied Irish Bank**
405 Park Avenue
New York, NY 10022
Tel. 212/339-8000

**American Express Co., Inc.**
International Bank
American Express Tower
New York, NY 10285-0001
Tel. 212/640-2000

**American Scandanavian
Banking Corp.**
437 Madison Ave.
New York, NY 10022
Tel. 212/371-1090

**Bank of Boston Corp.**
100 Federal Street
Boston, MA 02110-1898
Tel. 617/434-2200

**Bank of New York Co, Inc.**
48 Wall Street
New York, NY 10286-0001
Tel. 212/408-7000

**Bank of Tokyo Trust Co.**
100 Broadway
New York, NY 10005-1995
Tel. 212/766-3400

**BankAmerica**
201 California St.
San Francisco, CA 94111-5083
Tel. 415/445-4000

**Bankers Trust Co.**
280 Park Avenue
New York, NY 10017-1270
Tel. 212/250-2500

**Banque National de Paris**
BNP International
Financial Services
499 Park Avenue
New York, NY 10022
Tel. 212/418-8200

**Barclays Bank of New York**
300 Park Ave.
New York, NY 10022-7455
Tel. 212/418-4600

**Brown Brothers
Harriman & Co.**
59 Wall Street
New York, NY 10005-2818
Tel. 212/483-1818

**Chemical Bank**
277 Park Avenue
2nd Floor
New York, NY 10172-0087
Tel. 212/310-6161

**Citicorp**
399 Park Avenue
New York, NY 10043-0001
Tel. 212/559-1000

**Continental Bank NA**
231 S. LaSalle St.
Chicago, IL 60697
Tel. 312/828-2345

**Credit Agricole**
520 Madison Ave., 8th Fl.
New York, NY 10022
Tel. 212/418-2200

**Credit Lyonnais
Securities USA**
CL Global Partners
95 Wall St.
New York, NY 10005
Tel. 212/428-6100

**Credit Suisse**
100 Wall Street
New York, NY 10005
Tel. 212/612-8000

**Creditanstalt-Bankverein**
245 Park Avenue
27th Floor
New York, NY 10167
Tel. 212/856-1000

**Dai-Ichi Kangyo Bank**
770 Wilshire Blvd.
Los Angeles, CA 90017-3897
Tel. 213/612-6400

**Deutsche Bank Capital Corp.**
31 W. 52nd Street
8th Floor
New York, NY 10019-6160
Tel. 212/474-7000

**Dillon, Read, and Co.**
535 Madison Avenue
New York, NY 10022-4266
Tel. 212/906-7000

**Dresdner Bank**
75 Wall St.
New York, NY 10005
Tel. 212/574-0100

**European American Bank**
EAB Plaza
Uniondale, NY 11555-0001
Tel. 212/557-3700

**Federal Reserve Bank
of New York**
Federal Reserve P.O. Station
33 Liberty St.
New York, NY 10045-1011
Tel. 212/720-500

**Fidelity Group**
Broad and Walnut
Philadelphia, PA 19109
Tel. 215/985-6000

**First Boston, Inc.**
55 E. 52nd St.
New York, NY 10055-0001
Tel. 212/909-2000

**First Interstate Bancorp**
633 W. 5th St., 72nd Floor
Los Angeles, CA 90017
Tel. 213/614-3001

**First National Bank
of Boston**
100 Federal Street
Boston, MA 02110
Tel. 617/434-2200

**French American Banking
Corporation**
200 Liberty Street
20th Floor
New York, NY 10281-1003
Tel. 212/978-5700

**Fuji Bank**
2 World Trade Center
79th Floor
New York, NY 10048
Tel. 212/898-9407

**Goldman, Sachs & Co.**
85 Broad Street
New York, NY 10004-2456
Tel. 212/902-1000

**Industrial Bank of Japan**
245 Park Avenue
22nd Floor
New York, NY 10167-0038
Tel. 212/557-3500

**J.P. Morgan & Co., Inc.**
60 Wall Street
New York, NY 10260-0060
Tel. 212/483-2323

**Keefe, Bruyette, and Woods**
2 World Trade Center
85th Floor
New York, NY 10048-0203
Tel. 212/323-8300

**Kidder Peabody and Co.**
10 Hanover Square
New York, NY 10005-3592
Tel. 212/510-3000

**Kleinwort, Benson, Inc.**
200 Park Avenue
New York, NY 10166-0005
Tel. 212/983-4000

**Long-Term
Capital Management**
Greenwich Capital Markets
600 Steamboat Road
Greenwich, CT 06830
Tel. 203/861-2663

**Manufacturers
Hanover Corp.**
270 Park Avenue
New York, NY 10017-2040
Tel. 212/270-6000

**Marine Midland Bank**
237 Main St.
Buffalo, NY 14203-2702
Tel. 716/841-2424

**Mellon Bank Corporation**
Mellon Bank Center
Pittsburgh, PA 15258-0001
Tel. 412/234-5000

**Merrill Lynch & Co., Inc.**
250 Veseu Street
World Financial Building
North Tower
New York, NY 10081-1331
Tel. 212/449-9836

**Mitsubishi International Corp.**
520 Madison Ave., 42nd Fl.
New York, NY 10022-4223
Tel. 212/605-2000

**Morgan Guaranty Trust Company of New York**
60 Wall Street
New York, NY 10260-0023
Tel. 212/483-2323

**Morgan Stanley Group**
1251 Ave. of the Americas
New York, NY 10020-1181
Tel. 212/703-7105

**National Westminster Bank**
175 Water Street
New York, NY 10038-4987
Tel. 212/602-1000

**Nordic American Bankir Corporation**
600 5th Avenue
New York, NY 10022
Tel. 212/645-4220

**Normura Securities**
2 World Financial Center
Bldg. B
New York, NY 10281-1198
Tel. 212/667-9300

**Northern Trust**
50 LaSalle St.
Chicago, IL 60675-0001
Tel. 312/630-6000

**Paine-Weber Group**
1285 Ave. of the Americas
New York, NY 10019-6093
Tel. 212/713-2000

**Philadelphia National Bank**
5th & Market Streets
Philadelphia, PA 19101-0001
Tel. 215/973-8400

**Republic New York Corp.**
425 5th Avenue
New York, NY 10018-2790
Tel. 212/525-6225

**Salomon Brothers Inc.**
7 World Trade Center
New York, NY 10048-1196
Tel. 212/783-7000

**Sanwa Bank California**
444 Market St.
San Francisco, CA 94111-5381
Tel. 415/772-8200

**Shawmut National Corporation**
One Federal Street
Boston, MA 02211-0001
Tel. 617/292-2000

**Smith Barney**
1345 Ave. of the Americas
New York, NY 10105-0216
Tel. 212/399-6000

**Societe Generale Financial Corp.**
50 Rockefeller Center
New York, NY 10020
Tel. 212/698-0500

**Sumitomo Bank of California**
320 California St.
San Francisco, CA 94104
Tel. 415/445-8000

**Tokai Bank**
534 W. 6th Street
Los Angeles, CA 90014
Tel. 213/972-0200

**Wells Fargo Bank**
20 Montgomery St.
San Francisco, CA 94163
Tel. 415/396-2392

**Western Bancorporation**
1251 Westwood Blvd.
Los Angeles, CA 90024
Tel. 310/477-2401

# CONSULTING

**American Management Systems**
1777 N. Kent Street
Arlington, VA 22209
Tel. 703/841-6000

**Andersen Consulting**
69 Washington St.
Chicago, IL 60602
Tel. 312/580-0069

**Bain and Co.**
2 Copley Place
Boston, MA 02117
Tel. 617/572-2000

**Booz, Allen, and Hamilton**
101 Park Avenue
New York, NY 10178
Tel. 212/697-1900

**Boston Consulting Group**
1 Exchange Pl.
Boston, MA 02109
Tel. 617/973-1200

**Data Resources, Inc.**
24 Hartwell Avenue
Lexington, MA 02173
Tel. 817/863-5100

**Deloitte and Touche**
1 World Trade Center
Suite 9300
New York, NY 10048
Tel. 212/839-6600

**Ernst and Young**
277 Park Ave.
New York, NY 10172
Tel. 212/773-3000

**Frost and Sullivan**
106 Fulton Street
New York, NY 10038
Tel. 212/233-1080

**Hay Group**
229 S. 18th Street
Philadelphia, PA 19103
Tel. 215/875-2300

**Hewitt Associates**
100 Half Day Road
Lincolnshire, IL 60015
Tel. 312/295-5000

**Hill and Knowlton**
420 Lexington
New York, NY 10017
Tel. 708/295-5000

**Jones Lang Wooton USA**
101 E. 52nd St.
New York, NY 10022
Tel. 212/688-8181

**A.T. Kearney**
222 S. Riverside Plaza
Chicago, IL 60606
Tel. 312/648-0111

**Arthur D. Little Inc.**
25 Acorn Park
Cambridge, MA 02140
Tel. 617/864-5770

**McKinsey and Co. Inc.**
55 E. 52nd Street
New York, NY 10022
Tel. 212/446-7000

**Mercer Consulting Group**
1166 Ave. of the Americas
New York, NY 10036
Tel. 212/345-4500

**KPMG Peat-Marwick**
767 5th Avenue
New York, NY 10153
Tel. 212/909-5000

**Price Waterhouse**
1251 Ave. of the Americas
New York, NY 10020
Tel. 212/819-5000

**Kurt Salmon Associates**
1355 Peachtree St., NE
Atlanta, GA 30309
Tel. 404/892-0321

**Theodore Barry & Assoc.**
1520 Wilshire Blvd.
Los Angeles, CA 90017
Tel. 213/413-6080

**Towers, Perrin, Foster, and Crosby**
245 Park Avenue, 18th Fl.
New York, NY 10167
Tel. 213/309-3400

# LAW

**Cleary, Gottlieb, Steen, and Hamilton**
One Liberty Plaza
New York, NY 10006
Tel. 212/225-2000

**Coudert Brothers**
200 Park Avenue
New York, NY 10166
Tel. 212/880-4400

**Covington and Burling**
1201 Pennsylvania Ave., NW
Washington, DC 20004
Tel. 202/662-6000

**Debevoise & Plimpton**
875 Third Avenue
New York, NY 10022
Tel. 212/909-6000

**Gibson, Dunn, and Crutcher**
333 S. Grand Avenue
Los Angeles, CA 90071
Tel. 213/229-7631

**Mudge, Rose, Guthrie, Alexander, and Ferdon**
2121 K Street, NW, Suite 700
Washington, DC 20037
Tel. 202/429-9355

**Patton, Boggs, and Blow**
2550 M Street, NW, Suite 800
Washington, DC 20037
Tel. 202/457-6000

**Pennie and Edmonds**
1155 Ave. of the Americas
New York, NY 10036
Tel. 212/790-9090

**Sullivan & Cromwell**
125 Broad Street
New York, NY 10004
Tel. 212/558-4000

**White and Case**
1155 Ave. of the Americas
New York, NY 10036
Tel. 212/819-8200

# COMMUNICATIONS, MEDIA, JOURNALISM

## ■ Broadcasting

**Cable News Network**
100 International Blvd.
Atlanta, GA 30303
Tel. 404/827-1500

**Capital Cities/ABC, Inc.**
77 W. 66th St.
New York, NY 10023
Tel. 212/456-7777

**CBS Inc.**
51 W. 52nd Avenue
New York, NY 10019
Tel. 212/975-4321

**National Broadcasting Company (NBC)**
30 Rockefeller Plaza
New York, NY 10012
Tel. 212/664-4444

**Radio Free Europe/Radio Liberty, Inc.**
Production Center
1201 Connecticut Ave., NW
Washington, DC 20036
Tel. 202/457-6900

**Turner Broadcasting System**
One CNN Center
100 International Blvd.
Atlanta, GA 30303
Tel. 404/827-1700

■ **Magazines**

**Business International**
215 Park Avenue
New York, NY 10003
Tel. 212/460-0600

**Business Week**
1221 Ave. of the Americas
New York, NY 10020
Tel. 212/512-2511

**Diplomatic World Bulletin**
99 Wall Street
New York, NY 10005

**The Economist**
111 W. 57th St.
New York, NY 10019
Tel. 212/541-5730

**Forbes, Inc.**
60 5th Avenue
New York, NY 10011
Tel. 212/620-2200

**Foreign Affairs Journal**
58 E. 68th Street
New York, NY 10021
Tel. 212/734-0400

**Fortune Magazine**
Time and Life Building
Rockefeller Center
New York, NY 10020
Tel. 212/522-1212

**National Geographic**
17th and M Streets, NW
Washington, DC 20036
Tel. 202/857-7000

**Newsweek, Inc.**
444 Madison Avenue
New York, NY 10022
Tel. 212/350-4000

**Time, Inc.**
Time and Life Building
Rockefeller Center
New York, NY 10020
Tel. 212/522-1212

**U.N.I.C.E.F. News**
United Nations
New York, NY 10017

■ **Motion Pictures & TV Production**

**Columbia Pictures**
711 5th Avenue
New York, NY 10022
Tel. 212/751-4400

**Tri-Star Pictures**
711 5th Avenue
New York, NY 10022
Tel. 212/751-4400

**Viscom International**
350 5th Avenue
Suite 8208
New York, NY 10118

**Warner Communications Co.**
239 Lorraine Ave.
Upper Montclair, NJ 07043
Tel. 201/746-7900

## ■ Newspapers

**Christian Science Monitor**
1 Norway St.
Boston, MA 02115
Tel. 617/450-2000

**Gannett**
1100 Wilson Blvd.
Arlington, VA 22234
Tel. 703/284-6000

**Hearst Corporation**
959 8th Avenue
New York, NY 10019
Tel. 212/649-2000

**Knight-Ridder Newspapers**
One Herald Plaza
6th Floor
Miami, FL 33132
Tel. 305/376-3800

**Los Angeles Times**
Times Mirror Square
Los Angeles, CA 90053
Tel. 213/237-5000

**New York Times**
229 W. 43rd St.
New York, NY 10036
Tel. 212/556-1234

**Wall Street Journal**
Dow Jones and Co.
200 Liberty St.
New York, NY 10281
Tel. 212/416-2000

**Washington Post**
1150 15th St., NW
Washington, DC 20071
Tel. 202/334-6000

## ■ News Services

**Associated Press**
50 Rockefeller Plaza
New York, NY 10020
Tel. 212/621-1500

**Foreign Press Association**
110 E. 59th St.
New York, NY 10022
Tel. 212/826-4452

**Reuters Information Services**
Fleet Street
London EC4P4AJ, England

**United Press International**
1400 I St., NW, Suite 800
Washington, DC 20005
Tel. 202/898-8000

# TRANSLATING AND INTERPRETING

**All-Languages Services, Inc.**
545 Fifth Avenue
New York, NY 10017
Tel. 212/986-1688

**Berlitz Translation Services**
257 Park Ave. South
New York, NY 10010
Tel. 212/777-7878

**Lindner Translations, Inc.**
29 Broadway
New York, NY 10006
Tel. 212/213-9881

**Rennert Bilingual Translations**
2 West 45th St., 5th Fl.
New York, NY 10036
Tel. 212/819-1776

**Translation Aces, Inc.**
29 Broadway
New York, NY 10006
Tel. 212/269-4660

**Translation Company
of America**
10 West 37th St., 3rd Floor
New York, NY 10018
Tel. 212/563-7054

**University Language
Services, Inc.**
517 West 113th Street
Suite 52
New York, NY 10025
Tel. 212/316-5581

# TRAVEL

## ▪ Associations

**American Society of
Travel Agents**
1101 King St., Suite 200
Alexandria, VA 22314
Tel. 703/739-2782

**Association of Retail
Travel Agents**
25 South Riverside Avenue
Croton, NY 10520
Tel. 914/271-9000

**Hotel Sales and Marketing
Association International**
1300 L St., NW, Suite 800
Washington, DC 20005
Tel. 202/789-0089

**Society of Incentive
Travel Executives**
271 Madison Avenue
New York, NY 10016
Tel. 212/889-9340

## ▪ Airlines

**American Airlines Inc.**
P.O. Box 619616, MG3K28
DFW Airport
Dallas, TX 75261
Tel. 817/963-1234

**Continental Airlines, Inc.**
2929 Allen Parkway
Houston, TX 77019
Tel. 713/834-5000

**Delta Airlines**
Hartsfield International Airport
P.O. Box 20532
Atlanta, GA 30320
Tel. 404/715-2600

**Northwest Airlines**
Minneapolis-St. Paul
International Airport
St. Paul, MN 55111
Tel. 612/726-2111

**Trans World Airlines, Inc.**
100 South Bedford Road
Mt. Kisco, NY 10549
Tel. 914/242-3000

**United Airlines, Inc.**
1200 E. Algonquin Rd.
Elk Grove Village, IL 60007
Tel. 708/952-4000

**Virgin Atlantic**
96 Morton Street
New York, NY 10014
Tel. 212/206-6612

# ▪ Cruiselines

**Clipper Cruise Line**
7711 Bonhomme Avenue
St. Louis, MO 63105
Tel. 314/727-2929

**Commodore Cruise Line**
800 Douglas Rd.
Coral Gables, FL 3313
Tel. 305/529-3000

**Cunard Line, Ltd.**
555 Fifth Avenue
New York, NY 10017
Tel. 212/880-7500

**Norwegian Cruise Lines**
95 Merrick Way
Coral Cables, FL 33134
Tel. 305/447-9660

**Royal Caribbean Cruise Line**
1050 Caribbean Way
Miami, FL 33132
Tel. 305/379-2601

**Sun Line Cruises**
1 Rockefeller Plaza
New York, NY 10020
Tel. 800/872-6400

# ▪ Auto Companies

**Avis Rent-A-Car
Systems, Inc.**
900 Old Country Rd.
Garden City, NY 11530-2181
Tel. 516/222-3000

**Budget Rent-A-Car Corp.**
4255 Naperville Rd.
Lisle, IL 60532
Tel. 708/955-1900

**Hertz Corp.**
225 Brae Blvd.
Park Ridge, NJ 07656-1870
Tel. 201/307-2000

**Thrifty Rent-A-Car
System, Inc.**
5350 E 31st St.
Tulsa, OK 74135
Tel. 918/665-3930

# ▪ Travel Agencies

**Arrington Travel Center**
55 West Monroe St.
Suite 2450
Chicago, IL 60603
Tel. 312/726-4900

**Austin Travel Corporation**
219 South Service Road
Plainview, NY 11803
Tel. 516/752-9100

**Corporate Travel Services**
300 Lakeside Dr,. Suite 250
Oakland, CA 94612
Tel. 510/832-3100

**Crimson Travel Service, Inc.**
39 J.F.K. Street
Cambridge, MA 02138
Tel. 617/868-2600

**Garber Travel Service, Inc.**
1047 Commonwealth Ave.
Boston, MA 02215
Tel. 617/787-0600

**Morris Travel—Ask
Mr. Foster**
240 East Morris Avenue
Salt Lake, City, UT 84115
Tel. 801/487-9731

**Northwestern Business Travel**
7250 Metro Blvd.
Minneapolis, MN 55439
Tel. 612/921-3700

**Omega World Travel**
5203 Leesburg Pike
Two Skyline Plaza
Falls Church, VA 22041
Tel. 703/998-2990

**Rosenbluth Travel**
1515 Walnut St.
Philadelphia, PA 19102
Tel. 215/563-1070

**Sunbelt Travel**
909 E. Las Colinas Blvd.
Irving, TX 75039
Tel. 214/401-0210

**Travel and Transport**
9777 M Street
Omaha, NE 68127
Tel. 402/592-4100

**Wagons—Lits Travel, USA**
7812 McEwen Rd.
Dayton, OH 45459
Tel. 513/435-7397

■ **Hotels**

**Clarion Hotels & Resorts**
10750 Columbia Pike
Silver, Spring, MD 20901
Tel. 301/593-5600

**Club Mediterranee** (French)
40 West 57th St.
New York, NY 10019
Tel. 212/977-2100

**Hilton International**
605 3rd Avenue
New York, NY 10158
Tel. 212/973-2200

**Holiday Inns, Inc.**
3 Ravinia Drive
Suite 2000
Atlanta, FL 30346
Tel. 404/604-2000

**Hyatt Hotels Corp.**
200 W. Madison Ave.
Madison Plaza
Chicago, IL 60606
Tel. 312/750-1234

**Inter-Continental Hotels Corp.**
1120 Avenue of the Americas
New York, NY 10036
Tel. 212/852-6400

**ITT-Sheraton**
60 State St.
Boston, MA 02109-6002
Tel. 617/367-3600

**Marriott Corp.**
10400 Fernwood Rd.
Bethesda, MD 20817
Tel. 301/380-9000

**Meridien Hotels**
888 7th Ave, 27th Floor
New York, NY 10016-4895
Tel. 212/956-3501

**Nikko Hotels International**
1700 Broadway
New York, NY 10019
Tel. 212/765-4890

**Omni Hotels International**
500 Lafayette Rd.
Hampton, NH 03842-3625
Tel. 603/926-8911

**Pan Pacific Hotels**
1717 West Street
Anaheim, CA 92802
Tel. 714/999-0990

**Ramada, Hospitality
& Franchise**
3838 E. Van Buren
Phoenix, AZ 85008
Tel. 602/273-4000

**Regent International Hotels**
132 S. Rodeo Dr.
Beverly Hills, CA 90212
Tel. 310/275-8858

**Westin Hotels & Resorts**
2001 6th Avenue
Seattle, WA 98121
Tel. 206/443-5000

### ▪ Incentive Travel Wholesalers

**Carlson Marketing Group**
111 N. Main St.
Dayton, OH 45402-1709
Tel. 513/226-5000

**Maritz Travel**
1395 N. Highway Dr.
Fenton, MO 63099-0000
Tel. 314/827-2284

# FOREIGN FIRMS IN THE U.S.

**BASF Corp.** (German)
*chemicals, paints, inks*
8 Campus Dr.
Parsipanny, NJ 07054
Tel. 201/397-2700

**British Petroleum
Exploration, Inc.**—*oil*
5151 San Felipe
Houston, TX 77056
Tel. 713/552-8500

**Casio Inc.** (Japanese)—*watches,
computers, electronics*
570 Mt. Pleasant Ave.
Dover, NJ 07801
Tel. 201/361-5400

**Daimler-Benz
North American Corp.**
*autos*
375 Park Avenue
New York, NY 10152
Tel. 212/308-3622

**Fiat USA** (Italian)—*autos*
777 Terrace Ave.
Hasbrouck Heights, NJ 07604
Tel. 201/393-4000

**Heineken** (Dutch)
*beverages*
Van Munching & Company
1270 Ave. of the Americas
New York, NY 10020
Tel. 212/332-8500

**Hitachi** (Japanese)
*electronics, chemicals,
construction*
Hitachi America, Ltd.
50 Prospect Ave.
Tarrytown, NY 10591
Tel. 914/332-5800

**Hyundai** (Korean)—*autos, ships,
computers, and construction*
1 Bridge Plaza North
Fort Lee, NJ 07024
Tel. 201/592-7766

**Matsushita** (Japanese)
*electronics*
9401 Grand Ave.
Franklin Park, IL 60131
Tel. 708/451-1200

**Michelin** (French)—*rubber
products and travel guides*
Patewood Industrial Park
P.O. Box 19001
Greenville, SC 29602
Tel. 803/458-5000

**NEC** (Japanese)-*computers
and electronics*
NEC America
8 Old Sod Farm Road
Melville, NY 11747
Tel. 516/753-7060

**Nestle Food Corp.** (Swiss)
*coffee and food products*
1st Ave.
South Dayton, NY 14138
Tel. 716/988-3224

**Perrier Group** (French)—*bottled*
*water and fitness equipment*
Great Waters of France
777 W. Putnam Ave.
Greenwich, CT 06830
Tel. 203/531-4100

**Sony** (Japanese)—*electronics,*
*consumer products, and*
*motion pictures*
Sony Corporation of America
9 West 57th St.
New York, NY 10019
Tel. 212/371-5800

**Toshiba** (Japanese)
*computers, electronics,*
*nuclear products*
Toshiba America
82 Totowa Avenue
Wayne, NJ 07470
Tel. 201/628-8000

**Yamaha** (Japanese)—*sports*
*goods, electronics, music*
Yamaha International
6660 Orangethorpe Ave.
Buena Park, CA 90622
Tel. 714/522-9011

# 6

# CONTRACTING & CONSULTING FIRMS

$T$ he private contracting and consulting firms outlined in this chapter are the major recipients of government contracts and international funding. These firms provide technical assistance and other services to developing countries in Asia, the Pacific, Africa, Eastern Europe, the former Soviet Union, the Middle East, Latin America, and the Caribbean. They include everything from large construction and engineering firms involved in building roads, dams, and pharmaceutical plants to accounting firms, agricultural development specialists, health training groups, and telecommunication experts.

While some of these firms—especially those in engineering, construction, and accounting—also operate in North America and Europe, most are oriented toward solving the infrastructural and managerial problems of developing Third and Fourth World countries. In contrast to government agencies and United Nations organizations, which are primarily involved in defining problems and funding projects, these firms are involved in the day-to-day implementation of projects at the local level. They build roads, construct factories, initiate health programs, experiment with new crops, organize agricultural cooperatives, promote privatization and small business enterprises, and provide technical assistance in developing information and communication systems.

The firms identified in this chapter more or less operate abroad. Some assign 70 percent of their staff abroad while others have 70 percent of their staff based in the United States.

## NEW CONTRACTING FRONTIERS

Most contractors and consultants identified in this chapter are dependent on public financing of foreign aid and international assistance programs. As a major funding source, the U.S. Agency for International Development (USAID) focuses most of its resources on Latin America, Africa, and Asia. In 1992, for example, USAID awarded 5,689 contracts which totalled over $8.4 billion. They were distributed as follows:

| Region | Awards | Value of Awards |
|---|---|---|
| United States | 597 | $ 641,037,932.47 |
| Europe | 308 | 739,077,739.98 |
| Near East | 286 | 604,680,735.20 |
| Asia | 964 | 1,293,918,621.58 |
| Latin America | 1,524 | 1,439,174,626.28 |
| Africa | 1,312 | 1,312,798,030.21 |
| South Pacific | 19 | 24,603,039.00 |
| Worldwide | 679 | 2,328,170,133.78 |
| TOTAL: | 5,689 | $ 8,383,460,858.50 |

While these figures also include awards to private voluntary organizations, nonprofit organizations, and education institutions, a large percentage of this funding went to private contractors and consultants.

During the past few years a great deal of U.S. government money has begun to flow into Eastern Europe and the former Soviet Union via U.S.-based contractors and consultants. These countries are the new frontiers for international consulting work. Indeed, in 1992 alone, USAID earmarked more than $720 million in contracts—or 8 percent of all contracts it awarded worldwide—for countries in Eastern Europe and the former Soviet Union:

| | |
|---|---|
| Albania | $3.9 million |
| Bulgaria | $21.7 million |
| Czechoslovakia | $54.4 million |
| Eastern Europe Regional | $176.4 million |
| Former Soviet Union | $99.1 million |
| Hungary | $69.5 million |
| Poland | $276.5 million |
| Romania | $15.4 million |
| Yugoslavia | $3.5 million |

As parts of Eastern Europe and the former Soviet Union continued to disintegrate in 1993 and 1994, more and more aid should increase to this part of the world throughout the 1990s. A larger number of contractors and consultants should extend their operations into these newly developing countries.

Most of the contracts earmarked for Eastern Europe and the former Soviet Union focus on privatizing state owned industries; increasing the capacity of government ministries; installing new accounting and information processing systems; responding to emergencies; extending humanitarian assistance; restructuring agriculture; extending managerial expertise; developing legal systems; establishing investment programs; managing energy systems; and providing medical assistance.

The contracting and project challenges tend to be unique in this post-Cold War part of the world. USAID in 1991, for example, awarded a $2.9 million three-year contract to "Provide Vocational Training to Former Political Prisoners and Their Families." In response to Romania's run-away population growth, USAID awarded a $3 million contract to "Provide Romanian Health Care Provider Skills Required for Effective Family Planning Services." During the next few years more and more contracts should be awarded in the areas of small business development, environmental protection, vocational training, telecommunications, and public administration.

## STRATEGIES

Getting a job with a contracting and consulting firm requires a thorough understanding of the organizations and their skill requirements. Many organizations, such as engineering, construction, and accounting firms, are primarily concerned with recruiting individuals who have specific technical skills relevant to the work of the organization rather than knowledge of specific countries, exotic foreign language abilities, or extensive international experience. Other firms, such as those specializing in tropical agriculture, community development, population planning, rural health systems, and education, tend to recruit individuals who have a great deal of international experience as well as knowledge of specific countries. Many of these firms require candidates to have exotic combinations of language and work skills and Third World experience.

Given the project-by-project nature of these firms' work, most contracting and consulting firms encourage individuals to directly submit information on their skills and qualifications. Most of the firms maintain resume banks, computerized personnel files, or "resource rosters". Information on qualified candidates is kept on file and referred to when staffing needs occur. Firms use these resource rosters frequently given the nature of the contracting business. Therefore, you may want to send your resume to several firms which appear to be relevant to your interests and skills.

Many of the companies identified in this chapter compete with as well as work closely with counterpart organizations outlined in Chapters 7, 8, and 9. Private voluntary organizations (PVOs), nonprofit corporations, and university research centers share many of the same funding sources as the private contracting and consulting firms. Therefore, you may want to examine these firms in reference to the organizations in these other chapters. As you will quickly discover, the organizations in this and the next three chapters constitute an important "network" of international development organizations. Individuals who work for PVOs often find employment with nonprofit corporations and private contracting and consulting firms. After all, they engage in similar work and recruit individuals with similar international skills.

The abbreviations appearing in the descriptions of each firm refer to many of the organizations identified in Chapters 2 and 3 on the Federal government and international organizations. As you will quickly discover, the United States Agency for International Development (USAID) is the major funding source for most of these organizations. United Nations agencies (United Nations Development Programme [UNDP], World Health Organization [WHO]), as well as the World Bank (IBRD), International Monetary Fund (IMF), and several regional financial institutions also provide funding for these firms. If you are serious about working for an international contractor, you should first understand the nature of their international work and the way they are funded. As we outlined in *The Complete Guide to International Jobs and Careers*, international contracting and consulting firms have their own peculiar way of hiring and managing staffs at home and abroad. They offer rich opportunities to work in some of the most exciting international job and work settings today.

# THE ORGANIZATIONS

## Abt Associates, Inc.
4800 Montgomery Ave.
Suite 600
Bethesda, MD 20814
Tel. 301/913-0500
Fax 301/913-9061

Provides technical assistance in the areas of agriculture, health, and economic and urban development. Maintains a full-time staff in the U.S. of 373 and a long-term staff abroad of 4. Operates projects in Africa, Asia, Latin America, the Caribbean, Middle East, North Africa, and Portugal. Major clients include: USAID, The World Bank, African Development Bank, CARE, United Nations, and foreign governments. Previous projects included: "Agricultural Policy Analysis Project" (Worldwide, USAID, $10.8 million), "Agricultural Policy Implementation Project" (Tunisia, USAID, $3.1 million), and "Agricultural Planning and Analysis" (Sri Lanka, Government of Sri Lanka, $1.5 million).

## Advanced Systems Development, Inc.
2800 Shirlington Rd.
Suite 800
Arlington, VA 22206
Tel. 703/998-3900
Fax 703/824-5699

Provides information management system, engineering, and computer services. Has 8(a) status. Maintains a full-time U.S. staff of 90. Major client is the Department of Defense (Navy and Army).

## AER Enterprises
P.O. Box 6207
East Brunswick, NJ 08816
Tel. 908/254-6930
Fax 908/254-6812

Specializes in conference planning relating to technology transfer. Maintains a full-time staff in the U.S. of 4. Major clients include the U.S. Government, Government of the People's Republic of China, McGraw-Hill, and Pasha Publications. Previous projects included: "Transfer Technology from China to the U.S." (China, $20 million), "Fourth Pacific Rim Coal Conference" (Columbia, $500,000), and "Power Generation" (Singapore, $300,000).

## Aguirre International
411 Borel Avenue, Suite 402
San Mateo, CA 94402
Tel. 415/349-1842
Fax 415/513-6299
Branches: Mexico City and Washington, DC

Provides technical assistance in the areas of policy and development analysis; project design, development, and evaluation; human resource development; and program implementation. Has 8(a) status. Maintains a full-time staff in the U.S. of 35 and a long-term staff abroad of 7. Primarily operates in Latin America. Major clients include USAID, U.S. Department of Labor, U.S. Department of Education, and the U.S. Department of Energy. Previous projects included: "Translate Into Spanish, Publish, and Disseminate U.S. Technical Information" (Latin America, USAID, $9.2 million) and "Assess Effectiveness of Central American Peace Scholarship Program" (Central America, USAID, $2.7 million).

## Allied Signal Technical Services Corporation
1 Bendix Road
Columbia, MD 21045-1897
Tel. 410/964-7000
Fax 410/730-6775

A major international engineering firm providing comprehensive engineering, electronic, computer, and telecommunications services. Maintains a full-time staff in the U.S. of 6,600 and long-term staff abroad of 600. Operates in Asia, Latin America, Middle East, Europe, Australia, New Zealand, and Canada. Major clients include USAID, USIA, NASA, Department of Defense, Department of Energy, Federal Aviation Administration, U.S. Department of Agriculture, Defense Nuclear Agency, Government of Saudi Arabia, and numerous commercial firms. Previous projects included "Provide Technical Support in Operating Air Navigation Support Services Programs in 50 Locations" (Saudi Arabia, Government of the Kingdom of Saudi Arabia, $609 million) and "Operate, Install, Maintain, and Repair Seismic Devices in 50 Countries for Earthquake Research" (Worldwide, U.S. Geological Survey, $3 million).

## American Manufacturers Export Group
11511 Katy Freeway
Suite 300
Houston, TX 77079
Tel. 713/558-0528
Fax 713/558-8530

Performs feasibility studies and designs, implements, and evaluates Commodity Import Programs and development projects that have commodity components. Also provides extensive training and procurement services. Has 8(a) status. Operates a full-time staff in the U.S. of 9 and a long-term staff abroad of 118. Conducts projects in Africa, Asia, Latin America, the Caribbean, the Middle East, and North Africa. Major client is USAID. Previous projects in Afghanistan ($38.9 million), "Humanitarian Commodity Export Program", and Indonesia ($1.8 million), "Applied Agriculture Research Project."

## AMEX International, Inc.
1725 K Street, NW
Suite 402
Washington, DC 20006
Tel. 202/429-0222
Fax 202/429-1867

Provides three types of technical assistance: policy analysis, program and project design and evaluation, and development management. However, nearly 98 percent of business involves the procurement and shipment of agricultural commodities under the P.L. 480 program for Morocco, Zaire, and Ghana. Classified as an 8(a) firm. Operates with a full-time staff in the U.S. of 13 and a long-term staff abroad of 6. Major clients include USAID, the World Bank, and UNDP. Experienced in managing small projects in Bangladesh ("Bangladesh Agriculture Sector Analysis") and Nigeria ("National Technical Cooperation Assessments and Programs").

## Ammann & Whitney Consulting Engineers, Inc.
96 Morton St.
New York, NY 10014
Tel. 212/524-7200
Fax 212/524-7215

Specializes in the design, construction, and management of bridges, highways, airports, and mass transit facilities. Maintains a full-time U.S. staff of 309 and a long-term staff abroad of 45. Operates in Africa, Asia, Latin American, Middle East, North Africa, Western Europe, and Puerto Rico. major clients include the U.S. Department of State, U.S. Corps of Engineers, U.S. Information Agency, and several host country governments. Previous projects included: "IBS Radio Relay Station" (Middle East, International Broadcast Systems, $220.7 million), "Bandung Bypass Highway" (Indonesia, Indonesian Government, $97 million), and "Caracus Embassy" (Venezuela, Department of State, $25 million).

## Arkel International, Ltd.
1048 Florida Boulevard
Baton Rouge, LA 70802
Tel. 504/343-0525
Fax 504/336-1849

Offers engineering, construction, and factory management services. Specializes in sugar production and refining, petro chemical industry, sulfur recovery from hydrocarbons, fertilizers, pulp and paper industry, alcohol production, agricultural development, material handling systems, and oil and gas transmission. Maintains a full-time staff in the U.S. of 50 and a long-term staff abroad of 600. Operates in Africa, Asia, North Africa, and Canada. Major clients include Export-Import Bank, USAID, U.S. Army Corps of Engineers, Government of Egypt, and private companies in Kenya, Philippines, Ivory Coast, and the Sudan. Previous major projects included: "Rehabilitation and Expansion of Nzola Sugar Factory" (Kenya, Export-Import Bank, $28 million) and "Aircraft Maintenance Facilities" (Sudan, U.S. Army Corps of Engineers, $7 million).

## Arthur Andersen and Company
1666 K Street, NW
Washington, DC 20006
Tel. 202/862-3100
Fax 202/785-4689

An international accounting firm providing accounting/audit services, management information consulting, tax analyses, and professional educational services. Maintains a full-time staff in the U.S. of 24,160 and a long-term staff abroad of 21,845. Operates 159 offices in 47 countries of Africa, Asia, Latin America, the Middle East, Australia, Canada, and Western Europe. Major clients include USAID, the World Bank, Asian Development Bank, African Development Bank, UNDP, and hundreds of banks, commercial firms, and government agencies. Previous projects included: "Formulation and Monitoring of Public Investment Program" (Philippines, Government of the Philippines) and "Study of Government Accounting and Auditing Modernization" (Indonesia, World Bank and Government of Indonesia).

## Associates in Rural Development
110 Main Street
Fourth Floor
Burlington, VT 05401
Tel. 802/658-3890
Fax 802/658-4247

Provides technical assistance in agriculture and rural development, natural resources management, environmental protection, energy planning and technology, management and institutional development, and water and sanitation. Maintains a full-time staff in the U.S. of 35 and a long-term staff abroad of 35. Major clients include USAID, FINNIDA, Club du Sahel, World Bank, Asian Development Bank, Inter-American Development Bank, CARE, UNFAO, UNDP, UNOCF, and OECD. Operates projects in Africa, Asia, Latin America, the Caribbean, Middle East, North Africa, and Europe with some of the largest previous projects done worldwide ($8 million) for "Decentralization; Finance and Management Project", Pakistan ($5 million) for "Assist Implementation of Command Water Management Project," and Haiti ($5 million) for "Targeted Watershed Management Project."

## Atkinson, Guy F. Construction Co.
1001 Bayhill Drive, Suite 200
San Bruno, CA 94066
Tel. 415/876-1000
Fax 415/876-1678

A major international construction firm involved in building tunnels, dams, power plants, harbor projects, highways, bridges, airports, transit systems, paper mills, and commercial and institutional buildings. Maintains a full-time staff in the U.S. of 1,326 and a long-term staff abroad of 321. Operates in Latin America, the Caribbean, Middle East, Australia, and Canada. Major clients are several private companies. Previous projects included: "Macagua II Hydroelectric Project" (Venezuela, Private Export Financing Co., $320 million) and "Pulp Mill Expansion" (Canada, private funds, $162 million).

## Aurora Associates
1015 18th St., NW
Suite 400
Washington, DC 20036
Tel. 202/463-0950
Fax 202/659-2724

Specializes in providing assistance in two areas: management of computer services and automatic data processing facilities; and management of training programs for international students. Has 8(a) status. Maintains a full-time staff in the U.S. of 120 and a long-term staff abroad of 20. International contracts valued at $7 million. Operates in Africa, Asia, and North Africa. Major clients include USAID, U.S. Department of Labor, U.S. Department of State, U.S. Department of Justice, and the U.S. General Accounting Office. Previous projects included: "Provide Training for Disadvantages South Africans Scholarship Program" (South Africa and U.S., USAID, $4.5 million) and "Provide Support to South African Participants in American Colleges and Universities" (U.S., USAID, $2.5 million).

## Automation Research Systems, Ltd.
4480 King Street, Suite 500
Alexandria, VA 22302
Tel. 703/820-9000
Fax 703/820-9106

Specializes in providing technical services in two areas: integrated computer systems and customized software; and engineering and technical support. Has 8(a) status. Maintains a full-time staff in the U.S. of 305 and a long-term staff abroad of 20. Operates projects in the U.S., Korea, and Germany. Major international clients include USAID, Department of Defense (Army), and U.S. Department of State. Contracts valued at $17.7 million. Previous projects included: "Theater Automation Command and Control System" (Korea, Dept. of the Army, $8.1 million), "U.S. Department of State/Security" ($3.7 million), and "Assist Agency With Program and Support to Office of Private and Voluntary Cooperation" (Worldwide, USAID, $2.8 million).

## Bechtel Group, Inc.
P.O. Box 19365
San Francisco, CA 94119
Tel. 415/768-1234
Fax 415/768-9038

A major international construction firm specializing in all aspects of designing and constructing basic industrial plants—fossil and nuclear power, hydropower, mining and metals, petrochemical, refining, pipeline, chemical, food, and paper. Also involved in projects dealing with water use and conservation, pollution control, hazardous waste cleanup, asbestos abatement, rapid transit, airport development, hotels, factories, and commercial construction. Maintains a full-time staff in the U.S. of 18,000. Operates worldwide, including Western and Eastern Europe and the former Soviet Union. Major clients include USAID, U.S. Trade and Development Program, World Bank, African Development Bank, EEC, OECF, European Investment banks, and host country governments. Previous projects included: "Damletta Combined Cycle Project" (Egypt, African Development Bank and World Bank, $270 million) and "Shoubrah El-Kheima Unit 4 Thermal Power Project" (Egypt, USAID, Africa Development Bank, EEC, European Investment Bank, OECF, $156 million).

## R. W. Beck & Associates
2101 Fourth Avenue
Suite 600
Seattle, WA 98121-2317
Tel. 206/441-7500
Fax 206/441-4962

An major engineering and construction firm providing a wide range of technical assistance services in the areas of civil, mechanical, electrical, sanitary, and structural engineering, computer systems, economics, environmental, and construction management. Maintains a full-time staff in the U.S. of 5573. Operates in Asia, Latin America, the Caribbean, the Middle East, Canada, and New Zealand. Major clients include host country governments. Previous projects included: "Design of Diesel Generating Station" (Cayman Islands, Government of Cayman Islands) and "Review of Entire Electric Utility Industry for Transfer to Private Sector" (New Zealand, Government of New Zealand).

## Louis Berger International, Inc.
100 Halsted St.
East Orange, NJ 07019
Tel. 201/678-1960
Fax 201/672-4284

Provides services in the areas of engineering and architectural design, economic analyses, agricultural and rural development, environmental and natural resources management, transportation, and irrigation systems. Maintains a full-time staff in the U.S. of 450 and a long-term staff abroad of 1260. Operates in Africa, Asia, Latin America, the Caribbean, Middle East, North Africa, and Europe. Major clients include USAID, World Bank, African Development Bank, UNDP, Asian Development Bank, Caribbean Development Bank, and Inter-American Development Bank. Previous projects included: "Assist Liberia in Managing Finances" (USAID, $6.5 million), "Field Tested Feasibility of Renewable Energy Application With Egyptian Organizations" (USAID, $4.7 million), and "Increase Institutional Capability of Department of Irrigation, Hydrology, Meteorology" (Nepal, USAID, $2.4 million).

## Birch & Davis Associates, Inc.
8905 Fairview Road, Suite 300
Silver Spring, MD 20910
Tel. 301/589-6760
Fax 301/650-0398

U.S. staff of 150 and 3 abroad. Provides management consulting services in the areas of health and management information systems.

## Black and Veatch International
1500 Meadow Lake Parkway
P.O. Box 8405
Kansas City, MO 64114
Tel. 913/339-8700
Fax 913/339-8559

A major engineering-architectural firm providing electrical power generation, environmental engineering, and advanced energy technology services. Maintains a worldwide staff of over 3,000. Operates in Africa, Asia, Latin America, the Caribbean, Middle East, North Africa, Europe, the former Soviet Union, Japan, Australia, New Zealand, Greenland, and Canada. Major clients include USAID, World Bank, U.S. Export-Import Bank, and numerous host country governments and private companies. Previous projects included: "Rehabilitation and Expansion of Cairo Wastewater System" (Egypt, USAID/ODA, $14.6 million) and "Robe River, Cape Lambert Power Station" (Australia, GHD-B&V).

## Booz-Allen and Hamilton, Inc.
4330 East-West Highway
Bethesda, MD 20819
Tel. 301/951-2200
Fax 301/951-2383

A major management consulting firm providing technical assistance in the areas of information systems, tax administration, transportation planning, banking, environment, financial management, public administration, private sector development, and labor force analysis. Maintains a full-time staff in the U.S. of 2700 and a long-term staff abroad of 1500. Operates in Africa, Asia, Latin America, the Middle East, and North Africa. Major international clients include USAID and host country governments. Previous projects included: "Excise Tax Procedures and Systems" (Puerto Rico) and "Tax Reform Study" (Puerto Rico).

## John T. Boyd Company
400 Oliver Building
Pittsburgh, PA 15222
Tel. 412/562-1770
Fax 412/562-1953

U.S. staff of 54. Provides engineering, mining, environmental, and marketing, and financial services.

## Boyle Engineering Corp.
1501 Quail Street
P.O. Box 3030
Newport Beach, CA 92658-9020
Tel. 714/476-3300
Fax 714/721-7141

Provides complete engineering and architectural services in the areas of water supply, sewage, irrigation, and environment. Maintains a full-time staff in the U.S. of 500. Operates in Africa, Asia, Latin America, the Caribbean, the Middle East, Canada, and Western Europe. Major clients include host country governments and private firms.

## Buchart-Horn, Inc.
55 South Richland Avenue
York, PA 17404
Tel. 717/843-5561
Fax 717/845-3703

Offers engineering services in the areas of civil, sanitary, environmental, structural, electrical, mechanical engineering as well as architectural, land survey, landscape architecture, and solid/hazardous waste services. Maintains a full-time staff in the U.S. of 372 and a long-term staff abroad of 18. Operates in Columbia,

Saudi Arabia, Germany, and Greece. Major clients include the U.S. Army Engineer Division, Europe. Previous U.S. Army-funded projects included: "Military Community Master Planning/Mapping/Water and Electrical Studies" (Germany) and "Campbell Barracks Gymnasium Renovation" (Germany).

## Burns and Roe Enterprises, Inc.
800 Kinderkamack Rd.
Oradell, NJ 07649
Tel. 201/265-2000
Fax 201-599-2958

An architectural design and construction engineering firm focusing on electricity generation facilities. Maintains a full-time U.S. staff of 950 and a long-term staff abroad of 50. Operates in Asia, Latin America, the Caribbean, the Middle East, Australia, and Europe. Major clients include the Work Bank, USAID, U.S. Department of Defense, U.S. Department of Energy, Asian Development Bank, and host government agencies. Previous projects included: "North Bangkok Station Rehabilitation Study" (Thailand) and "Review of Guangzhou Pumped Storage Plant" (China).

## CACI International, Inc.
1100 N. Glebe Road
Arlington, VA 22201
Tel. 703/841-7800
Fax 703/841-7882

Specializes in providing information systems, advanced technologies, software development, and marketing services in the fields of defense, aerospace, communications, transportation, finance, and retailing. Maintains a full-time staff in the U.S. of 2,350 and a long-term staff abroad of 150, with 45 offices in North America and Europe. Operates projects Canada, Ireland, the Netherlands, Sweden, the United Kingdom.

## Camp Dresser and McKee International, Inc.
Ten Cambridge Center
Cambridge, MA 02142
Tel. 617/621-8181
Fax 617/577-7504

A major engineering firm specializing in water supply issues, wastewater, hazardous/industrial/solid wastes, agriculture and irrigation, utilities, and environmental planning. Maintains a full-time staff in the U.S. of 1900 and a long-term staff abroad of 36. Operates in Africa, Asia, the Pacific Islands, Latin America, the Caribbean, Middle East, North Africa, and Australia. Major clients include USAID, World Bank, Asian Development Bank, DECF, and the Government of Singapore. Previous projects included: "Greater Cairo Wastewater Project" (Egypt, USAID, $30 million), "Water and Sanitation for Health II

Project" (Worldwide, USAID, $25 million), "Irrigation Support Project for Asia/Near East" (USAID, $15 million).

## Carter & Burgess, Inc.
3880 Hulen Street
Ft. Worth, TX 76107
Tel. 817/735-6000
Fax 817/735-6148

An engineering design and construction management firm providing technical assistance in the areas of mechanical, electrical, civil, and structural engineering, land use planning, landscape architecture, and surveying. Maintains a full-time staff in the U.S. of 215. Operates projects in Nigeria, Taiwan, Latin America, the Middle East, and Spain. Major clients include U.S. government agencies, host country governments, and major corporations such as ARAMCO, General Dynamics, and IBM.

## CBI Industries, Inc.
800 Jorie Blvd.
Oak Brook, IL 60521-2268
Tel. 708/572-7000
Fax 708/572-7405

The Chicago Bridge and Iron Company (CBI) is a construction firm providing design, engineering, fabrication, project management, and general contracting services in the areas of forest product industries, water and wastewater treatment plant equipment, petrochemicals, oil, and gas. Maintains a full-time staff in the U.S. of 8,000 and a long-term staff abroad of 4,000. Operates in Africa, Asia, Latin America, the Middle East, Australia, Canada, and Western Europe.

## Checchi and Company Consulting, Inc.
1730 Rhode Island Ave., NW
Washington, DC 20036
Tel. 202/452-9700
Fax 202/466-9070

Specializes in agricultural and rural development, management training, project planning, investment analysis, feasibility studies, and infrastructure appraisal. Maintains a full-time staff in the U.S. of 25 and a long-term staff abroad of 25. Operates in Africa, Asia, Pacific Islands, Latin America, the Caribbean, Middle East, and North Africa. Major clients include USAID, World Bank, Asian Development Bank, and the U.S. Department of Treasury. Previous projects included: "Technical Assistance to Strengthen Bangladesh National Agricultural Research System" (USAID, $10.7 million), "Help Ministry of Education Design and Implement Training Programs" (Oman, USAID, $7.6 million), and "Strengthen Policy Analysis Capability in Agricultural Sector" (Sudan, USAID, $3 million).

## Chemonics International
2000 M Street, NW
Suite 200
Washington, DC 20036
Tel. 202/466-5340
Fax 202/331-8202

Provides technical assistance services to USAID in the areas of agriculture (policy and planning, farming systems research/extension, on-farm water management, rice production, livestock, seed technology, and agricultural engineering), agribusiness (food/fiber processing, marketing, agrochemicals, and business/financial management), natural resources (soil/water conservation/management, range management, and forestry), and rural development (infrastructure, cooperatives, information systems, and public administration). Maintains a full staff in the U.S. of 65 and a long-term staff abroad of 130. Recent international contracts totalled nearly $52 million. Operates in over 40 countries in Africa, Asia, Latin America, the Caribbean, Middle East, and North Africa. Previous projects included: $7.2 million for "Central American Non-Traditional Agricultural Export Support" and $7 million for "Egypt Local Development II—Rural Sector."

## Clapp and Mayne, Inc.
1606 Ponce de Leon Avenue
San Juan, Puerto Rico 00909
Tel. 809/721-3800
Fax 809/721-3812

Provides technical assistance in the areas of development administration, agriculture and rural development, education, health management, economic development, and personnel administration. Operates with a full-time U.S. staff of 10 and a long-term staff abroad of 11 with contracts valued at $11.5 million. Operates projects in Africa, Asia, Latin America, the Caribbean, the Middle East, and North Africa. Previous projects included "El Salvador Health Delivery Systems" ($3.8 million) and "Strengthening Democratic Institutions in Honduras" ($2 million).

## Computer Dynamics, Inc.
4452 Corporation Lane, Suite 300
Virginia Beach, VA 23462
Tel. 804/490-1234
Fax 804/490-8353

Specializes in integrating computer systems, developing software, and manufacturing computer hardware. Has 8(a) status. Maintains a full-time staff in the U.S. of 475 and a long-term staff abroad of 20. Operates in Korea, Japan, the Philippines, Bermuda, Cuba, Panama, and the Azores. Major client is the U.S. Department of Defense, Dependent Schools Programs ($20 million contract).

## COMSIS Corporation
8737 Colesville Road
Silver Spring, MD 20910
Tel. 301/588-0800
Fax 301/588-5922

U.S. staff of 200. Provides a variety of specialized transportation services, from mass transit to aviation planning.

## Conservation International
1015 18th St., NW, Suite 1000
Washington, DC 20036
Tel. 202/429-5660
Fax 202/887-5188

Provides technical assistance in the areas of marine resources and conservation. Recent projects included: "Provide Assistance to Sustainable Resource Management" (Guatemala, USAID, $2.8 million) and "Implement Montes Azules Biosphere Management Program in Chiapas, Mexico" (USAID, $577,000).

## Consoer, Townsend, and Envirodyne Engineers, Inc.
303 East Wacker Dr., Suite 600
Chicago, IL 60601
Tel. 312/938-0300
Fax 312/938-1109

Provides engineering and construction services relating to water resources, wastewater collection and treatment, solid waste management, transportation, and architecture. Maintains a full-time staff in the U.S. of 530 and a long-term staff abroad of 5. Operates in Africa, Asia, Latin America, the Middle East, and France. Many clients include the U.S. Army Corps of Engineers, private firms, and host country governments. Previous projects: "General Consultant to Puerto Rico Aqueduct and Sewer Authority" (PRASA, $10.5 million) and "Solid Waste Master Plan for Metropolitan Manila" (Philippines, USAID-TDP, $750,000).

## Construction Control Services Corporation
115 West Main Street
Durham, NC 27701
Tel. 919/682-5741
Fax 919/683-3072

Provides a full range of construction coordination and management services for clients. Has 8(a) status. Maintains a full-time staff in the U.S. of 138 and a long-term staff abroad of 75. Operates in Chad, Mali, Afghanistan, India, Pakistan, Mexico, and Egypt. Major clients include USAID and the African Development Bank. Previous projects included: "Road Resources Management" (Pakistan, USAID, $6.5 million), "Assist in Construction of Warehouses and Social Infrastructure Building in New Villages" (Mali, USAID, $2.9 million), and "Afghan Construction Logistics Union" (Afghanistan, USAID, $2.5 million).

## Coopers and Lybrand
1251 Avenue of the Americas
New York, NY 10020
Tel. 212/536-2000
Fax 212/536-3500

One of the oldest (since 1898) and most respected international firms specializing in audit, accounting, tax, information systems, business planning, and resource productivity. Maintains a full-time staff in the U.S. of 15,000 and a long-term staff abroad of 45,000. Operates in nearly 100 countries. Major funding comes from USAID and host country organizations. Sample contracts include: "Assist AID in Studying the Financial Status of the Rural Electrification Program in Bangladesh" (USAID, $245,816) and "Assist USAID Sudan to Conduct Study of Railway Corporations Early Retirement Program" (USAID, $86,000).

## Creative Associates International, Inc.
5301 Wisconsin Ave., NW 700
Washington, DC 20015
Tel. 202/966-5804
Fax 202/363-4771

U.S. staff of 50 and 200 abroad. Provides technical assistance in the several areas of educational development. USAID is major funding source. Recent projects include "Provide Funding for the Resettlement of Salvadoran Displaced Families" (USAID, $5.2 million) and "Support to Tertiary Education of Black South Africans and Selected Institutions for Positions of Leadership" (USAID, $8.5 million).

## Damnes and Moore
911 Wilshire Blvd., Suite 700
Los Angeles, CA 90017
Tel. 213/683-1560
Fax 213/628-0015

7101 Wisconsin Ave., Suite 700
Bethesda, MD 10814-4870
Tel. 301/652-2215
Fax 301/656-8059

Specializes in environmental and earth sciences, with emphasis on water resources development and environmental pollution control. Maintains a full-time staff in the U.S. of 2121 and a long-term staff abroad of 450. Operates projects in Africa, Asia, the Pacific, Latin America, the Caribbean, Middle East, North Africa, Western Europe, Australia, New Zealand, Antarctica, and Canada. Major clients include USAID, Inter-American Development Bank, World Bank, and numerous host country governments and private firms. Previous projects included: "Design and Installation of a Hydrometerological Monitoring Network and Water

Resource Surveys for Five Rep. Wadis" (Saudi Arabia, Kingdom of Saudi Arabia, $15 million), "Environmental Baseline and Impact Assessment Studies for Ruwals Industrial Complex" (Abu Dhabi, United Arab Emirates, $4 million), and "Senegal River Upper Valley Master Plan and Fiscal Allocation Study" (Senegal, Mali, Mauritania, USAID/OMVS, $3.5 million).

## Deleuw, Cather International Ltd.
1133 15th St., NW
Washington, DC 20005-2701
Tel. 202/775-3300
Fax 202/775-3422

A major international engineering and construction firm specializing in highways, railroads, rapid transit systems, marine and air terminals, parking garages, municipal water and sewage systems, community planning and development, and industrial and commercial complexes. Maintains a full-time staff in the U.S. of 893 and a long-term staff abroad of 269. Operates in Africa, Asia, Latin America, the Caribbean, Middle East, and North Africa. Major clients include USAID, Asian Development Bank, and World Bank. Previous projects included: "Provide Engineering Construction Supervision for Transportation and Roads Improvement Program" (United Arab Emirates, Emirate of Abu Dhabi, $100 million), "Kuwait Motorway System-Design/Construction Supervision" (Kuwait, Ministry of Public Works, $15 million), and "Taipei MRT System—Design Consultant" (Taiwan, Taiwan Department of Rapid Transit Systems, $11.2 million).

## Deloitte and Touche
1001 Pennsylvania Ave., NW
Suite 350N
Washington, DC 20004-2505
Tel. 202/879-5600
Fax 202/879-5309

Provides technical assistance in the areas of management information systems, financial information management, private enterprise development, financial institutions development, marketing services, and agricultural and rural development. Maintains a full-time staff in the U.S. of 9500 and a long-term staff abroad of 17,000. Operates projects in Africa, Asia, Latin America, the Caribbean, Middle East, and North Africa. Major clients include USAID, World Bank, IMF, Overseas Private Investment Corporation, Canadian International Development Agency, United Kingdom Overseas Development Agency, Inter-American Development Bank, African Development Bank, UNFAO, and the International Fund for Agricultural Development. Previous projects included: "Private Sector Services Project" (Jordan, USAID, $7.2 million), "Provide Technical Automation Support to AID'S Washington Bureaus and Overseas Missions" (Worldwide, USAID, $4.8 million), and "Kenya Rural Private Enterprise Project" (USAID, $2.2 million).

## Development Alternatives, Inc.
7250 Woodmont Ave.
Suite 200
Bethesda, MD 20814
Tel. 301/718-8699
Fax 301/718-7968

A high quality consulting/contracting firm providing technical assistance services in the areas of agriculture, natural resources, finance, management, and economics. Maintains a full-time staff in the U.S. of 69 and a long-term staff abroad of 46. Operates in Africa, Asia, Pacific Islands, Latin America, the Caribbean, Middle East, and North Africa. Major clients include USAID, African Development Bank, Asian Development Bank, World Bank, and United Nations Development Programme. Previous projects included: "Development Strategies for Fragile Lands Project" (Latin America/Caribbean, USAID, $12.9 million), "High Impact Agricultural Marketing and Production" (Eastern Caribbean, USAID, $7.5 million), "Mahawell Agricultural Development" (Sri Lanka, USAID, $7.7 million), and "Assist USAID/Pakistan to Facilitate the Resettlement of War Affected Afghans into Afghanistan" (Pakistan, USAID, $10.2 million).

## Development Assistance Corporation
1415 11th St., NW
Washington, DC 20001
Tel. 202/234-8842
Fax 202/234-5878

Provides technical assistance in the areas of agricultural productivity, seed multiplication, and economic and social development. Maintains a full-time staff in the U.S. of 85 and a long-term staff abroad of 6. Major clients include USAID, U.S. Department of Defense (Army), and the U.S. Department of Health and Human Services. Operates projects in Africa, Asia, Latin America, the Caribbean, and North Africa. Previous major projects included: "North Cameroon Seed Multiplication Project" ($4.9 million) and "Togo Child Survival Project" ($3.5 million).

## Development Associates, Inc.
1730 North Lymn St.
Arlington, VA 22209
Tel. 703/276-0677
Fax 703/276-0432

A well established and highly respected management and government consulting firm operating in Africa, Asia, the Pacific Islands, Latin American, the Caribbean, Middle East, and North Africa. Maintains a full-time staff in the U.S. of 100 and a long-term staff abroad of 11. Recent annual international contracts total nearly $50 million. Major clients include USAID, Department of Health and Human Services, Department of Education, Department of Agriculture, Department of Commerce, Department of Labor, Inter-American Bank, World Bank, United Nations, and many state and local governments, foundations, and foreign governments. Provides technical assistance in the areas of private sector promotion, health and nutrition, education, agriculture and rural development, public administration, urban and community development, drug and alcohol abuse problems, training development, population and family projects. Two of their largest projects included: $6.7 million for "Strengthen or Develop Capacity of Latin American Family Planning Programs" and $3.6 million for "Assist USAID Dominican Republic With Private Sector Growth and Development."

## Devres, Inc.
2426 Ontario Road, NW
Washington, DC 20009
Tel. 202/319-7400
Fax 202/319-7401

Offers technical assistance services in agriculture, rural development, private and public sector enterprise, health, nutrition, natural resource managements, development strategies, institutional development, education, and training. Operates with a full-time staff in the U.S. of 30 and a long-term staff abroad of 6 with projects in Africa, Asia, the Pacific Islands, Latin America, the Caribbean, Middle East, and North Africa. Some of the largest previous projects were in Morocco, Nepal, Belize, and Ecuador. International contracts valued at $9.5 million. Major clients include USAID and the U.S. Department of Health and Human Services. Some of their largest projects included: "Services in Biomedical Research" ($4.5 million) and "Export Credit Insurance Institution in Morocco" ($1.3 million).

## Dillingham Construction Corporation
5960 Inglewood Dr.
Pleasanton, CA 94566
Tel. 510/463-3300
Fax 510/463-1571

A major engineering and construction firm providing a wide range of technical assistance services in the areas of highways, bridges, locks, dams, canals, hydroelectric projects, commercial and residential buildings, military bases and airfields, marine structures and dredging, oil storage facilities, pulp and paper mills. Maintains a full-time staff in the U.S. of 1,500 and a long-term staff abroad of 150. Nearly 25% of their projects are located outside the U.S. Operates in Africa, Asia, the Pacific Islands, Latin America, the Caribbean, Middle East, Europe, Russia, and Australia. Major clients are the U.S. Army Corps of Engineers, host countries, and private companies.

## DPRA, Inc.

| 200 Research Drive | 1300 North 17th St., NW |
| Manhattan, KS 66502 | Rosslyn, VA 22209 |
| Tel. 913/539-3565 | Tel. 703/522-3772 |
| Fax 913/539-5353 | Fax 703/524-9415 |

Specializes in conducting studies relating to economics, environment, financial and regulatory analysis, industrial assessments, marketing research and statistics. Has conducted projects in over 60 countries. Major clients include USAID and the Environmental Protection Agency. Provides technical assistance in the areas of environmental regulation, water resources, agriculture, industry, and trade. Maintains a full-time staff in the U.S. of 150 and long-term staff about of 3. Operates in Africa, Asia, Latin America, the Caribbean, the Middle East, North Africa, Australia, New Zealand, and Western Europe. Major clients include USAID, the World Bank, the United Nations, and several government agencies. Previous projects included: "Kenya On-Farm Grain Storage" (USAID, $2 million).

## Dual, Inc.

2101 Wilson Blvd.
Suite 600
Arlington, VA 22201
Tel. 703/527-3500
Fax 703/527-0829

Specializes in providing services in the areas of program/project management and evaluation; family planning; management information systems; and automation planning, design, acquisition, and implementation. Has 8(a) status. Maintains a full-time staff in the U.S. of 280. Primarily operates in Asia, Latin America, and the Caribbean but also does some work in Portugal and France. Major clients include USAID, U.S. Navy, NASA, and the National Science Foundation. Previous contracts included: "Population Technical Assistance Project" (World-wide, USAID, $8.8 million) and "Strengthening Democratic Institutions Initiative" (Honduras, USAID, $1.5 million).

## Earth Satellite Corporation

6011 Executive Blvd.
Suite 400
Rockville, MD 20852
Tel. 301/231-0660
Fax 301/231-5020

U.S. staff of 50. Provides technical services relating to the application of remote sensing and geographic information systems technology to agricultural land use and geological problems.

## EBASCO Overseas Corporation

(sub. EBASCO Services Inc.)
2 World Trade Center
93rd Floor
New York, NY 10048-0752
Tel. 212/839-1000
Fax 212/839-3481

A major engineering and construction firm providing project management, engineering design, quality assurance, construction management, and plant services worldwide. Involved in the design and construction of nuclear power facilities, hydroelectric power generation, roads, airports, hazardous waste remediation, petrochemical, commercial buildings, tunnels, piers, defense, aerospace, telecommunications, and pharmaceuticals. Maintains a full-time staff in the U.S. of 6,300 and a long-term staff abroad of 61. Operates in Africa, Asia, Latin America, the Caribbean, the Middle East, Europe, Australia, and Canada. Major clients include USAID, World Bank, U.S. Department of State, host country governments, and private firms. Previous projects included: "Laguna Verde Nuclear Power Project" (Mexico, Comision Federal de Electridad, Mexico, $100 million), "Provide Assistance for Rural Electrification Project" (Pakistan, USAID, $19.7 million), and "C-130 Hangar and Utility Upgrade, Construction" (Egypt, U.S. Army Corps of Engineers, $12.3 million).

## Edison-Hubbard Corporation

2625 Barrington Court
Hayward, CA 94545
Tel. 510/784-0600
Fax 510/784-0760

U.S. staff of 12 and 18 abroad. Provides electrical utility services in developing countries.

## Empire Acoustical/McKeown Industries

89 Park Avenue West
Mansfield, OH 44902
Tel. 419/522-0800
Fax 419/522-7937

U.S. staff of 20 and 20 abroad. Provides engineering services relating to water treatment and environmental protection.

## Engineering-Science, Inc.
100 West Walnut St.
Pasadena, CA 91124
Tel. 818/440-6000
Fax 818/440-6195

Provides engineering and construction services relating to urban infrastructure, water systems, sewage treatment, flood control, and wastewater management. Maintains a full-time staff in the U.S. of 860 and a long-term staff abroad of 30. Operates in Asia, Latin America, the Caribbean, the Middle East, North Africa, Greece, and Portugal. Major clients include USAID and host country governments. Previous projects included: "Modernization of Kaohsiung Refinery Wastewater Management System" (Taiwan, local funds, $3 million), "Rural Water and Sanitation Project" (Philippines, USAID, $2.9 million), and "Colombo Sewerage Project" (Sri Lanka, World Bank, $2 million).

## Ernst & Young
3000 K Street, NW
Washington, DC 20007
Tel. 202/327-9300
Fax 202/956-6529

One of the largest international accounting and business advisory firms representing the merger of two "Big Eight" firms in 1989: Arthur Young & Co. with Ernst and Whinney. Maintains a full-time staff in the U.S. of 7,700 and a long-term staff abroad of 23,500. Has branch offers in 400 cities of 72 countries. Operates worldwide with a major presence in both developing and developed countries, including Europe, Australia, Canada, and the U.S. (92 cities). Major clients include USAID, World Bank, Asian Development Bank, Inter-American Development Bank, and numerous governments and private firms. Previous projects included: "Increase Use of Private Enterprise in Developing Countries" (Worldwide, USAID, $6.1 million), "Develop Programs to Develop Financial Markets" (Worldwide, USAID, $1.4 million), and "Technical Assistance for Rationalization and Privatization of Selected Government Activities" (Western Samoa, Asian Development Bank, $850,000).

## Executive Resource Associates
1850 Centennial Park Dr., Suite 300
Reston, VA 22091-1517
Tel. 703/716-0000
Fax 703/716-3000

Provides technical support and training services in facilities management and operations support, ADP security, organization and management support, international programs, system engineering, and human resources management. Has 8(a) status. Maintains a full-time staff in the U.S. of 400. Operates projects in Egypt and Saudi Arabia. International contracts valued at $58.9 million which represent a single USAID contract for "Automation Facilities Management, Technical Support, Mission Support and Directives Systems Maintenance". Also provides MIS training to USAID overseas missions and host country clients. Major clients include USAID, DOD (Navy), USIA, DOE, DDHS, Treasury (Customs), DOT (FAA), EPA, Commerce (NIST, NOAA), FEMA, DEA, and the VA.

## Fluor Corporation
3333 Michelson Dr.
Irvine, CA 92730
Tel. 714/975-2000
Fax 714/975-5271

A major engineering, construction, and technical service company providing a broad range of international services relating to industrial, power, and hydrocarbon plant operations. Maintains a full-time staff in the U.S. of 17,876. Operates in Asia, Latin America, the Middle East, Australia, Canada, and Western Europe. Major clients include numerous private firms and government agencies worldwide.

## Foster Wheeler International Corporation
1701 Pennsylvania Ave., NW
Washington, DC 20006
Tel. 202/298-7750
Fax 202/342-0597

Offers engineering and construction services relating to industrial process plants such as petroleum refining, petrochemicals, chemicals, fertilizers, pulp and paper, and pharmaceuticals. Maintains a full-time staff in the U.S. of 1200 and a long-term staff abroad of 7000. Operates in Africa, Asia, Latin America, the Caribbean, the Middle East, North Africa, European, and the USSR. Major clients include the World Bank, USAID, Export-Import Bank, and numerous private companies. Previous projects included: "Project Management Contractor-National Fertilizer Corporation" (Thailand, USAID, USTDP, Export-Import Bank, $5 million) and "Afsin-Elbistan Power Project, Engineering and Construction" (Turkey, World Bank, Export-Import Bank).

## Frederic R. Harris, Inc.
300 East 42nd St.
New York, NY 10017
Tel. 212/973-2900
Fax 212/953-0399

An engineering firm specializing in transportation and related systems. Maintains a full-time staff in the U.S. of 800 and a long-term staff abroad of 100. Operates in Africa, Asia, Latin America, the Caribbean, the Middle East, and North Africa. Major clients include USAID, the World Bank, African Development Bank, Inter-American Development Bank, and numerous U.S. and host country government agencies. Previous projects included: "Fourth Highway Project" (Pakistan, World Bank, $7 million) and "Pasni Fisheries Harbour" (Pakistan, ADB, $2 million).

## The Futures Group, Inc.
1050 17th St., NW
Suite 1000
Washington, DC 20036
Tel. 202/775-9680
Fax 202/775-9694

Offers technical assistance services in the areas of family planning, health, and policy analysis. Maintains a full-time staff in the U.S. of 80 and a long-term staff abroad of 12. Operates in Africa, Asia, the Pacific Islands, Latin America, the Caribbean, Middle East, and North Africa. Major clients include USAID and the United Nations. Previous projects included: "Deliver Affordable Contraceptives and Inform Potential Users about Correct Use" (Worldwide, USAID, $33 million), "Resources for Awareness of Population Impact on Development" (Worldwide, USAID, $12.6 million), and "Assist LDC Institutions in Promoting, Developing, and Implementing Population Policies" (Worldwide, USAID, $7.9 million).

## Gannett Fleming Engineers, Inc.
P.O. Box 67100
Harrisburg, PA 17106-7100
Tel. 717/763-7211
Fax 717/763-8150

Provides architectural and engineering services relating to transportation, environmental control, water treatment, solid waste management, and rural development. Maintains a full-time staff in the U.S. of 1,000 and a long-term staff abroad of 30. Operates in Africa, Latin America, the Caribbean, and Saudi Arabia. Major clients include the World Bank, African Development Bank, United Nations, USAID, and numerous commercial firms and U.S. government agencies. Previous projects included: "Implement road Construction and Equipment Maintenance Project" (Cameroon, World Bank, $5 million), "Provide Architect/Engineering Expertise for Restoring Regular Maintenance of Roads" (Chad, USAID, $4.6 million), and "Assist in Design of Resettlement Project" (Mali, USAID, $3 million).

## Gibbs and Hill, Inc.
11 Pennsylvania Plaza
New York, NY 10001
Tel. 212/216-6000
Fax 212/216-6650 and 212/216-6002

Provides engineering design and consulting services relating to combined cycle gas fired power plants, coal fired power plants, ports and harbors, mass transit systems, railway electrification, hazardous waste disposal, and environmental control. Maintains a full-time staff in the U.S. of 360 and a long-term staff abroad of 22. Operates in Asia, Latin America, the Middle East, North Africa, Kenya, Italy, and Spain. Major clients include the World Bank, USAID, Asian Development Bank, and several U.S. and host country government agencies. Previous projects included: "Assist in Implementing Guddu Power Plant Project" (Pakistan, USAID, $14.5 million) and "Engineering Services For GEC Systems Rehabilitation" (Guyana, Inter-American Development Bank, $2.5 million).

## Harza Engineering Company
233 South Wacker Drive
Chicago, IL 60606-6392
Tel. 312/831-3000
Fax 312/831-3999

Provides technical assistance services relating to water resources (electrical power, irrigation, drainage, flood control, water supply, pollution abatement), municipal public works, transportation, tunnels, solid waste disposal, telecommunications, mining and environmental sciences. Maintains a full-time staff in the U.S. of 500 and a long-term staff abroad of 105. Operates projects in Africa, Asia, Latin America, Middle East, and North Africa. Major clients include USAID, World Bank, InterAmerican Development Bank, Asian Development Bank, and host country governments and private firms. Previous projects included: "Egypt Main System Management" (USAID, $8.2 million), "Al Wehdah Dam Project" (Jordan, USAID/Government of Jordan, $7 million), and "Apply System Analysis Approach to Large Scale River Basin Development" (India, USAID, $3.4 million).

## Heery International, Inc.
999 Peachtree St., NE
Atlanta, GA 30367
Tel. 404/881-9880
Fax 404/875-1283

Provides architectural, engineering, construction, and planning services for all types of facilities—commercial, sports/recreation, educational, health, military, convention, and multi-use. Maintains a full-time staff in the U.S. of 405 and a long-term staff abroad of 59. Operates in Asia, Latin America, the Middle East, Canada, and Western Europe. Major clients include the U.S. Army Engineering Division, U.S. Army Corps of Engineers. Previous projects included: "Multi-

National Oil Company London Facilities Consolidation" ($27 million) and "Medical Contingency Complex" (Luxenbourg, U.S. Army Engineering Division, $14 million).

## Hellmuth, Obata, and Kassabaum, Inc.
1 Metropolitan Square
211 North Broadway
Sixth Floor
St. Louis, MO 63102
Tel. 314/421-2000
Fax 314/421-6073

Provides architectural and engineering services in numerous areas—facilities, urban, site development, and environment. Maintains a full-time staff in the U.S. of 930 and a long-term staff abroad of 9. Operates in Asia, Latin America, the Caribbean, the Middle East, Australia, and Western Europe. Major clients include host country governments. Previous projects included: "St. Enoch's Mall" (Scotland), "Turtle Beach Master Plan and Osaka Retirement Community" (Japan), and "Jamaica Hospital Restoration" (Jamaica).

## H-R International, Inc.
2045 Lincoln Hwy.
Edison Square North
Edison, NJ 08817
Tel. 908/287-2111, Fax 908/287-5252

Provides a full range of engineering and construction services in a variety of commercial development areas. Maintains a full-time staff in the U.S. of 400 and a long-term staff abroad of 25. Operates in the Philippines, Western Samoa, Aruba, Chile, Venezuela, Saudi Arabia, and the Virgin Islands. Major clients include numerous private companies and government agencies.

## ICF Kaiser Engineers Group, Inc.
1800 Harrison Street
Oakland, CA 94612
Tel. 510/419-6000
Fax 510/419-5355

Provides a wide range of management engineering, procurement, and construction services for environmental, transportation, advanced technology, industrial, and other infrastructure projects. Maintains a full-time staff in the U.S. of 1,550 and a long-term staff abroad of 50. Operates in Asia, Latin America, Middle East, North Africa, Europe, and Australia. Major clients include: U.S. government agencies, host country governments, and private firms. Previous projects included: "Taipei Rapid Transit System" (Taipei Municipal Government, $17 million), "Tin Processing Plant" (Portugal, SOMINCOR, $9 million), and "Neves-Corvo Copper Project" (Portugal, SOMINCOR, $6.2 million).

## Institute for International Research, Inc.
1815 N. Fort Myer Dr.
Suite 600
Arlington, VA 22209
Tel. 703/527-5546
Fax 703/527-4661

Provides technical assistance in the areas of education systems, communication, and human relations. Maintains a full-time staff in the U.S. of 40 and a long-term staff abroad of 5. Operates in Africa, Asia, Latin America, the Caribbean, Middle East, and North Africa. Main client is USAID. Previous projects included: "Improving the Efficiency of Educational Systems" (14 countries, USAID, $6.8), "Liberian Rural Communications Network" (USAID, $5.4 million), and "Honduras Primary Education Efficiency Project" (Honduras, $2 million).

## Institute for Resource Development
11785 Beltsville Drive
Calverton, MD 20705
Tel. 410/290-2800
Fax 410/572-0999

Provides technical assistance in the area of population planning and health. A subsidiary of Westinghouse Electric Company. Maintains a full-time staff in the U.S. of 80 and a long-term staff abroad of 5. Operates in Africa, Asia, Latin America, the Caribbean, Middle East and North America. Major client is USAID. Previous project included: "Train 29 Village Health Workers in Providing IEC in Family Planning" (West Africa, USAID, $70,000).

## International Resources Group
1400 I Street, NW
Suite 700
Washington, DC 20005
Tel. 202/289-0100
Fax 202/289-7601

Provides technical assistance in the areas of energy planning and policy, finance, natural resources, conservation, wildlife systems, and health care. Maintains a full-time staff in the U.S. of 30 and a long-term staff abroad of 10. Operates in Africa, Asia, Latin America, the Caribbean, Middle East and North Africa. Major clients include USAID, World Bank, and the Asian Development Bank. Previous projects included: "Energy Initiatives for Africa Project" (Africa, USAID, $5.9 million), "Morocco Energy Planning Project" (Morocco, USAID, $2.4 million), and "Technology Transfer and Development in Health" (Latin America Region, USAID, $2.0 million).

## International Science and Technology Institute
1129 20th St., NW
Suite 800
Washington, DC 20036
Tel. 202/785-0831
Fax 202/223-3865

Provides technical assistance in the areas of health, population, and nutrition planning and administration; private enterprise development; and environmental, energy, and nature resource development. Maintains a full-time staff in the U.S. of 89 and a long-term staff abroad of 30. Major clients include USAID, IBRD, and UNDP. Previous projects included: "Health Sector Financing" (Indonesia, USAID, $13.4 million), "Health Information Systems" (Worldwide, USAID, $6 million), and "Population Technical Assistance" (Worldwide, USAID, $3.6 million).

## IRI Research Institute, Inc.
169 Greenwich Ave.
Stamford, CT 06904-1276
Tel. 203/327-5985
Fax 203/359-1595

Specializes in providing technical assistance relating to agriculture: crop production, agribusiness, research, and marketing. Maintains a full-time staff in the U.S. of 10 and a long-term staff abroad of 8. Operates primarily in Latin America and the Caribbean but also has projects in Kenya, Bangladesh, Indonesia, Egypt, Oman, and Yemen Arab Republic. Previous projects included: "Assist USAID/Dominican Republic in Establishment of Agriculture Research Foundation" (USAID, $1.4 million) and "Agricultural Technology Development and Support" (Dominican Republic, USAID, $1.5 million).

## John Snow, Inc.
210 Lincoln Street
Boston, MA 02111
Tel. 617/482-9485
Fax 617/482-0617

1616 North Fort Myer Drive,
11th Floor
Arlington, VA 22209
Tel. 703/528-7474

One of the largest and most capable international companies providing technical assistance in developing countries relating to family planning, family health, nutrition, rural health systems, and education; water, sanitation, and tropical diseases; logistics and information systems; training and staff development; and research. Maintains a full-time staff in the U.S. of 120 and a long-term staff abroad of 17. Operates in Africa, Asia, Latin America, the Caribbean, Middle East, and North Africa. Engaged in joint contracts with PVOs and other private contractors. Major clients include USAID and UNHCR. Previous contracts included: "The Enterprise Program" (Worldwide, USAID, $27.8 million), "Resources for Child Health" (Worldwide, USAID, $17.4 million), and "Maternal and Neonatal Health and Nutrition Project" (Worldwide, USAID, $13.5 million).

## Juarez and Associates, Inc.
12139 National Blvd.
Los Angeles, CA 90064
Tel. 213/879-5899
Fax 213/479-1863

U.S. staff of 15 and 1 abroad. Provides research and management services relating to education, general management, urban studies, and human resource development. Recent project included: "Assist With Improvements in the Quality and Quantity of Maternal Health Services" (Guatemala, USAID, $300,000).

## The M.W. Kellogg Company
Three Greenway Plaza
Houston, TX 77046-0395
Tel. 713/960-2000
Fax 713/960-2032

One of the world's oldest (1901) and largest international engineering and construction firms engaged in the design and construction of processing and manufacturing projects around the world: chemical, petrochemical, fertilizer, gas processing, refining, and computer integrated manufacturing. A subsidiary of Dresser Industries, Inc. Maintains a full-time staff in the U.S. of 2898 and a long-term staff abroad of 580. Has branch offices in London, Cayman Islands, Washington, DC, Buenos Aires, Singapore, Beijing, Jakarta, and Kuala Lumpur. Major clients include all major companies in the U.S. as well as both public and private companies and governments abroad. Operates projects in more than 30 countries, including countries in Western and Eastern Europe, and on all but one continent. Previous projects included: "Fertilizer Complex: Operations, Maintenance and Training" (Nigeria, Federal Government of Nigeria, $800 million), "Ethylene Plant Expansion: Technology Package" (Saudi Arabia, Saudi Basic Industries Corp., $600 million), and "Methanol Complex: Operations and Maintenance" (Chile, Cape Horn Methanol, Inc., $300 million).

## KPMG Peat Marwick
767 Fifth Avenue, 47th Floor
New York, NY 10153
Tel. 212/909-5000
Fax 212/909-5200

U.S. staff of 30,000 and 60,000 abroad. Provides tax and management consulting services. Recent projects included: "Technical Services to Ministry of Finance in the Area of Tax Administration and Customs" (El Salvador, USAID, $4 million) and "Assist the Ministry of Privatization in Poland With Privatizing the Furniture and Particle Board Industry" (USAID, $1.3 million)

## Labat-Anderson, Inc.
2200 Clarendon Boulevard
Suite 900
Arlington, VA 22201
Tel. 703/525-9400
Fax 703/524-7668

Provides technical assistance services in agricultural research, analysis, and extension; natural resource and environmental planning; private sector and small enterprise strategy; resource development; health and child survival initiatives; and management information systems. Has 8(a) status. Maintains a full-time staff in the U.S. of 400 and a long-term staff abroad of 3. Major clients include USAID, Peace Corps, and the Department of State. Contracts valued at nearly $20 million. Operates in Africa, Asia, Latin America, North Africa, and the Middle East. Some of the largest previous contracts included: "Agricultural Production and Cereals Research/Extension Projects" (Niger, $3.8 million), "Computer Related Services for the Disaster Information Network" (Worldwide, $3.6 million), and "Peace Corps Training/Senegal" ($2.4 million).

## Arthur D. Little
25 Acorn Park
Cambridge, MA 02140
Tel. 617/864-5770
Fax 617/661-5830

Provides technical assistance in the areas of technology development, energy, financial planning, natural resource development, management, and infrastructure. Operates a full-time staff in the U.S. of 2,500. Operates in Africa, Asia, the Pacific Islands, Latin American, the Caribbean, Middle East, North Africa, Europe, Japan, and Canada. Major clients include USAID, World Bank, and host country governments. Previous projects included: "Assistance to EEGI in Preparing Investment Plan and Strategy for Short, Medium, and Long Term" (Ivory Coast, Government of Ivory Coast, $1.2 million) and "CNMI Seven-Year Strategic Development Plan" Northern Mariana Islands, Commonwealth of N. Mariana Islands, $200,000).

## Roy Littlejohn Associates, Inc.
1101 14th St, NW, Suite 1000, 10th Floor
Washington, DC 20005
Tel. 202/722-2446
Fax 202/842-0215

U.S. staff of 30 and 5 abroad. Provides technical assistance in the areas of manpower/economic development, program design, applied research, data processing, technology, and applied science relating to labor, health, welfare, education, public administration, agriculture, and tourism.

## Logical Technical Services Corporation
7250 Woodmont Ave.
Suite 340
Bethesda, MD 20814
Tel. 301/652-2121
Fax 301/951-9624

Provides technical, software, and hardware support services relating to information services and technical publications. Maintains a full-time staff in the U.S. of 150. Operates projects in Africa, Asia, Latin America, and the Caribbean. Major clients include USAID. Previous project included: "Operate and Maintain a Comprehensive Facility for Handling USAID Development" (USAID, $23.4 million).

## Lummus Crest, Inc.
1515 Broad St.
Bloomfield, NJ 07003
Tel. 201/893/1515
Fax 201/893-2000

Provides engineering and construction services relating to chemical, petrochemical, and refinery plants. Maintains a full-time staff in the U.S. of 1 and a long-term staff abroad of 1,800. Operates in Africa (Nigeria), Asia, Latin America, Middle East, Western and Eastern Europe, the USSR, and Japan. Major clients include governments and private companies. Recent projects include: "Safanlya Gosp IV Offshore Facilities" (Saudi Arabia, ARAMCO, $650 million), "Copene Ethylene Complex" (Brazil, Copene-Petroquimica do Nordeste S.A., $400 million), and "Zhong Yuan Ethylene/Polyethylene Facility" (China, Zhong Yuan Petrochemical United Corp., $180 million).

## Management Systems International
600 Water St., SW, NBU 7-7
Washington, DC 20024
Tel. 202/484-7170
Fax 202/488-0754

Provides technical assistance in the areas of small enterprise development, institutional strengthening, information utilization, and project design, implementation, and evaluation. Maintains a full-time U.S. staff of 65 and along-term staff abroad of 3. Operates in Africa, Asia, Pacific Islands, Latin America, the Caribbean, Middle East, North Africa, Portugal, and Puerto Rico. Major clients include USAID, The World Bank, United Nations, and various U.S. government agencies. Previous projects included: "Immunization and Oral Rehydration Services Project" (Guatemala, USAID, $2 million), "Senegal Community and Enterprise Development Project" (USAID, $1.1 million), and "Small Project Support" (Zaire, USAID, $900,000).

## Mathtech, Inc.
5111 Leesburg Pike, Suite 702
Falls Church, VA 22041
Tel. 703/824-0800
Fax 703/671-6208

U.S. staff of 60 and 1 abroad. Provides technical assistance on energy issues in developing countries.

## Medical Service Corporation International
1716 Wilson Blvd.
Arlington, VA 22209
Tel. 703/276-3000
Fax 703/276-3017

Provides technical assistance in the areas of health career management, information systems, training, vector borne disease control, and program management. Maintains a full-time staff in the U.S. of 50 and a long-term staff abroad of 20. Operates in Africa, Asia, Latin America, the Caribbean, Middle East, North Africa, Australia, and Hungary. Major clients include USAID, and the U.S. Department of Health and Human Services. Previous projects included: "Improve Vector Control Programs and Reduce Incidence of Vector Diseases for LDC Populations" (Worldwide, USAID, $7.9 million), "Health Systems Support" (El Salvador, USAID, $3.4 million), and "Rural Health Support Project" (Sudan, USAID, $2.3 million).

## Meta Systems, Inc.
58 Charles St., 3rd Floor
Cambridge, MA 02141
Tel. 617/491-1001
Fax 617/621-0674

U.S. staff of 15. Provides technical services related to economic and engineering analysis, strategic planning, and policy analysis.

## Metcalf & Eddy International, Inc.
30 Harvard Mill Square
Wakefield, MA 01880
Tel. 617/246-5200
Fax 617/245-6293

Provides extensive capabilities in the areas of water and wastewater treatment, including the design and construction of wastewater systems, and defense communication systems. Maintains a full-time staff in the U.S. of 1,463 and a long-term staff abroad of 47. Operates in Africa, Asia, Latin America, the Caribbean, Middle East, North Africa, Europe, Antarctica, Arctic, Australia, and Puerto Rico. Major clients include USAID, U.S. Air Force, and the Government of Egypt. Previous projects included: "Alexandria Wastewater Program" (Egypt, USAID, $1 billion), "Peace Shield C31 Facility" (Saudi Arabia, USAF Logistics Command, $900 million), and "Wastewater Program Management" (Puerto Rico, Puerto Rico Aqueduct & Sewer Authority, $180 million).

## MMM Design Group
229 West Bute Street
Norfolk, VA 23510
Tel. 804/623-1641
Fax 804/623-5809

Provides a wide range of architecture, planning, and consulting engineering services. Maintains a full-time staff in the U.S. of 120 and a long-term staff abroad of 50. Operates in Africa, Asia, the Caribbean, the Middle East, North Africa, the Western Europe. Major clients include the World Bank, USAID, and several U.S. government agencies. Previous projects included "800 Car Parking Garage" (Italy, U.S. Navy, $8 million) and "Command, Control, and Communications Complex" (Italy).

## Montgomery Watson, Inc
250 North Madison Ave.
Pasadena, CA 91101
Tel. 818/796-9141
Fax 818/449-3741

An international engineering and construction firm providing a full range of services involved in designing, constructing, and managing water and wastewater systems in more than 40 countries. Maintains a full-time staff in the U.S. of 1,130 and a long-term staff abroad of 11. Operates in Africa, Asia, Latin America, the Caribbean, Middle East, and Europe. Major clients include USAID, Asian Development Bank, IBRD, and numerous governments and private companies. Previous projects included: "Canal Cities Water and Wastewater Construction Management Services" (Egypt, USAID, $5.8 million), "Training and Procurement for Reconstructing GEDAREF Water System" (Sudan, USAID, $2.7 million), and "Water and Wastewater Sector Institutional Development for Water Quality Monitoring" (Jordan, USAID, $1.5 million).

## Morrison-Knudsen Corporation
P.O. Box 73
Boise, ID 83729
Tel. 208/386-5000
Fax 208/386-7186

Provides a full range of engineering and construction services relating to transportation, water resources, defense systems, nuclear and hazardous wastes, power plants, railroads, and aircraft. Maintains a full-time staff in the U.S. of

13,500 and a long-term staff abroad of 500. Major clients include numerous host country governments. Previous projects included: "Itaipu Hydroelectric Development Power Plant/Concrete Earth Dam" (Brazil, Itaipu Binacional Authority, $49.8 million), "Inga-Shaba Technical Assistance Generation and Transmission" (Zaire, Soc. Nat. de Electricite-SNEL, $37.3 million), "Santa Luzia Steel Fabrication & Galvanization/Tower" (Brazil, various clients, $26.1 million), and "Road Construction in South Cotabao" (Philippines, USAID, $40.2 million).

## Morrison-Maierle/CSSA, Inc.
910 Helena Avenue
Helena, MT 59601
Tel. 406/442-3050
Fax 406/442-7862

U.S. staff of 125 and 3 abroad. Provides engineering consulting services in a variety of areas. Recent project involved: "Engineering and Construction Inspection Services" (Philippines, USAID, $4.2 million).

## Robert R. Nathan Associates, Inc.
2101 Wilson Blvd., Suite 1200
Arlington, VA 22201-3062
Tel. 703/516-7700
Fax 703/351-6162

Provides technical assistance in the areas of agricultural development, urban planning, small-scale enterprise development, macro-economic policy, and financial infrastructure. Maintains a full-time staff in the U.S. of 70 and a long-term staff abroad of 22. Operates in Africa, Asia, the Pacific Islands, Latin America, the Caribbean, Middle East, North America, and Europe. Major clients include USAID, UNDP, FAO, and the Asian Development Bank. Previous major projects included: "Agricultural Training, Planning, and Institutional Development" (Zambia, USAID, $8.8 million), "Promote Process of Small Business/Micro-Enterprise Development" (Worldwide, USAID, $6.8 million), "Provide Technical Services for Public Management and Policy Planning Project" (Barbados, USAID, $5.4 million).

## A. L. Nellum and Associates
1900 L Street, NW, Suite 405
Washington, DC 20036
Tel. 202/466-4920
Fax 202/466-4745

Trains U.S. Peace Corps Volunteers as extension workers in natural resource and environmental conservation. Operates in Africa, the Caribbean, Latin America, and the Philippines.

## New Jersey Marine Sciences Consortium
Building 22
Fort Hancock
Highlands, NJ 07732
Tel. 908/872-1300
Fax 908/291-4483

Provides technical assistance in the areas of marine and coastal science and technology. Maintains a full-time staff in the U.S. of 30. Operates primarily in the Middle East (Egypt and Israel). Major client is USAID. Previous projects included: "Cooperative Marine Technology Program for the Middle East" (USAID, $14 million) and "Support Middle East Peace Process by Increasing Contact and Cooperation Between Egyptian and Israeli Scientists" (USAID, $2.7 million).

## Robert D. Niehaus, Inc.
5951 Encina Road, Suite 105
Santa Barbara, CA 93117
Tel. 805/681-7300

U.S. staff of 10. Provides economic and environmental consulting services to international development projects.

## The Ralph M. Parsons Company
100 W. Walnut Street
Pasadena, CA 91124
Tel. 818/440-2000
Fax 818/440-2630

One of the largest international engineering and construction firms. Offers a full range of services to government, industry, and commerce. Has completed nearly 7,000 projects in more than 90 countries, from transportation systems to power plants. Maintains a full-time staff in the U.S. of 3290 and a long-term staff abroad of 596. Operates in Africa, Asia, the Pacific Islands, Latin America, the Caribbean, Middle East, North Africa, Europe, the USSR, and Australia. Major clients include several U.S. government agencies as well as foreign governments and major corporations. Previous projects included: "Yanbu Industrial City" (Saudi Arabia, Government of Saudi Arabia, 30 year project involving several billion dollars) and "Royal Country Club Resort Development wan" (Taiwan, private, $300 million).

## Parsons Brinckerhoff International, Inc.
One Penn Plaza
New York, NY 10119
Tel. 212/465-5000
Fax 212/465-5096

Provides planning, engineering, and architectural services relating to transportation, construction, industrial complexes, environmental protection, energy, water resources, urban and regional planning, and agricultural systems. Maintains a full-time staff in U.S. of 2,100 and a long-term staff abroad of 480. Operates in Africa, Asia, Latin America, the Caribbean, Middle East, North Africa, Europe, and the former Soviet Union. Major clients include USAID, the World Bank, and host country government. Previous projects included: "Karachi Mass Transit Study for Karachi Development Authority" (Pakistan, Karachi Special Development Programme/ World Bank, $1.3 million) and "Perform Post-Award and Construction Surveillance/Inspection Services for Port of Kismayo Port Rehabilitation Project" (Somalia, USAID, $600,000).

## Payette Associates Inc.
285 Summer St.
Boston, MA 02210
Tel. 617/342-8200
Fax 617/342-8202

Provides planning, design, construction services for research and health care projects. Maintains a full-time staff in the U.S. of 145. Operates in Guinea-Bissau, Korea, Pakistan, and Egypt. Major funding source is the Aga Khan Foundation. Previous projects included: "Aga Khan University Hospital and Medical College" (Pakistan, Aga Khan Foundation, $300 million) and "Armed Forces Medical City" (Pakistan, $50 million).

## Planning and Development Collaborative Inc. (PADCO)
1012 N Street, NW
Washington, DC 20001
Tel. 202/789-1140
Fax 202/789-0242

Provides technical assistance in the areas of housing and urban development, regional and rural development, financial management, human resource development, and project/program evaluation. Maintains a full-time staff in the U.S. of 20 and a long-term staff abroad of 7. Operates in Africa, Asia, Latin America, the Caribbean, Middle East, and North Africa. Major clients include USAID, Asian Development Bank, World Bank, and the United Nations. Previous projects included: "Assist in Planning, Implementation, Monitoring, and Evaluation of Rapati Zone Rural Area Development Project" (Nepal, USAID, $7.4 million), "Assist AID's Office of Housing and Urban Problems With

Implementation of Shelter-Related Issues and Problems" (Worldwide, USAID, $2.4 million), and "Advisory Services in Housing Policy to Ministry of Housing" (Jamaica, USAID, $1.9 million).

## Pragma Corporation
116 E. Broad Street
Falls Church, VA 22046
Tel. 703/237-9303
Fax 703/237-9326

Offers management consulting services in the areas of agriculture and rural development, family planning, health, financial management, private sector development, training/education, industrial development and finance, microcomputer applications, and information systems. Maintains a full-time staff in the U.S. of 30 and a long-term staff abroad of 27. Major clients include USAID, World Bank, InterAmerican Development Bank, IFAD, OAS, and Peace Corps. Operates in Africa, Asia, Latin America, the Caribbean, Middle East, and North Africa with its largest contacts for Burkina Faso, Burma, Zaire, Kenya, and Benin. Some of the largest previous contracts in Kenya ($5.3 million) for "Provide Training Program to Strengthen Kenya's Leadership for National Development", the U.S. ($4.5 million) for "Provide Support Services for Economic and Social Data System", and Burma ($4.2 million) for "Coordinate Placement, Monitoring, and Administration of Burmese."

## Price Waterhouse
1801 K Street, NW
Washington, DC 20006
Tel. 202/296-0800
Fax 202/466-3918, 296-2785

Operating since 1849, this is one of the world's premier accounting and management consulting firms with 416 offices operating in over 100 countries. Maintains a full-time staff in the U.S. of more than 13,000 and a long-term staff abroad of more than 26,000. Provides extensive services to both business and government. Previous technical assistance projects included: institutional strengthening; operational audits; strategic planning; management information systems; financial and economic analysis; management sciences and economics; public utility management; transportation planning and management; project and program monitoring and evaluation; private and public sector analysis; privatization; training and human resource development; financial markets strengthening; trade and development; and training and technology transfers. Operates in Africa, Asia, the Pacific Islands, Latin America, the Caribbean, Middle East, North Africa, Eastern Europe, and the USSR. Major clients include USAID, World Bank, United Nations, Inter-American Development Bank, foreign governments, and private companies. Previous projects included: "Kenya Agricultural Research Institute" (USAID, $12 million), "Financial Sector Development Project" (Worldwide, USAID, $10.7 million), and "Kenya Agricultural Management Project" (Kenya, USAID, $3.5 million).

## Price, Williams, and Associates, Inc.
8484 Georgia Ave., Suite 400
Silver Spring, MD 20910
Tel. 301/565-9700
Fax 301/585-4318

U.S. staff of 100. Provides data processing, software utilization, strategic planning, and management information systems services.

## RDA International, Inc.
801 Morey Dr.
Placerville, CA 95667
Tel. 916/622-8800
Fax 916/626-7391

Provides technical assistance in the areas of fisheries, aquaculture, and natural resources. Maintains a full-time U.S. staff of 10 and a long-term staff abroad of 21. Operates in Africa, Asia, Latin America, the Caribbean, and Oman. Major clients include USAID and FUSADES. Previous projects included: "Oman Fisheries Development" (Sultanate of Oman, USAID and Oman Government, $7.7 million) and "Rural Development Study: Shrimp Aquaculture, Fresh-Water Prawns, Aquarium Fish, Tourism, Land Information System, Wood Production, Rattan" (Belize, USAID, $375,000).

## Resources Conservation Company
3006 Northup Way
Bellevue, WA 98004-1407
Tel. 206/828-2400
Fax 206/828-0526

U.S. staff of 85. Provides technical services relating to evaporative water treatment systems for recycling wastewater.

## Resources Management International
2000 L St., NW
Washington, DC 20036
Tel. 202/223-1020
Fax 202/775-5199

U.S. staff of 4 and 60 abroad. Provides consulting services in a variety of areas, such as agriculture, education, and energy, primarily in Asia, Eastern Europe, and the former Soviet Union. Recent major projects include: "Improve Industrial Energy Efficiency and Reform Energy Price Systems in Eastern Europe" (USAID, $2.3 million) and "Analysis of the Heating System Energy Efficiency in Byelorus, Ukraine, and Armenia" (USAID, $6.3 million).

## Ronco Consulting Corporation
1995 University Ave., Suite 330
Berkeley, CA 94704
Tel. 510/526-8290
Fax 510/848-1983

Specializing in providing a full range of agricultural, energy, private sector, human resource, family planning, and food aid services. Maintains a full-time staff in the U.S. of 20 and a long-term staff abroad of 25. Operates in Africa, Asia, Latin America, the Caribbean, Middle East, and North Africa. Major clients include USAID and UNFAO. Previous major projects included: "Develop Capacity of Institutions and Agencies in Mid-East/North Africa to Design Family Planning Service Training" (Worldwide, USAID, $5.9 million), "Commodity Export Project" (Pakistan, USAID, $5.2 million), and "Promote/Strengthen Private Agricultural Production Organizations Project" (Bolivia, USAID, $4.7 million).

## H. K. Schueler International, Ltd.
150 Fifth Avenue
New York, NY 10011-4377
Tel. 212/645-1900
Fax 212/645-2662

U.S. staff of 6. Procures and supplies medical and laboratory products for international health organizations, PVO's, and NGO's.

## Servicios Tecnicos del Caribe
Ave. Ponce De Leon 1605-Pda. 23
Santurce, Puerto Rico 00909

Provides agricultural development services primarily in Latin America and the Caribbean. Has 8(a) status. Maintains a full-time staff in the U.S. of 20 and a long-term staff abroad of 10. Major clients are USAID and the World Bank. Previous major projects included: "Design, Coordinate, and Complete the Proposed Economic Studies" (Panama, USAID, $2.9 million) and "Assist With Implementation of Agrarian Reform Program" (El Salvador, USAID, $1.5 million).

## Sheladia Associates, Inc.
15825 Shady Grove Rd., Suite 100
Rockville, MD 20850
Tel. 301/590-3939
Fax 301/948-7174

Provides technical assistance in the areas of water resources, transportation, and communication systems. Maintains a full-time U.S. staff of 186 and a long-term

CONTRACTING AND CONSULTING FIRMS

staff abroad of 23. Operates in Africa, Asia, Latin America, Middle East, and North Africa. Major clients include USAID, U.S. Department of State, and other consulting firms. Previous projects included: "Irrigation Systems Management Project" (Sri Lanka, USAID, $4.7 million), "Watershed Development Project" (Cape Verde, USAID, $2.4 million), and "Assist in Implementing Soil/Water Conservation Program and Food Aid Assistance Program" (Cameroon, USAID, $2.1 million).

## John Short and Associates, Inc.
10227 Wincopin Circle
Suite 400
Columbia, MD 21044
Tel. 301/964-2811
Fax 301/964-0598

Provides a wide-range of health care management and consulting services, such as public health, primary care, nursing, population and family planning, research, evaluation, health finance, business, and marketing. Maintains a full-time staff in the U.S. of 429 and a long-term staff abroad of 6. Operates in Africa, Asia, Latin America, the Caribbean, Middle East, and North Africa. Major clients include USAID and numerous government agencies and private firms. Previous projects included: "Increase Allocation of Private Sector Resources to Family Planning and Birthspacing in Private Homes" (Worldwide, USAID, $5.5 million), "Jordan Primary Health Care Nursing Development Program" (Jordan, USAID, $3.4 million), and "Technical Assistance in Family Planning for Enterprise Project" (Worldwide, USAID, $2.4 million).

## Wilbur Smith Associates, Inc.
NCNB Tower—Gervais St. 1301/P.O. Box 92
Columbia, SC 29201
Tel. 803/738-0580
Fax 803/251-2064

U.S. staff of 600 and 100 abroad. Provides international consulting services relating to engineering, architecture, planning, and economics.

## Sparks Commodities, Inc.
889 Ridge Lake Blvd.
Memphis, TN 38120
Tel. 901/766-4600
Fax 901/766-4402

U.S. staff of 100. Specialties in providing food and agriculture services.

## Stanley Consultants, Inc.
Stanley Building
Muscatine, IA 52761

U.S. staff of 350 and 10 abroad. Provides engineering and consultative services relating to a wide range of engineering issues.

## Stetson-Harza
181 Genesee Street
Utica, NY 13501
Tel. 315/797-5800
Fax 315/797-8143

Provides architectural and engineering services relating to chemical, systems, building, civil, and water resources engineering. Maintains a full-time staff in the U.S. of 180. Operates in Korea, Italy, West Germany, and Puerto Rico. Major clients are U.S. Army Engineers and private companies. Previous projects included: "Design/Engineering Non-Beta Lactam Manufacturing Plant" (Puerto Rico, Bristol-Myers Co, $30 million) and "Provide Comprehensive Master Plan for Vicenza Military Community" (Italy, U.S. Army Engineers, $1.1 million).

## STV Engineers, Inc.
11 Robinson St.
Pottstown, PA 19464
Tel. 610/326-4600
Fax 610/326-3833

A major international engineering, architectural, planning, construction management, management consulting, and interior design firm. Maintains a full-time staff in the U.S. of 1100 and a long-term staff abroad of 50. Operates in Africa, Asia, Latin America, the Caribbean, the Middle East, and Western Europe. Major clients include USAID, U.S. Department of State, numerous other U.S. government agencies, private firms, and host country governments. Previous projects included: "Second Manila Port Project" (Philippines, Government of the Philippines, $3 million), "Awaran-Turbot Road" (Pakistan, USAID, $2 million), and "Services at Foreign Service Posts Worldwide" (Africa, Europe, U.S. Department of State, $2 million).

## TAMS Consultants, Inc.
655 Third Avenue
New York, NY 10017
Tel. 212/867-1777
Fax 212/697-6354

A full service international engineering, architecture, planning, and environmental consulting firm specializing in projects relating to airports, natural resource management, highways, ports, transportation planning, urban development, waste, and water resources. Maintains a full-time staff in the U.S. of 450 and a long-term staff abroad of 25. Operates in Africa, Asia, Latin America, the Caribbean, the Middle East, North Africa, Australia, Portugal, and the Slovac Republic. Major clients include the World Bank, Inter-American Development Bank, USAID, and host country governments. Previous projects included: "Daule Peripa Hydroelectric Project" (Ecuador, IADB, $19 million), "Casa de Piedra Hydroelectric Project" (Government of Argentina, $16 million), and "Kordofan Feeder Roads Project" (Sudan, USAID, $12.2 million).

## Thunder and Associates
719 Price Street
Alexandria, VA 22314
Tel. 703/684-5584
Fax 703/684-3954
72144.3635@compuserve.com

Provides management training and organizational development and technical assistance to governments, especially in computer applications. Has a staff of 20 in Virginia and 20-30 in its field office in Kenya. Operates in Asia, Africa, and the former Soviet Union. USAID is a major contract source. Previous projects included: "Senior Management Survey to Determine Future Directions of the Agency" (USAID, $130,000) and "Development Mission Orders and Procedures" (USAID, $130,000).

## Training Resources Group
909 North Washington Street
Suite 305
Alexandria, VA 22314
Tel. 703/548-3535
Fax 703/836-2415

U.S. staff of 25. Provides management training, train the trainers, and cross-cultural training services. Recent project included: "Conduct Management Training Program" (worldwide, USAID, $762,000)

## TransCentury Corporation
1901 North Fort Myer Drive
Arlington, VA 22209
Tel. 703/351-5500
Fax 703/351-5507

Specializes in providing technical assistance to Third World countries in a wide range of program areas, from accounting to management and training. Operates in Africa, Asia, Latin America, the Caribbean, and Middle East. Maintains a full-time staff in the U.S. of 15 and a long-term staff abroad of 25. Major clients include USAID, Ford Foundation, and host country governments. Previous projects included: "Swaziland Manpower Development Project Interrelated Project Elements" (USAID, $11.1 million) and "Child Survival Project" (Egypt, USAID, $2 million).

## Triton Corporation
1010 Wayne Avenue
Suite 300
Silver Spring, MD 20910
Tel. 301/565-4020
Fax 301/565-5112

U.S. staff of 200 and 5 abroad. Provides management consulting services relating to organizational infrastructure and social marketing of contraceptives.

## Tropical Research and Development, Inc.
7001 SW 24th Ave.
Gainesville, FL 32607
Tel. 904/331-1886
Fax 904/331-3284

Provides technical assistance in the areas of natural resource development, marine culture, fisheries and coastal management, crop, livestock and forest production, water resource management, and integrated regional development. Maintains a full-time U.S. staff of 37 and a long-term staff abroad of 7. Operates in Africa, Asia, Latin America, the Caribbean, Jordan, Italy, and Puerto Rico. Major clients include USAID, InterAmerican Development Bank, U.S. Navy, FUSADES, FAO, and universities. Previous projects included: "Associated High Valleys Technical Assistance" (Bolivia, USAID, $900,000) and "Development Strategies for Fragile Lands" (Latin America/Caribbean, USAID, $745,000).

## TVT Associates
503 Capitol Ct., NE
Suite 300
Washington, DC 20002
Tel. 202/547-4550
Fax 202/547-7082

U.S. staff of 10. Provides technical assistance in the areas of rural development, small enterprise development, income generation, agri-business, investment promotion, and evaluation. Recent project included: "Monitoring and Evaluating Senegal African Economic Policy Program" (Senegal, USAID, $153,000)

## University Research Corporation
7200 Wisconsin Ave.
Suites 500 & 600
Bethesda, MD 20814
Tel. 301/654-8338
Fax 301/654-5976

Provides technical assistance in the areas of family planning, health care, and rural health delivery systems. Maintains a full-time staff in the U.S. of 200 and a long-term staff abroad of 10. Operates in Africa, Asia, Latin America, the Caribbean, the Middle East, and North Africa. Major clients include USAID, United Nations, U.S. Peace Corps, Organization of American States, and several U.S. government agencies. Previous projects included: "Primary Health Care Operations Research" (Worldwide, USAID, $10.5 million), "Improve Cost-Effectiveness of Family Planning/Maternal Child Health Service Delivery Systems in Asia" (USAID, $6.6 million), and "Somalia Family Health Services Project" (USAID, $4.2 million).

## Washington Consulting Group
20036 DuPont Circle, NW
Washington, DC 20036
Tel. 202/797-7800
Fax 202/797-7806

Provides technical assistance in the areas of aviation, computer technology, quantitative studies, and technical publications. Maintains a full-time staff in the U.S. of 500. Has 8(a) status. Operates projects in Africa, Asia, Latin America, the Caribbean, Middle East, and North Africa. Major clients include USAID, World Bank, UNDP, USDA, 8 other government departments, National Institutes of Health, and commercial clients. Previous large projects in Indonesia ($13.4 million), "Health Sector Financing" and Senegal ($8.7 million), "Senegal Family Health and Population."

## Wimberly Allison Tong and Goo
2222 Kalakaua Avenue Penthouse
Honolulu, HI 96815
Tel. 808/922-1253
Fax 808/922-1250

Provides architecture and planning services dealing with hotels, resorts, rapid transit, waterfront development, and environmental projects. Maintains a full-time staff in the U.S. of 180. Operates in Asia, the Pacific Islands, Middle East, Mexico, Australia, New Zealand, Western Europe, and the former Soviet Union. Major clients include private firms and host country governments. Recent projects include: "Surfers Paradise Resort Hotel" (Australia, $170 million), "Hyatt Nusadua" (Bali, $70), and "Ramada Goa" (India, $30 million).

# 7

# PRIVATE VOLUNTARY ORGANIZATIONS (PVOs)

*P*rivate voluntary organizations (PVOs)—also frequently referred to as non-governmental organizations (NGOs)—function similarly to nonprofit corporations and contracting firms. Often competing for the same public and private funding source, they operate projects and manage staffs at the field level in poor Third and Fourth World countries. They primarily provide assistance to various disadvantaged groups in developing countries. They work in rural villages, urban slums, and remote areas.

## ORIENTATION

PVOs are especially noted for helping the poorest and most distressed groups in developing countries—groups government agencies, international organizations, businesses, and contracting firms are not well equipped to help. A disproportionate number of PVOs focus on child survival, refugee and disaster relief, self-help income generation, enterprise development, vocational training, agriculture and food production, population planning, communications, social welfare, environment and natural resource management, housing, health care, and community development, and women in development efforts for the very poor and destitute. Few if any are involved in creating physical infrastructure or managing technical and marketing programs, although many of their activities support these other efforts that are largely dominated by the private contracting and consulting firms outlined in Chapter 6.

Many of these organizations have religious affiliations, such as the Adventist Development and Relief Agency International, Catholic Relief Services, and Lutheran World Relief, Inc.. These groups are closely linked to the missionary activities of U.S.-based Christian churches.

In many respects, PVOs are modern-day missionaries who are less motivated by an evangelical zeal to save souls than by a commitment to humanity—help the very poor move into the mainstream of development. These organizations appeal to a certain type of person who still has a missionary zeal to improve the conditions of poor people throughout the world. Individuals working for PVOs tend to be dedicated to certain human values and committed to helping others; few are motivated by money. Working conditions for employees of these organizations can be difficult and pay is often low. Noted for people-to-people contact at the community level, PVO work tends to generate a certain sense of personal satisfaction and accomplishment that is hard to match in the counterpart work of businesses, government agencies, or international organizations.

While many of these groups are funded by individual and corporate contributions, most also receive contracts and grants from government agencies and foundations. Some of the more enterprising child survival groups, such as Save the Children Foundation, Foster Parents Plan, and Christian Children's Fund, also operate individual "sponsorship" programs for generating income.

PVOs are increasingly playing a major role in developing countries. Funding agencies view these groups as most capable of making a difference in developing countries. Given their great strengths—extensive field operations, commitment to change, adaptability, innovation, performance—PVOs have increasingly become favorite target organizations for key funding organizations such as USAID and the United Nations. These organizations are committed to expanding the community-based operations of PVOs in Third and Fourth World countries. Consequently, many of these organizations may experience significant growth during the coming decade.

PVOs have traditionally operated in the poorest countries of Sub-Saharan Africa, Asia, the Caribbean, and Central and South America. Within the past four years, however, many of these groups have extended their operations into the former communist countries of Eastern Europe and the former Soviet Union. For the first time in more than 50 years, numerous PVOs provide assistance in such familiar and unfamiliar places as Albania, Armenia, Belarus, Bosnia-Hercegovina, Bulgaria, Croatia, Czech Republic, Estonia, Georgia, Hungary, Kazakhstan, Kyrgyzstan, Latvia, Lithuania, Moldova, Poland, Romania, Russia, Serbia, Slovak Republic, Tajikistan, Turkmenistan, and the Ukraine.

## STRATEGIES

Many PVOs are headquartered in New York City and Washington, DC and operate field staffs throughout the developing world. In contrast to other types of organizations in development, PVOs tend to have a larger proportion of staff working in the field than at headquarters. Therefore, if you are interested in working on development projects in the poor countries of Asia, Africa, and Latin America, many of the PVOs outlined in this chapter may be your perfect choice for targeting a job search.

PVOs should be approached in the same manner as private contracting and consulting firms and nonprofit corporations: identify those organizations that interest you, send a copy of your resume to their resource bank (usually operated by the Personnel or Human Resource Development Department), monitor job vacancy announcements appearing in major publications, and network for information, advice, and referrals amongst individuals related to the organization.

In contrast to many other organizations operating in developing countries, it is often easier to break into the international job market via PVOs and nonprofit corporations than through government agencies, international organizations, businesses, and private contracting and consulting firms. Many of these organizations offer volunteer opportunities which enable inexperienced individuals to acquire valuable international experience which may turn into full-time employment. As we will see in Chapter 11, many of these same organizations offer internships.

# THE ORGANIZATIONS

## Accion International/AITEC

130 Prospect Street
Cambridge, MA 02139
Tel. 617/492-4930
Fax 617/876-9509

733 15th St., NW, 7th Fl.
Washington, DC 20005
Tel. 202/393-5113
Fax 202/393-5115

U.S. staff of 14 and 10 abroad. Dedicated to eliminating hunger and poverty in the Americas by promoting small-scale economic activities amongst low-income groups in South and Central American, the Caribbean, and the southwestern United States. Operates with a $4 million annual budget.

## Adventist Development and Relief Agency International

12501 Old Columbia Pike
Silver Spring, MD 20904
Tel. 301/680-6380
Fax 301/680-6370

Sponsored by the Seventh-Day Adventist Church. Provides technical assistance in the areas of education, agriculture, health care, community development, social welfare, and disaster relief in Africa, Asia, Latin America, and the Middle East. Maintains a full-time staff in the U.S. of 45 and a long-term staff abroad of 130. Funded through donations from individuals, corporations, and foundations as well as USAID. Recent projects include: "Medical Care and Relief or Children Who are Victims of Civil Strife" (Nicaragua, USAID, $2.5 million), "Assist in Design for Food for Peace Programs" (Worldwide, USAID, $1.8 million), and "Enhancing the Micro-Medium Small Business Sector" (Worldwide, USAID, $1.7 million).

## The African-American Institute

833 United Nations Plaza
New York, NY 10017-3509
Tel. 212/949-5666
Fax 212/682-6174

1625 Mass. Ave., NW, #210
Washington, DC 20036
Tel. 202/667-5636
Fax 202/265-6332

U.S. staff of 80 and 46 abroad. Promotes development in Africa and greater understanding between Americans and Africans. Conducts programs on economic recovery and growth, education, policy analysis, outreach, and women in development. Its program representatives operate in 24 African countries. Operates with a $28 million annual budget.

### African Medical and Research Foundation
420 Lexington Ave., Suite 244
New York, NY 10170
Tel. 212/986-1835
Fax 212/599-5074

U.S. staff of 5 and 650 abroad. Provides primary health care services in rural areas of Africa. Conducts education and training programs, conducts research, produces health materials, and operates "flying doctor" teams and mobile medical units. Operates with a $2 million annual budget.

### African Wildlife Foundation
1717 Massachusetts Ave., NW, Suite 602
Washington, DC 20036
Tel. 202/265-8394
Fax 202/265-2361

U.S. staff of 11 and 30 abroad. Promotes wildlife preservation through education and training programs in Africa.

### Africare, Inc.
440 R Street, NW
Washington, DC 20001
Tel. 202/462-3614
Fax 202/387-1034

Provides assistance to Africa in the areas of water resources, agriculture and food production, education, construction, medical care, health services, and refugee assistance. Maintains a full-time staff in the U.S. of 35 and a long-term staff abroad of 90. Funded by USAID and numerous corporations, foundations, and host country governments. Previous projects included: "Provide Support to Africare's Implementation of Quaddal Rural Development Project" (Chad, USAID, $2.8 million), "Assist Food Crop Producers in Timbuktu Region Over 3 Year Period" (Mali, USAID, $1.7 million), and "Strengthen, Diversify, and Expand Economic Activities of Small/Medium Scale Entrepreneurs" (Malawi, USAID, $1.5 million). Operates with a $15 million annual budget.

### Aga Kahn Foundation
1901 L Street, NW, Suite 700
Washington, DC 20036
Tel. 202/293-2537
Fax 202/785-1752

U.S. staff of 6 and 120 abroad. Promotes social development among low-income groups in Asia and Africa. Supports programs in education, agriculture and food production, and public health. Operates with a $2.7 million annual budget.

## Alan Futtmacher Institute

111 5th Avenue
New York, NY 10003
Tel. 212/254-5656
Fax 212/254-9891

2010 Massachusetts Ave., NW
Washington, DC 20036
Tel. 202/296-4012
Fax 202/223-5756

Conducts research, policy analysis, and public education programs to disseminate information on reproductive health rights. Supports family planning efforts. Operates with a $4.2 million annual budget.

## America-Mideast Educational and Training Services, Inc.

1100 17th St., NW
Suite 300
Washington, DC 20036
Tel. 202/785-0022
Fax 202/822-6563

A 195-member educational organization that administers educational exchange, grant, and scholarship programs as well as provides technical assistance in the areas of manpower development, educational reform, and vocational and legal development. Maintains a full-time U.S. staff of 80 and a long-term staff abroad of 60. Operates only in the Middle East and North Africa. Major clients include USAID, USIA, the World Bank, Educational Testing Services, and host country governments. Previous projects included: "Cyprus American Scholarship Program" (USAID, $45.9 million), "Partners for International Education and Training" (Middle East and North Africa, USAID, $26.2 million), and "West Bank/Gaza Human Resources Development Project" (USAID, $5.6 million).

## America's Development Foundation

101 North Union Street, Suite 200
Alexandria, VA 22314
Tel. 703/836-2717
Fax 703/836-3379
Network E-Mail: Peacenet,
Sprintnet: adf@igc.org

Promotes the international development of democracy and respect for human rights. Provides technical assistance to private sector organizations. Sponsors programs on institutional development, civic education, electoral processes, and human rights. Recent projects included: "Implement the Umbrella Management Unit of the Democracy Enhancement Project" (Haiti, USAID, $4.6 million) and "Implement a Program for Democracy Development in Panama" (Panama, USAID, $240,000). Operates with a $2 million annual budget.

## American Council for Nationalities Services
95 Madison Avenue
3rd Floor
New York, NY 10016
Tel. 212/532-5858
Fax 212/532-8558

Serves as the national organization for a network of 40 community supported social service agencies committed to responding to the needs of immigrants and refugees. Monitors refugee movements throughout the world and informs the public and policy makers about world refugee issues. Operates with a $7.5 million annual budget.

## American Friends Service Committee (AFSC)
1501 Cherry Street
Philadelphia, PA 19102
Tel. 215/241-7150 or 7141
Fax 215/241-7026

A Quaker organization committed to alleviating human suffering and promoting global peace. Programs focus on integrated community development, agricultural production, cooperative organization, construction, public health services and refugee assistance. Staff and volunteers in Africa, Latin America, the Middle East and Southeast Asia. Although no specific degrees are required, a minimum of a Bachelor's degree is generally expected. Work experience related to areas of programs, experience living/working in a developing country and a service ideal are most important. Primarily funded through private grants, contributions, bequests, and investments. Operates with a $27 million annual budget.

## American Institute for Free Labor Development
1015 20th Street, NW
Washington, DC 20036
Tel. 202/659-6300
Fax 202/872-0618

Provides technical assistance to developing democratic trade unions in Latin America. Sponsored by the AFL-CIO, it works with local trade unions to provide training and planning for the economic development of the region. Maintains a full-time staff in the U.S. of 57 and a long-term staff abroad of 22. Major clients include USAID and the National Endowment for Democracy. A Bachelor's degree may be accepted and training/experience in trade unions, industrial relations, economic development and Latin America is helpful. Previous projects included: "Provide Technical Assistance for Development of Democratic Trade Union Movement" (USAID, $49.9 million), "El Salvador Land Reform" (USAID, $11.7 million), and "Support Training of Labor Leaders to Better Service Unions, Federations, and Better Membership" (USAID, $5.6 million).

## American Jewish Joint Distribution Committee, Inc.

711 Third Avenue
10th Floor
New York, NY 10017
Tel. 212/687-6200
Fax 212/370-5467

Provides relief, reconstruction, and rehabilitation and supports development projects in Europe and the developing world. Involved in community development, education, disaster relief, health care, refugee services, and social welfare projects. Supports the work of the United Nations in human rights, assists overseas Jewish communities, and helps Israel protect its existence. Conducts programs in Central and South America, Eastern Europe, Russia and the Commonwealth of Nations, Europe, Middle East, South Asia, Southeast Asia, and Sub-Saharan Africa. Operates field offices in Argentina, Austria, France, Israel, and Italy. Major funding comes through the United Jewish Appeal along with some government contracts and grants. A Master's degree in public administration, social work or areas relating to human services or planning and program management is preferred as is experience in Jewish community services. Language of the country in which one would be stationed plus previous work abroad may be required. Operates with a $70 million annual budget.

## American Jewish World Service

15 West 26th Street
9th Floor
New York, NY 10010
Tel. 212/683-1161
Fax 212/683-5187

Supports programs and NGO projects that develop the education and skills of women, ethnic minorities, and the rural poor. Programs include education, micro-enterprise development, disaster relief, and sustainable agriculture. Operates with a $2.2 million annual budget.

## American Near East Refugee Aid, Inc.

1522 K Street, NW, Suite 202
Washington, DC 20005
Tel. 202/347-2558
Fax 202/682-1637

Provides direct financial and technical assistance to Palestinian refugees and other needy individuals in the Arab world. Supports economic and social development through education, public health, vocational training, and municipal and agricultural cooperatives. Includes field offices in Israel and Gaza. Operates with a $6 million annual budget.

## American ORT Federation (Education for Life)

817 Broadway                              2025 I Street, NW, Suite 320
New York, NY 10003-4756                   Washington, DC 20006
Tel. 212/677-4400                         Tel. 202/293-2560
Fax 212/979-9545                          Fax 202/293-2577

Provides technical assistance for human resource development, education, health care, transportation, agricultural and rural development, manufacturing and mining, public and private service enterprises, and urban development. Operates a worldwide network of vocational and technical education programs. Maintains a full-time U.S. staff of 40 and long-term staff abroad of 8,000. Major funding comes form USAID, CIDA, the World Bank, and the Swiss Development Corporation. Previous projects included: "Expand and Strengthen Capability to Implement Development Projects in Zaire" (USAID, $5 million), "Lake Chad Agricultural Development and Farmer Training" (Chad, USAID, $3.5 million), and "Provide Vocational Training to Former Political Prisoners and Their Families" (Albania, USAID, $2.9 million). Operates with a $13 million annual budget.

## American Red Cross International Services

18th and D Streets, NW
Washington, DC 20006
Tel. 202/639-3319 or 202/737-8300
Fax 202/347-4486

Provides relief to disaster victims and refugees, development assistance, primary health care and education, HIV/AIDS education, blood collection and processing, and capacity building assistance. Collaborates with 150 National Red Cross and Red Crescent societies throughout the world. Recent projects include: "Provide Emergency Medical Program to the Newly Independent States" (former Soviet Union, USAID, $850,000), "Support Emergency Medical Relief Assistance and Strengthen the Lebanese Red Cross Programs" (Lebanon, USAID, $2.1 million), and "Provide Disaster Assistance to Ethiopia for the Displaced Persons Program" (Ethiopia, USAID, $1.5 million). Operates with a $1.6 billion annual budget.

## American Refugee Committee

2344 Nicollet Avenue, Suite 350
Minneapolis, MN 55404-3305
Tel. 612/872-7060
Fax 612/872-4309

Provides medical care, training, and other assistance to refugees and other displaced persons. Operates programs in Southeast Asia, Sub-Saharan Africa, and Eastern Europe and field offices in Cambodia, Malawi, Somalia, Thailand, and Croatia. Recent project includes: "Provide Support for the Humanitarian Aid to Children of Cambodia Program" (Cambodia, USAID, $500,000). Operates with a $3.5 million annual budget.

## AmeriCares Foundation
161 Cherry Street
New Canaan, CT 06840
Tel. 203/966-5195
Fax 203/972-0116

Provides international relief by soliciting donations of medicines, medical supplies, and other materials from American companies and delivering them to health and welfare professionals in the U.S. and 60 other countries. Also provides training and conducts research. Maintains a full-time staff in the U.S. of 20. Operates in the Caribbean, Central and South America, Sub-Saharan Africa, Asia, South Asia, Southeast Asia, Middle East, Eastern Europe, and the former Soviet Republics. Major funding sources are USAID, CARE, Knights of Malta, and private companies. Previous projects included: "Conduct Field Trials on New Medical Treatment for Control/Prevention of Leprosy" (Central America, Panama, USAID, $800,000) and "Assist USAID/Afghanistan With Support for Medical Refresher Course for Afghans" (Afghanistan, USAID, $469,900). Operates with a $160 million annual budget.

## Amigos de las Americas
5618 Star Lane
Houston, TX 77057
Tel. 713/782-5290
Fax 713/782-9267

Provides leadership and development opportunities for young people and public health assistance in Latin America with volunteers who focus on sanitation projects, human immunization, dental screening, and rabies inoculation for animals. Maintains a full-time U.S. staff of 15 and numerous volunteers abroad. Operates only in the Caribbean (Dominican Republic) and Latin America (Brazil, Costa Rica, Ecuador, Honduras, Mexico, Paraguay). Funded through private contributions. Operates with a $2 million annual budget.

## Asian-American Free Labor Institute
1125 15th St., NW
Suite 401
Washington, DC 20005
Tel. 202/737-3000
Fax 202/785-0370

Helps develop trade unions in the Middle East, Asia, and the Pacific. Conducts programs in communications, community development, and education. Maintains a full-time U.S. staff of 21 and a long-term staff abroad of 6. Major funding sources are USAID, USIA, and NED. Major recent project includes: "Support Program to Strengthen Free and Democratic Trade Unions" (Near East Region, USAID, $10 million).

## Baptist World Alliance
6733 Curran Street
McLean, VA 22101
Tel. 703/790-8980
Fax 703/893-5160

Works with Baptist communities throughout the world in extending assistance to poor and disadvantaged peoples. Sponsors programs in agricultural assistance, community development, disaster relief and rehabilitation, and fellowship. Operates programs in the Caribbean, Central and South America, Eastern Europe, former Soviet republics, Middle East, South and Southeast Asia, and Sub-Saharan Africa. Operates with a $2.5 million annual budget.

## Bread for the World
802 Rhode Island Avenue, NE
Washington, DC 20018
Tel. 202/269-0200
Fax 202/529-8546

A 45,000-member Christian organization with a staff of 70 dedicated to fighting world hunger and poverty. Lobbies members of Congress, campaigns to reduce hunger, promotes peace and development, and conducts the Bread for the World program. Operates with a $3 million annual budget.

## Brother's Brother Foundation
824 Grandview Avenue
Pittsburgh, PA 15211-1442
Tel. 412/431-1600
Fax 412/431-9116

U.S. staff of 6. Promotes preventive medicine and provides medical care and emergency relief to disaster areas throughout the world. Donates medical, educational, agricultural, and nutritional resources. Operates programs in the Caribbean, Central and South America, Eastern Europe, former Soviet republics, Asia, and Sub-Saharan Africa. Operates with a $70 million annual budget.

## Catholic Relief Services (CRS)
209 W. Fayette Street
Baltimore, MD 21201
Tel. 410/625-2220
Fax 410/234-3186

The relief and development agency of the U.S. Catholic Church which is the official overseas aid and development agency of the United States Catholic Conference. Operates relief and self-help development programs in 68 countries in the areas of community development, housing, education, agriculture, health care, and social welfare. Maintains a full-time staff in the U.S. of 180 and a long-term staff abroad of 1400. Operates in Africa, Asia, the Pacific Islands, Latin America, the Caribbean, the Middle East, North Africa, Italy, and Poland. Major funding sources include USAID, European Economic Community, National Council of Catholic Women, Church of Jesus Christ of Latter-Day Saints, foundations, corporations, and others. Major recent projects include: "Provide Rural Development III Program in West Bank/Gaza" (USAID $3.8 million), "Provide Emergency Relief Services to Displaced Persons" (Lebanon, USAID, $3.1 million), and "Relief Program for Children Who Are Victims of Civil Strife" (Nicaragua, USAID, $3 million).

## Center for International Development & Environment
World Resources Institute
1709 New York Ave., NW
Suite 700
Washington, DC 20006
Tel. 202/638-6300
Fax 202/638-0036

Provides technical support and policy advice on sustainable development to developing countries desiring to better manage their natural resources. Disseminates information on development and environment issues. Operates programs in Central and South America, South and Southeast Asia, North Africa, and Sub-Saharan Africa. Operates with a $3 million annual budget.

## Centre for Development and Population Activities
1717 Massachusetts Ave.
Suite 202
Washington, DC 20036
Tel. 202/667-1142
Fax 202/332-4496

Provides technical assistance in the areas of population and family planning, women in development, maternal health, child survival, and community development. Maintains a full-time staff in the U.S. of 36. Operates in Sub-Saharan Africa, North Africa, South Asia, Central and South America, the Middle East, and Eastern Europe. Major funding sources include USAID, INFPA, USA For Africa, and several foundations. Recent major projects include: "Extending Family Planning Services Through Third World Managers" (Worldwide, USAID, $6.7 million), "Family Health Services/Family Life Education" (Nigeria, USAID, $1.5 million), and "Management Training and Technical Cooperation With NGO's" (Worldwide, UNFPA, $827,000). Manages field offices in Egypt, India, Kenya, Nepal, and Romania. Operates with a $5 million annual budget.

## Childreach

155 Plan Way
Warwick, RI 02886-1099
Tel. 401/738-5600
Tel. 800/444-7918
Fax 401/738-5608

P.O. Box 804
804 Quaker Lane
East Greenwich, RI 02818
Tel. 401/826-2500
Fax 401/826-2680

The U.S. member of PLAN International, this is a sponsorship organization linking caring people in the U.S. with children and their families in developing countries. Assists needy children and their families. Promotes self-help programs in health, nutrition, education, livelihood, community development, construction, agriculture, enterprise development and management, social welfare, and population and family planning, and environment and national resource management. Provides assistance to more than 660,000 families, in 28 countries of Africa, Asia, Latin America, and the Caribbean. Has regional offices in Ecuador, Guatemala, India, Kenya, the Philippines, and Senegal and works with over 100 field offices of PLAN International. Operates with a $32 million annual budget.

## Children's Survival Fund, Inc.

P.O. Box 3127
Carbondale, IL 62902
Tel. 618/549-7873
Fax 618/549-8320

Attacks hunger, disease, and suffering afflicting millions of children around the world. Sponsors programs in disaster and emergency relief, education, medicine, and public health. Operates programs in the Caribbean, Central and South America, Eastern Europe, the former Soviet republics, the Middle East, South and Southeast Asia, and North and Sub-Saharan Africa. Operates with a $4 million annual budget.

## Christian Children's Fund, Inc.

2821 Emerywood Parkway, P.O. Box 26484
Richmond, VA 23261
Tel. 804/756-2700
Fax 804/756-2718

Provides monthly support through individual sponsors for more than 700,000 children in over 40 developing countries. Assistance focuses on disaster relief, community development, cooperatives, housing, family planning services, medicine, public health, education, agriculture, vocational and nutritional training, and social welfare. Maintains full-time staff in the U.S. of 160 and long-term staff abroad of 400. Operates projects and field offices in Sub-Saharan Africa, South and Southeast Asia, Central and South America, Eastern Europe, and the Caribbean. Major funding comes from sponsorships, private donations, and grants. Projects primarily involve sponsoring individual children. Operates with a $110 million annual budget.

## Church World Service
475 Riverside Drive
New York, NY 10115-0050
Tel. 212/870-2257
Fax 212/870-2055

Provides disaster relief, rehabilitation, agriculture, food productions, health, nutrition, education, family planning, housing, social welfare and community development assistance in Africa, Asia, the Pacific Islands, Latin America, the Caribbean, Eastern Europe, the former Soviet republics, and the Middle East. Maintains a full-time U.S. staff of 179 and a long-term staff abroad of 23. Major funding sources include USAID, CARE, United Nations agencies, and private foundations and contributions. A graduate degree in business, medicine, or international affairs and expertise in development technology, water resources, forestry or cross cultural administration/management are preferred. Recent projects include: "Support Primary Health Care and Development Program" (Indonesia, USAID, $218,015) and "Support Management and Monitoring of Distribution of Emergency Food Aid" (Sudan, USAID, $29,500). Operates with a $48 million annual budget.

## Compassion International
3955 Cragwood Drive
P.O. Box 7000
Colorado Springs, CO 80933-7000
Tel. 719-594/9900
Fax 719/594-6271

An Inter-denominational organization focusing on child development through relief services. Primarily operates a monthly sponsorship program for needy children. Maintains a full-time staff in the U.S. of 170 and a long-term staff abroad of 274. Operates in Africa, Asia, the Pacific Islands, Latin America, and the Caribbean. Major funding comes from numerous individual and corporation donations.

## Cooperative Housing Foundation, Inc.
P.O. Box 91280
Washington, DC 20090-1280
Tel. 301/587-4700
Fax 301/587-2626

U.S. staff of 20 and 10 abroad. Provides technical assistance relating to shelter, community improvement, and employment generation programs for low-income groups in developing countries.

## Cooperative for American Relief
## Everywhere, Inc (CARE)

151 Ellis Street                          2025 I Street, NW
Atlanta, GA 30335                         Washington, DC 20006
Tel. 404/681-2552                         Tel. 202/223-2277
Fax 404/577-6271                          Fax 202/296-8695

Provides emergency relief for disaster victims and sponsors programs to improve
nutrition, health, employment, and education of the poor worldwide. Maintains
a full-time staff in the U.S. of 200 and a long-term staff abroad of 6,250. Major
funding sources include donations from numerous individuals, foundations,
corporations, and others as well as grants from USAID. Operates projects in
North Africa, Sub-Saharan Africa, Asia, the Pacific, Latin America, the
Caribbean, Eastern Europe, former Soviet republics, and the Middle East. A
Bachelor's degree and overseas work experience of Master's degree in an
international field or experience in a project related area and speaking ability in
a foreign language—usually French or Spanish—required. Previous projects
included: "Implement Community Water Systems Development Project" (Haiti,
USAID, $7.9 million), "Increase CARE's Ability to Design, Implement, and
Evaluate Field Projects Leading to Creation of Rural Capital" (Worldwide,
USAID, $71 million, and "Support Coordination and Logistical Movement of
Emergency Relief Food and Supplies" (Mozambique, USAID, $6.6 million).
Conducts operations from 58 overseas field offices. Operates with a $500 million
annual budget.

## Coordination in Development (CODEL)

475 Riverside Drive, Rm. 1832
New York, NY 10115
Tel. 212/870-3000
Fax 212/870-3545

U.S. staff of 10. An ecumenical consortium promoting collaboration development
efforts of member agencies in developing countries.

## Delphi International

1090 Vermont Avenue, NW
7th Floor
Washington, DC 20005
Tel. 202/898-0950
Fax 202/842-0885

Promotes understanding and cooperation between the United States and other
countries. Sponsors programs for youth, women, urban poor, the elderly, and
disabled in the areas of education and training, community development, and
citizen and student exchange. Operates with a $7.7 million annual budget.

## Direct Relief International
27 S. La Patera Lane
Santa Barbara, CA 93117-3251
Tel. 805/964-4767
Fax 805/681-4838

U.S. staff of 8. Provides medical supplies and personnel to health care programs worldwide. Assists victims of war, poverty, and natural and civil disasters through donations of phamaceuticals, medical supplies, and medical equipment. Operates programs in the Caribbean, Central and South America, Eastern Europe, the former Soviet republics, the Middle East, Pacific Islands, East and Southeast Asia, and Sub-Saharan Africa. Operates with a $11 million annual budget.

## The Episcopal Church of the U.S.A.
## Episcopal Migration Ministries
The Episcopal Church Center
815 Second Avenue
New York, NY 10017
Tel. 212/922-5407
Fax 212/949-6781

Provides training and development assistance in the areas of management and community development as well as relief and rehabilitation assistance. Maintains a full-time staff in the U.S. of 220 and a long-term staff abroad of 120. Operates in Africa, Latin America, the Caribbean, and the Philippines. Major funding provided by the Episcopal Church but also includes some assistance from USAID and private foundations. Previous projects included: "Procure Architectural/Engineering and Construction Services for Facility Upgrade at Cuttingham University" (Liberia, USAID, $1.4 million). Operates from a combined annual domestic and foreign missionary budget of $63 million.

## Esperanca, Inc.
1911 West Earll Drive
Phoenix, AZ 8015
Tel. 602/252-7772
Fax 602/340-9197

U.S. staff of 6 and 20 abroad. Provides primary health, rural development, and community organization assistance. Recent projects include: "Support the Seperanca Child Survival Agreement in Bolivia" (USAID, $705,000), "Provide Assistance for the Construction of a Training Center" (Brazil, USAID, $500,000), and "Provide Support for a Program Entitled 'South-South' Human Health Resource Development" (Latin American Regional, USAID, $600,000).

## Food for the Hungry, Inc.
7729 E. Greenway Rd.
Scottsdale, AZ 85260
Tel. 602/998-3100 or 800/2HUNGER
Fax 602/998-4806

Provides assistance in the areas of rural development and food-for-work programs as well as relief and rehabilitation programs in emergency aid and disaster situations. Sponsors programs in community development, water resources, income generation, food production, and agriculture. Maintains a full-time staff in the U.S. of 12 and a long-term staff abroad of 525. Operates in Sub-Saharan Africa, Asia, Central and South America, Eastern Europe, and the Caribbean. Major funding comes from USAID and the United Nations High Commission for Refugees. Operates with a $30 million annual budget.

## Food for the Poor
550 Southwest 12th Ave.
Deerfield Beach, FL 33442
Tel. 305/427-2222
Fax 305/570-7654

Operates humanitarian and developmental assistance programs relating to food, clothing, medicine, social development, and self-sufficient economic development. Maintains a full-time U.S. staff of 120 and a long-term staff abroad of 60. Major funding comes from private donations.

## Foundation for International Community Assistance
901 King Street, Suite 400
Alexandria, VA 22314
Tel. 703/836-5516
Fax 703/836-5366

Promotes self-help and self-sustaining economic development among the poor by administering revolving loans through community banks. Sponsors programs in enterprise development and credit loans and women in development in the Caribbean, Central and South America, and Sub-Saharan Africa. Operates with a $3.5 million annual budget.

## Foundation for the Peoples of the South Pacific
3550 Afton Road
San Diego, CA 92123
Tel. 619/279-9820
Fax 619/637-9107

U.S. staff of 8 and 100 abroad. Sponsors programs in community development, construction, cooperatives and credit loans, environment and natural resource management, food production and agriculture, nutrition and public health, and women in development. Recent projects include: "Support the Stable Transition of Newly-Emerging Democracies to Market-Based, Pluralistic Societies-NIS" (former Soviet Union, USAID, $600,000), "Provide Support to Conserve, and Sustain the Tropical Rainforests as Renewable Resources That are Profitable" (Fiji, USAID, $640,000), and "Establish a New child Survival Project Which Aims to Reduce Infant Mortality and Morbidity in Vanuatu" (Vanuatu, USAID, $855,000). Operates with a $3.5 million annual budget.

## Freedom From Hunger
1644 DaVinci Court
Davis, CA 95617
Tel. 916/758-6200
Fax 916/758-6241

U.S. staff of 20. Supports programs relating to food, educational, nutritional, and community health problems in developing countries. Operates programs and field offers in Bolivia, Burkina Faso, Honduras, Ghana, Mali, and Thailand. Recent five-year funded project: "Provide Support for the Freedom From Hunger Foundation and Program" (Free World, USAID, $3.8 million). Operates with a $3 million annual budget.

## Goodwill Industries of America, Inc.
9200 Wisconsin Avenue
Bethesda, MD 20814-3896
Tel. 301/530-6500
Fax 301/530-1516

Provides vocational rehabilitation services and employment opportunities through technical assistance and training for people with disabilities and special needs. Conducts programs for information exchange and referral, international visitors, partnership with industry, and technical assistance. Supports programs in the Caribbean, Central and South America, Asia, Eastern Europe, Russia, and Sub-Saharan Africa. Operates with a $7 million annual budget.

## Habitat for Humanity International
121 Habitat Street
Americus, GA 31709
Tel. 912/924-6935
Fax 912/924-6541

A Christian housing ministry involved in improving the housing conditions of poor people in developing countries through construction, rehabilitation, and innovative financing arrangement. Maintains a full-time U.S. staff of 490 and a long-term staff abroad of 85. Operates in Africa, Asia, the Pacific Islands, Latin America, and the Caribbean. Receive funding from private donations.

## Heifer Project International, Inc

1015 South Louisiana St., P.O. Box 808
Little Rock, AR 72203
Tel. 501/376-6836
Fax 501/376-8906

Assists developing countries in establishing community-based livestock and
poultry operations. Activities include dairy projects, poultry cooperatives,
marketing training, veterinary training, and aquaculture models. Also sponsors
projects for women in development, nutrition, community development, and
environment and national resource management. Maintains a full-time staff in the
U.S. of 125 and a long-term staff abroad of 10. Operates projects in Sub-Saharan,
Africa, Asia, the Pacific, the Caribbean, Middle East, Central and South America,
and Eastern Europe. Major funding comes through donations and USAID. A
graduate degree in animal husbandry or veterinary medicine is required;
knowledge of French, Spanish or Arabic is useful among with work in developing
countries. Operates with a $10 million annual budget.

## Helen Keller International

90 Washington Street
15th Floor
New York, NY 10006
Tel. 212/943-0890
Fax 212/940-1220

Offers technical assistance to governments that wish to integrate eye care into
community-level health care. Emphasizes the prevention of nutritional blindness
and trachoma, and the restoration of sight through cataract surgery. Maintains a
full-time staff in the U.S. of 34 and a long-term staff abroad of 16. Operates in
Africa, South and Southeast Asia, the Pacific Islands, South America, Mexico,
the Caribbean, and Morocco. A degree in international affairs or public health or
an MD, MPH or PhD are useful. Foreign language helpful and work experience
in the Third World or in public health is required. Major funding provided by
USAID and private donations. Previous projects included: "Vitamin A Technical
Assistance Program" (Worldwide, USAID, $5 million), "Blindness Prevention
Matching Grant" (Worldwide, USAID, $2.6 million), and "Vitamin A Interven-
tion Programs—Child Survival" (Bangladesh, Haiti, Indonesia, Niger, Philippines,
USAID, $1.8 million). Operates with a $8 million annual budget.

## HIAS (Hebrew Immigrant Aid Society)

333 Seventh Avenue
New York, NY 10001-5004
Tel. 212/967-4100
Fax 212/967-4442

Provides services for Jewish refugees and migrants. Also provides under
contractual arrangements similar services for non-Jewish refugees and migrants.
Operates programs in migration and refugee affairs and monitoring and advocacy.

Has programs in the Caribbean, Central and South American, Europe, the former Soviet republics, and Middle East. Operate with a $14 million annual budget.

## High/Scope Educational Research Foundation
60 North River Street
Ypsilanti, MI 48198
Tel. 313/485-2000
Fax 313/485-0604

U.S. staff of 49. Promotes learning and development of children. Recent project includes: "Support Activities of Inter-Agency Consultative Group in Early Childhood Development" (US, USAID, $594,200).

## The Hunger Project
One Madison Avenue
New York, NY 10010
Tel. 212/532-4255
Fax 212/532-9785

Promotes leadership, youth, and information dissemination programs to end hunger throughout the world. Has field offices in Australia, Japan, Europe, South Asia, and Senegal. Operates with a $4.5 million annual budget.

## Institute of Cultural Affairs
629 East Fifth Street
New York, NY 10009-6824
Tel. 212/673-5984
Fax 212/505-1548

Provides training and planning assistance for grassroots development programs in research, education, and community development. Has programs in Australia, Central and South America, Europe, Eastern Europe, Asia, Sub-Saharan Africa, and Egypt. Operates with a $2 million annual budget.

## Institute of International Education
809 United Nations Plaza
New York, NY 10017
Tel. 212/883-8200
Fax 212/984-5452

Provides technical assistance in the area of educational development through the support of training and education efforts. Administers the Fulbright Program for USIA. Maintains a full-time staff in the U.S. of 329 and a long-term staff abroad of 40. Operates in Africa, Asia, Latin America, the Caribbean, and Egypt. Major clients include USIA, USAID, the World Bank, Inter-American Development

Bank, and private foundations. Previous projects included: "Energy Training" (Worldwide, USAID, $36 million), "Assist Agency With Training for the Disadvantaged South Africans Scholarship Program" (USAID, $21 million), and "Fulbright and Humphrey Program" (Worldwide, USIA, $27.6 million).

## Interchurch Medical Assistance, Inc.
Blue Ridge Building
College Avenue, P.O. Box 429
New Windsor, MD 21776
Tel. 410/635-8720
Fax 410/635-8726

Staff of 7 in U.S. only. Procures and distributes medical supplies for overseas health care ministries of Protestant Churches and U.S. relief organizations. Operates programs in emergency and disaster assistance and medicine and public health. Has programs in the Caribbean, Central and South America, Eastern Europe, the former Soviet republics, the Middle East, Africa, the Pacific, and Asia. Operates with a $17 million annual budget.

## International Aid, Inc.
17011 W. Hickory
Spring Lake, MI 49456
Tel. 616/846-7490
Fax 616/846-3842

This Christian relief and development agency provides food, health, and hope to the needy through a network of more than 500 relief organizations, NGOs, and churches in over 140 countries. Conducts programs in disaster and emergency relief, medicine and public health, and material aid. Has programs in Central and South America, Europe, the former Soviet republics, the Middle East, the Pacific, Asia, and Sub-Saharan Africa. Operates with a $25 million annual budget.

## International Catholic Migration Commission
1319 F Street, NW, Suite 820
Washington, DC 20004
Tel. 202/393-2904
Fax 202/393-2908

Coordinates international Catholic assistance to refugees, migrants, and displaced persons through a network of 70+ national affiliates. Promotes the implementation of major programs for refugees, migrants, and displaced persons. Has programs in Central and South America, Europe, Russia, Turkey, North Africa, Asia, and Sub-Saharan Africa. Operates with a $25 million annual budget.

## International Center for Research on Women
1717 Massachusetts Avenue, NW
Suite 302
Washington, DC 20036
Tel. 202/797-0007
Fax 202/797-0020

Conducts research and disseminates information on the role of women in development. Has programs in the Caribbean, Central and South America, the Middle East, Africa, and Asia. Operates with a $3 million annual budget.

## International Development Enterprises
710 Kipling Street
Suite 204
Lakewood, CO 80215
Tel. 303/232-4336
Fax 303/232-8346

U.S. staff of 4 and 154 abroad (4 expats and 150 locals). Promotes projects for developing self-sustaining business enterprises amongst Third World entrepreneurs.

## International Executive Service Corps
8 Stamford Forum
P.O. Box 10005
Stamford, CT 06904-2005
Tel. 203/967-6000
Fax 203/324-2531

Promotes the development of private enterprise in the host nation by upgrading management skills, improving basic technologies and increasing management skills, improving basic technologies and increasing the productivity of businesses in the developing world. Participants selected by IESC work on short-term assignments as unpaid volunteers, although travel and living expenses are paid. Maintains a full-time staff in the U.S. of 60 and a long-term staff abroad of 40. Operates in Africa, Asia, Latin America, the Caribbean, the Middle East, North Africa, Hungary, and Poland. Individuals must be retired experts in their business field and willing to share their knowledge on a volunteer basis. Major funding comes through USAID, 180+ corporate sponsors, and numerous private donors. Previous USAID-funded projects included: "Furnish Business/Management Expertise to Business and Other Institutions" (Worldwide, $47.9 million) and "Provide Technical Services to Solve Broad Range of Technical and Managerial Problems" (Egypt, $1.5 million).

## International Eye Foundation
7801 Norfolk Avenue
Bethesda, MD 20814
Tel. 301/986-1830
Fax 301/986-1876

U.S. staff of 7 and 12 abroad. Assists developing countries in establishing health care systems that stress the prevention and cure of blindness. Has field offices and programs in the Caribbean, Central America, Sub-Saharan Africa, and Bulgaria. Operates with a $2.2 million annual budget.

## International Institute of Rural Reconstruction
475 Riverside Drive, Room 1270
New York, NY 10115
Tel. 212/870-2992
Fax 212/870-2981

U.S. staff of 5 and 140 abroad. Conducts leadership training, field operations, applied research, and international extension. Conducts programs in agriculture and food production, community development, cooperatives and credit loans, development education, enterprise development and management, environment and natural resource management, medicine and public health, nutrition, and population and family planning. Has programs in Guatemala, China, India, Southeast Asia, and Sub-Saharan Africa. Operates with a $3 million annual budget.

## International Medical Corps
5933 West Century Blvd., Suite 310
Los Angeles, CA 90045
Tel. 310/670-0800
Fax 310/670-0125

Provides medical assistance and training to the most difficult devastated regions throughout the world. Sponsors programs in public health care, training, and education in Afghanistan, Pakistan, Angola, Bosnia, Cambodia, Namibia, and Somalia. Operates with a $10 million annual budget.

## International Planned Parenthood Federation/Western Hemisphere Region, Inc.
902 Broadway, 10th Floor
New York, NY 10010
Tel. 212/995-8800
Fax 212/995-8853

A federation of 45 family planning associations in Latin America and the Caribbean. Provides family planning information and services. Maintains a full-time staff in the U.S. of 60. Major funding sources include USAID, UNFPA, and many private foundations. Previous USAID-funded projects included: "Population and Family Planning" (Ecuador, $10.5 million), "Support Expansion and Improvement of Family Planning Programs in Latin America and the Caribbean" ($9.8 million), and "Private Sector Family Planning Project" (Haiti, $6.5 million).

## International Reading Association
800 Barksdale Road
Newark, DE 19714-8139
Tel. 302/731-1600
Fax 302/731-1057

Functions as a clearinghouse for disseminating reading research and promoting literacy levels worldwide. Works with more than 1,200 councils and national affiliates in 90 countries. Operates with a $8 million annual budget.

## International Rescue Committee
386 Park Avenue South
New York, NY 10016
Tel. 212/679-0010
Fax 212/689-5459

Provides emergency relief, public health, medical, educational, and resettlement programs for refugees and maintains health care programs in refugee camps with emphasis toward training of refugee health workers. Operates programs in Asia, Eastern Europe, Sub-Saharan Africa and Central America. Major funding through private donations. A graduate degree in medicine, nursing, public health, immunology, infectious diseases or nutrition is required. Medical personnel should have strong backgrounds in public health and experience in developing world health care is essential. A Third World language is useful, but not required. Operates with a $55 million annual budget.

## International Voluntary Services, Inc.
1424 16th Street, NW, Suite 204
Washington, DC 20036
Tel. 202/387-5533
Fax 202/387-4234

U.S. staff of 10 and 3 abroad. Volunteer technicians assist with community development, cooperatives, agriculture and food production, health care, and micro-enterprise development. Operates projects in Bolivia, Ecuador, Bangladesh, Thailand, Vietnam, and Zambabwe and field offices in Bangladesh and Ecuador. Operates with a $2 million annual budget.

## Laubach Literacy International
1320 Jamesville Ave.
P.O. Box 131
Syracuse, NY 13210
Tel. 315/422-9121
Fax 315/422-6369

Promotes the development of adult literacy programs in developing countries. Maintains a full-time U.S. staff of 110. Has projects in Haiti, Mexico, Guatemala, South America, South and Southeast Asia, and Sub-Saharan Africa. Major funding provided by U.S. Department of Education, American Library Association, and numerous private foundations. Operates with a $11 million annual budget.

## Lutheran Immigration and Refugee Service

390 Park Avenue South
New York, NY 10016
Tel. 212/532-6350
Fax 212/683-1329

122 C Street, NW, Suite 300
Washington, DC 20001
Tel. 202/783-7509
Fax 202/783-7502

Promotes resettlement, advocacy, and immigration services for refugees and immigrants. Involved in recruitment and training, finding foster homes, processing refugees, and supporting programs for asylum seekers. Administered from the U.S. and Hong Kong. Operates with a $9 million annual budget.

## Lutheran World Relief, Inc.
390 Park Avenue South
New York, NY 10016
Tel. 212/532-6350
Fax 212/213-6081

Promotes integrated community development projects which are usually operated through counterpart church-related agencies in the areas of disaster relief, refugee assistance, and social and economic development. Has projects in water resources, reforestation, land reclamation, construction and engineering, small business development nutrition, medical assistance, health practices, disaster relief, education, public administration, social welfare, and family planning. Maintains a full-time staff in the U.S. of 26 and a long-term staff abroad of 17. Operates projects in Sub-Saharan Africa, Asia, Central and South America, and the Middle East. Major funding support comes from USAID, Lutheran churches, CROP, Interfaith Hunger Appeal, and many individual contributors. Previous projects included: "Provide Support for LWR's development Assistance Program" (Worldwide, USAID, $2.3 million), "Safafi Soils Lab/Seed Production" (Madagascar, LWR, $394,702), and "Support a Program to Enable Poor Communities to Meet Their Own Needs as Lutheran World Relief Partners" (Worldwide, USAID, $2.5 million). Operates with a $24 million annual budget.

## MAP International
2200 Glynco Parkway, P.O. Box 50
Brunswick, GA 31521-0050
Tel. 912/265-6010 or 800/225-8550
Fax 912/265-6170

Helps developing countries design, implement, and evaluate community development projects focusing on food production, water resources, health services, nutrition education, and disaster and emergency relief. Maintains a full-time staff in the U.S. of 80 and a long-term staff abroad of 15. Operates in Sub-Saharan Africa, Asia, Central and South America, the Caribbean, Eastern Europe, the former Soviet republics, and the Pacific. A graduate degree in international public health, education or medicine useful. Foreign language, especially French or Spanish, are helpful, but not required. A minimum of three years work in medicine, health, or education in a developing country is necessary for employment. Major funding provided by private contributions. Operates with a $50 million annual budget.

## Mennonite Central Committee
21 South 12th St.
Akron, PA 17501
Tel. 717/859-1151
Fax 717/859-1151

Functions as the cooperative relief service, and development agency of North American Mennonite and Brethren in Christ churches. Provides disaster relief and development assistance in the areas of education, agriculture, housing, health care, and crafts development. Maintains a salaried staff in North America of 275 as well as 660 volunteers (289 overseas and 271 in North America). Operates in Africa, Asia, Latin America, the Caribbean, the former Soviet republics, the Middle East, Europe, and Canada. Major funding comes form individual and corporate contributions.

## Mercy Corps International
3030 SW First Avenue
Portland, OR 97201
Tel. 503/242-1032
Fax 503/223-0501
E-Mail mercycorps @ igc.apc.org (PeaceNet)

Provides agricultural development assistance, primary health care, education, and emergency relief services. Conducts programs in agriculture and food production, community development, development education, disaster and emergency relief, medicine and public health, and migration and refugee services. Operates in Central America, Eastern Europe, the former Soviet republics, the Middle East, Asia, and Sub-Saharan Africa. Operates with a $20 million annual budget.

## National Cooperative Business Association
1401 New York Ave., NW, Suite 1100
Washington, DC 20005
Tel. 202/638-6222
Fax 202/638-1374

Provides technical assistance in the areas of income-generation, business development, agriculture, rural development, and cooperatives in developing countries. Maintains a full-time U.S. staff of 39 and a long-term staff abroad of 26. Operates in Africa, Asia, Latin America, the Caribbean, the Middle East, and North Africa. Major funding source is USAID. Previous projects included: "Assist Agricultural Production Support Project" (Niger, $3 million), "Support National Cooperative Business Association to Initiate Project in Developing Countries" (Worldwide, $2.8 million), and "Assist in Cooperatives Development" (Equatorial Guinea, $21 million).

## National Council for International Health
1701 K Street, NW, Suite 600
Washington, DC 20006
Tel. 202/833-5900
Fax 202/833-0075

U.S. staff of 11. This membership organization promotes international health through a wide range of information and education activities. Conducts programs in education and training for health professionals and serves as a public policy advocacy group. Operates with a $1.4 million annual budget.

## National Council of Negro Women/
## International Division
1667 K Street, NW, Suite 700
Washington, DC 20004
Tel. 202/659-0270 or 202/659-0006
Fax 202/785-8733

Promotes improved socio-economic conditions for women. Conducts institutional development, education, and women in development programs in Egypt, Botswana, Senegal, and Zimbabwe. Operates with a $4 million annual budget.

## National Rural Electric Cooperative Association
1800 Massachusetts Ave., NW
Washington, DC 20036
Tel. 202/857-9500
Fax 202/857-4863

Provides rural electrification specialists to assist developing countries expand and improve their rural electrical systems. Maintains a full-time staff in the U.S. of

400 and a long-term staff abroad of 30. Operates in Africa, Asia, the Pacific Islands, Latin America, the Caribbean, and the Middle East. Major funding provided by USAID, the World Bank, and donors. Previous projects included: "Assist in Establishment of Rural Electrification" (Bangladesh, USAID, $13 million), "Provide Advisory Services in Rural Electrification" (El Salvador, USAID, $10 million), and "Assist in Implementation of Rial Electric Cooperative System" (Guatemala, USAID, $5 million).

## National Wildlife Federation
1400 16th St., NW
Washington, DC 20036
Tel. 202/797-6800
Fax 202/797-6646

The world's largest organization of private citizens promoting the conservation of natural resources. Maintains a full-time staff in the U.S. of 650. Operatives throughout the world. Major funding sources includes USAID, U.N. Environmental Programme, and many private foundations, corporations, and individuals.

## The Nature Conservancy
1815 North Lynn Street, Suite 400
Arlington, VA 22209
Tel. 703/841/5300
Fax 703/841-1283

Identifies, protects, and manages natural land areas for the purpose of preserving biological diversity. Maintains a full-time staff in the U.S. of 1,086 and a long-term staff abroad of 2. Operates in the Caribbean and Latin America. Major funding comes from USAID and private donations. Previous project included: "Conservation of Biological Diversity and Rational Use of Natural Resources in the Peruvian Central Jungle" (Peru, USAID, $200,000).

## OIC International (Opportunities Industrialization Centers International, Inc.)
240 West Tulpehocken Street
Philadelphia, PA 19144
Tel. 215/842-0220
Fax 215/849-7033

Assists local communities and government in creating nonformal skills training institutions. Conducts programs in agriculture and food production, enterprise development and management, and vocational and technical training. Operates in Belize, Poland, United Kingdom, the Philippines, and several countries in Sub-Saharan Africa. Maintains a full-time U.S. staff of 26 and a long-term staff abroad of 5. Major funding provided by USAID, CIDA, United Nations agencies, U.S. Peace Corps, Japanese Overseas Volunteer Service, and numerous other volunteer and private groups. Previous projects included: "Support for Recipient to Develop and Implement Local Non-Formal Skills Training Programs" (Sub-Saharan Africa, USAID, $19.2 million) and "Sierra Leone Small Enterprise Development and Training Initiative" (USAID, $3.6 million). Operates with a $9 million annual budget.

## Operation USA
8320 Melrose Avenue
Los Angeles, CA 90069
Tel. 213/658-8876
Fax 213/653-7846

Provides disaster relief assistance, trains health workers, and supports health care and children's programs in the Caribbean, Central and South America, the Middle East, Asia, and Sub-Saharan Africa. Operates with a $4 million annual budget.

## Opportunity International
360 Butterfield Rd.
Suite 110
Elmhurst, IL 60126
Tel. 708/279-9300
Fax 708/279-3107

U.S. staff of 13 and 20 abroad. Formerly known as the Institute for International Development. Promotes job-creation for the poor in Africa, Asia, and Latin America. Recent project includes: "Provide Support to Develop Indigenous Small and Micro Enterprise Development Agencies" (Worldwide, USAID, $2.3 million).

## Oxfam America
26 West Street                          4797 Telegraph Ave., Suite 201
Boston, MA 02111                        Oakland, CA 94609
Tel. 617/482-1211                       Tel. 510/652-4388
Fax 617/728-2584                        Fax 510/652-4497

Promotes self-reliant, participatory development among poor people through community development, education, food production, agriculture, public health, and material aid projects. Provides emergency and disaster relief. Operates in Sub-Saharan Africa, South and Southeast Asia, the Caribbean, and Central and South America. Major funding comes form private contributions. Operates with a $14 million annual budget.

## PACT (Private Agencies Collaborating Together)
1901 Pennsylvania Ave., NW, Suite 501
Washington, DC 20006
Tel. 202/466-5666
Fax 202/466-5669

A consortium for improving the lives of low-income individuals. Focuses on strengthening the programs of PVOs and NGOs through education, information, humanitarian assistance, coalition building, small grants, training, and technical assistance. Operates programs in Central and South American, Romania, the former Soviet republics, Southeast Asia, and Sub-Saharan Africa. Operates with a $7 million budget.

## Pan American Development Foundation
1889 F Street, NW, 8th Floor
Washington, DC 20006
Tel. 202/458-3969
Fax 202/458-6316

Provides technical assistance for improving the living standards of low income people in Central and South America and the Caribbean through private sector initiatives. Operates programs in disaster and emergency relief, enterprise development, environment and natural resource management, agriculture, material aid, and medicine and public health. Maintains a full-time staff in the U.S. of 26 and a long-term staff abroad of 50. Major funding provided by U.S. corporations, foundations, individuals, and USAID. Recent USAID funded projects include: "Promote Cash Cropping of Trees by Farmers, Extension" (Haiti, $12.6 million) and "Support Medical Care and Relief for Child Victims of Nicaraguan Civil Strife" (Nicaragua, $2 million). Operates with a $9 million annual budget.

## Partners of the Americas (National Association of the Partners of the Americas, Inc.)
1424 K Street, NW, Suite 700
Washington, DC 20005
Tel. 202/628-3300
Fax 202/628-3306

U.S. staff of 42 and 3 abroad. Promotes Inter-American friendship and cooperation between the United States, Latin America, and the Caribbean through technical training programs and economic and social development activities. Helps raise funds and promote technical assistance services of 45 volunteer Partners of Americas' committees located in 45 states. Links 45 state committees with 60 similar committees in Latin America and the Caribbean. Sponsors programs on agriculture and food production, citizen and student exchange, development education, environment and natural resource management, human resource development, public health and nutrition, and technical training. Operates with a $11 million annual budget.

## Pathfinder International
9 Galen Street, Suite 217
Watertown, MA 02172-4501
Tel. 617/924-7200
Fax 617/924-3833

Promotes population planning through innovative efforts to make fertility services more effective, less expensive, and more readily available to people in developing countries. Maintains a full-time staff in the U.S. of 57 and a long-term staff abroad of 12. Programs operate in the Caribbean, South American, Sub-Saharan Africa, Asia, and the Middle East. Most professional positions require a Master's Degree in public health or a Master's Degree in business with an emphasis in health. Related fields such as international affairs or geography would be considered for some positions. Preference given to candidates with experience in developing countries. Major funding provided by USAID and numerous private foundations. Previous USAID-funded projects included: "Provide Family Planning Assistance to LDC's" (Worldwide, $60 million), "Provide Financial and Advisory Services Support on Family Planning" (Bangladesh, $11.5 million), and "Family Health Initiatives" (Nigeria, $11 million). Operates with a $23 million annual budget.

## People to People Health Foundation, Inc (Project HOPE)
Health Sciences Education Center, Carter Hall
Millwood, VA 22646
Tel. 703/837-2100
Fax 703/837-1813

Provides education and training assistance in the areas of modern health science techniques, sanitation, nutrition, public health, biomedical engineering, and preventive medicine. Maintains a full-time staff in the U.S. of 140 and a long-term staff abroad of 250. Operates in Africa, Asia, Latin America, the Caribbean, Egypt, Poland, Portugal, Russia and the Commonwealth of Independent States. Major funding comes from USAID, Inter-American Development Foundation, Pan American Health Organization, and numerous foundations, corporations, and individual donors. Previous projects included: "Health Services Infrastructure and Training" (Grenada, $6.6 million), "Medical Assistance and Support to Hospitals in Poland" ($4 million), and "Support for Commodities and Operation Costs for Project HOPE Schools of Health Sciences" (Worldwide, $3.7 million).

## Phelps-Stokes Fund
10 East 87th Street
New York, NY 10128
Tel. 212/427-8100
Fax 212/876-6278

U.S. staff of 20 in New York and Washington. Promotes improvement of education for Africans, African-Americans, American Indians, and poor white Americans through scholarship programs, and study tours.

## Planned Parenthood Federation of America
810 Seventh Avenue
New York, NY 10019
Tel. 212/541-7800
Fax 212/245-1845

The international department, Family Planning International Assistance (FPIA), assists local organizations throughout the world design and initiate family planning projects, monitor project performance, and provide technical assistance. Maintains a full-time staff in the U.S. of 175 and a long-term staff abroad of 63. Although projects operate in 37 countries outside the U.S., staff are primarily posted in Thailand and Kenya. A Bachelor's degree is required; a graduate degree is preferred for employment. A specialization in public or business administration is desirable. Fluency in French, Spanish or Arabic is often required. Work experience in developing countries and involvement in family planning and community health programs is desirable for positions posted abroad. Major funding provided by USAID, USIA, and the U.S. Department of Education. Previous projects included: "Epidemiology of Insulin Dependent Diabetes Mellitus" (Finland, Israel, Japan, U.S. National Institute of Health, $1.1 million) and "Curriculum Design and Development for Training Health Administrators in West Indies" (Barbados, Jamaica, Trinidad, USAID, $500,000).

## Planning Assistance, Inc.
1832 Jefferson Place, NW
Washington, DC 20036
Tel. 202/466-3290
Fax 202/466-3293

U.S. staff of 6 and 13 abroad. Provides training and technical assistance services to help organizations design and manage more efficient development programs in the areas of health, population/family planning, and food security/food aid management. Has programs in Haiti, Central America, South American, Turkey, and Sub-Saharan Africa. Operates with a $3 million annual budget.

## Population Action International
(formerly Population Crisis Committee)
1120 19th Street, NW
Suite 550
Washington, DC 20036
Tel. 202/659-1833
Fax 202/293-1795

This advocacy group promotes public awareness, understanding, and action toward reducing population growth rates in developing countries through voluntary family planning. Operates with a $4.5 million annual budget.

## Population Council
One Dag Hammarskjold Plaza
New York, NY 10017
Tel. 212/339-0500
Fax 212/755-6052

Primarily involved with population research and information dissemination, the Council assists decision makers and population professionals in developing countries to design, implement, and evaluate research and assistance programs. Maintains a full-time staff in the U.S. of 174 and a long-term staff abroad of 31. Operates projects in Africa, Asia, Latin America, the Caribbean, the Middle East, and North Africa. An advanced degree in demography, public health, economics, population or biomedicine is preferred; undergraduate work in public health, international relations, economic, sociology and demography is also useful. Previous work experience is usually required. Experience requirements vary with different departments. Major funding provided by USAID, CIDA, United Nations, and numerous private foundations, corporations, and individuals. Previous USAID-funded projects included: "Support Program in Family Planning Research and Services" (Worldwide, $37 million), "Carry Out Program to Improve Delivery, Use, and Effectiveness of Family Planning Services in Developing Countries (Worldwide, $23.5 million), and "Conduct Operations Research to Promote Family Planning Service" (Africa, $16.8 million).

## Program for Appropriate Technology in Health
4 Nickerson St.
Seattle, WA 98109-1699
Tel. 206/285-3500
Fax 206/285-6619

Promotes the availability, effectiveness, safety, and acceptance of health products and technologies in developing countries. Maintains a full-time staff in the U.S. of 115 and a long-term staff abroad of 50. Operates in Africa, Asia, Latin America, the Caribbean, and the Middle East. Major funding provided by USAID, United Nations, and numerous private foundations, corporations, and individuals. Previous projects: "Provide Support in Diagnostic Technology Development" (Worldwide, USAID, $5.1 million), "Healthtech" (Thailand, Indonesia, Kenya, Egypt, Guatemala, Pakistan, Malawi, Zimbabwe, USAID, $4.6 million), and "Support Program of Oral Rehydration Salt to Reduce Mortality and Morbidity Due to Diarrheal Dehydration" (Worldwide, USAID, $3.2 million).

## Project Concern International
3550 Afton Road
San Diego, CA 92123
Tel. 619/279-9690
Tel. 619/279-9690

U.S. staff of 44 and 15 abroad. Provides health care training and development programs in developing countries. Promotes basic, low-cost health care services.

Operates programs in community development, development education, population and family planning services, and public health and nutrition. Operates in Guatamela, Nicaragua, Bolivia, Mexico, Romania, Papua New Guinea, and Indonesia. Operates with a $12 million annual budget.

## River Blindness Foundation
14141 S.W. Freeway
Suite 6200
Sugar Land, TX 77478
Tel. 713/491-1600 or 800/755-3811
Fax 713/242-4353

Promotes the prevention of blindness caused by onchocerciasis through the distribution of Mectizan. Sponsors programs in development education, medicine and material aid, and public policy and advocacy. Operates in Guatemala, Mexico, South America, and Sub-Saharan Africa. Operates with a $4 million annual budget.

## Salvation Army World Service Office
615 Slaters Lane, P.O. Box 269
Alexandria, VA 22313
Tel. 703/684-5528
Fax 703/684-5536

U.S. staff of 12. Provides financial and personnel assistance for programs in education, community centers, disaster relief, health and medical services, agriculture, community development, and spiritual ministry. Operates programs on agriculture and food production, communications, community development, construction, cooperatives, disaster relief and reconstruction aid, education, material aid, medicine and public health, and social welfare. Has programs in the Caribbean, Central and South America, Europe, Eastern Europe, former Soviet republics, the Pacific, and South and Southeast Asia. Operates with a $18 million annual budget.

## Save the Children Federation, Inc.
| | |
|---|---|
| 54 Wilton Road | 333 East 43rd Street |
| Westport, CT 06880 | New York, NY 10017 |
| Tel. 203/221-4000 | Tel. 212/682-6881 |
| Fax 203/227-5667 | Fax 212/661-3438 |

Supports development projects aimed at helping children and their communities with programs in sustainable agriculture, natural resource management, education, economic opportunities, health care, emergency response. Maintains a full-time staff in the U.S. of 371 and a long-term staff abroad of 95. Operates in 35 countries in the Caribbean, Central and South America, the Middle East, Sub-Saharan and North Africa, Greece, and Asia. A Bachelor's degree, but preferably an advanced degree in an area pertinent to Third World development is useful.

Ability to speak French, Spanish, or Arabic is required. Work experience abroad is essential for overseas based positions. Major funding provided by sponsorship program, USAID, private foundations, corporations, and individual donors. Previous USAID-funded projects included: "Provide Emergency and Relief Assistance to Families Affected by War-Related Events" (Lebanon, $10.7 million), "Assist in Increasing Self-Reliance of Families Living in Low-Income Areas" (Worldwide, $6.2 million), "Support for Inland Transportation" (Ethiopia, $2.2 million). Operates with a $95 million annual budget.

### The Sierra Club
730 Polk Street
San Francisco, CA 94109
Tel. 415/776-2211
Fax 415/776-0350

This membership group seeks to stop the abuse of wilderness lands, save endangered species, and protect the global environment through grassroots conservation efforts and an extensive publication and information dissemination program. Operates programs in education, environment and natural resource management, and public policy and advocacy. Operates with $52 million annual budget.

### Sister Cities International
120 S. Payne St.
Alexandria, VA 22314
Tel. 703/836-3535
Fax 703/836-4815

U.S. staff of 10. Promotes the development of long-term relationships between sister cities as well as collaborate development efforts.

### Summer Institute of Linguistics
7500 W. Camp Wisdom Road
Dallas, TX 75236
Tel. 214/709-2400
Fax 214/709-2433

Conducts language research, bilingual educational projects, and literacy programs in 43 countries. Full-time staff in the U.S. of 1,500 and long-term staff abroad of 5,000. Major funding provided by 43 governments in the countries where projects operate.

## TechnoServe
49 Day St.
Norwalk, CT 06854-3106
Tel. 800/999-6757
Fax 203/838-6717

Helps low-income people develop their own community-based enterprises in the areas of primary agricultural production, crop processing, livestock development, and savings and credit programs. Maintains a full-time staff in the U.S. of 36 and a long-term staff abroad of 148. Operates in Central America, Peru, Poland, and Sub-Saharan Africa. Major funding source is USAID. Previous projects included: "Rural Private Enterprise" (Rwanda, $4 million), "Initiate Programs to Assist Small and Medium-Sized Enterprises" (Worldwide, $3.4 million), and "Management Assistance and Training to Agricultural Bank" (Sudan, $2.2 million). Operates with a $7 annual budget.

## Thomas A. Dooley Foundation/Intermed—USA
420 Lexington Ave., Suite 2428
New York, NY 10170
Tel. 212/687-3620
Fax 212/599-6137

U.S. staff of 10 and 5 abroad. Provides medical equipment, supplies, personnel, and training support for health services in developing countries with emphasis on self-help through education.

## Tolstoy Foundation, Inc.
200 Park Avenue South, 16th Fl.
New York, NY 10003-1522
Tel. 212/677-7770
Fax 212/674-0519

A humanitarian foundation that assists refugees and the elderly and infirmed. Conducts Russian cultural and educational programs. Operates programs in South America, Europe, and Russia. Operates with a $2.6 million annual budget.

## Unitarian Universalist Service Committee
130 Prospect Street
Cambridge, MA 02139-1813
Tel. 617/868-6600
Fax 617/868-7102

U.S. staff of 37. Promotes self-reliant development in the areas of public health, emergency relief, water resource development, vocational planning, leadership development, family planning, and child care. Operate programs in development education, education and training, medicine and public health, population and family planning, food production and agriculture, and environment. Operates with a $4 million annual budget.

## United Methodist Committee on Relief
General Board of Global Ministries
The United Methodist Church
475 Riverside Drive
Room 1374
New York, NY 10115
Tel. 212/870-3816 or 800/841-1235
Fax 212/870-3624

Focuses efforts on alleviating hunger and human suffering. Conducts programs in agriculture and food production, community development, nutrition, social welfare, disaster and emergency relief, migration and refugee services, and public policy and advocacy. Operates programs in the Caribbean, Central and South America, the Middle East, Egypt, and South and Southeast Asia. Operates with a $16 million annual budget.

## U.S. Catholic Conference Office of Migration and Refugee Services
3211 4th Street, NE                   902 Broadway, 8th Fl.
Washington, DC 20017-1194             New York, NY 10010-6093
Tel. 202/541-3220                     Tel. 212/614-1277
Fax 202/541-3399                      Fax 212/614-1201

Supports a network of 145 local Catholic diocesan resettlement offices in the United States that provide assistance for approximately one-third of all refugees admitted to U.S. annually. Operates with a $9 million annual budget.

## U.S. Feed Grains Council
1400 K Street, NW
Suite 1200
Washington, DC 20005
Tel. 202/789-0789
Fax 202/898-0522

Provides technical assistance to create, develop, and promote overseas markets for U.S. feed grains. Maintains a full-time staff in the U.S. of 38 and a long-term staff abroad of 60. Operates programs in 55 countries through a network of 13 overseas offices. Major funding sources include associations of grain producers.

## U.S. Committee for UNICEF

331 East 38th Street                    110 Maryland Avenue, NE
New York, NY 10016                      Washington, DC 20002
Tel. 212/686-5522                       Tel. 202/547-7946
Fax 212/779-1679                        Fax 202/543-8144

Supports UNICEF programs in over 120 developing countries. Helps raise funds and disseminate information about the needs of children worldwide. Programs encompass development education, emergency relief and material aid, medicine and public health, child survival, nutrition, social welfare, and women in development. Operates programs in Sub-Saharan Africa, Cambodia, El Salvador, and Mexico. Operates with a $38 million annual budget.

## Volunteers in Overseas Cooperative Assistance

50 F Street, NW
Suite 1075
Washington, DC 20001
Tel. 202/626-8750
Fax 202/783-7204

U.S. staff of 12. Provides short-term technical assistance for agricultural development through a Cooperative Assistance Program and a Farmer-to-Farmer Program.

## Volunteers in Technical Assistance (VITA)

1600 Wilson Blvd.
Suite 500
Arlington, VA 22209
Tel. 703/276-1800
Fax 703/243-1865

Provides information and assistance on appropriate technology to help small businesses, farmers, community workers, and government agencies in Africa, Asia, the Caribbean and Latin America. Maintains a full-time staff in the U.S. of 25 and a long-term staff abroad of 11. A Bachelor's degree in a technical field such as engineering is useful for volunteers as is knowledge of energy systems, agriculture, sanitation, or construction. French or Spanish competency is preferred; work experience abroad is not required to become a volunteer. Major funding comes from USAID, the United Nations, and numerous private foundations and corporations. Previous USAID-funded projects included: "Establish Programs and Systems to Support Expanded Agricultural Production" (Pakistan, $6 million), "Provide Technical Assistance for Post Harvest Food Systems Project" (Central African Republic, $4.3 million), and "Liberia Small and Medium Enterprise Development Project" ($3.2 million).

## Winrock International Institute
## For Agricultural Development
Petit Jean Mountain
Route 3, Box 376
Morrilton, AR 72110
Tel. 501/727-5435
Fax 501/727-5242

Seeks to alleviate poverty and hunger worldwide through agricultural, rural development, and environmental resources management assistance. Provides training, education, consultation, and project design services. Maintains a full-time staff in the U.S. of 165 and a long-term staff abroad of 54. Operates in Sub-Saharan Africa, Southeast Asia, Central and South America, the Caribbean, and the former Soviet republics. Major funding provided by USAID, the World Bank, African Development Bank, Asian Development Bank, and several private foundations. Previous projects included: "Enhance Capability of National Agricultural System to Conduct Research on High Priority Problems" (India, USAID, $12.7 million), "Forestry/Fuelwood Research and Development" (Pakistan, USAID, $8.3 million). Operates with a $35 million annual budget.

## World Concern
19303 Fremont Ave. North
P.O. Box 33000
Seattle, WA 98133
Tel. 206/546-7201
Fax 206/546-7269

A division of Crista Ministries, World Concern sends personnel, commodities, and funds to aid projects related to health, agriculture, animal husbandry, water development, education, economic development, refugee aid, community development, and emergency relief. Maintains a full-time staff in the U.S. of 35 and a long-term staff abroad of 118. Operates in Sub-Saharan Africa, Asia, the Pacific, Central and South America, the Caribbean, Europe, Eastern Europe, and the former Soviet republic. Major funding provided by CRISTA Ministries, USAID, and many corporations and individual donors. Operates with a $15 million annual budget.

## World Council of Credit Unions
P.O. Box 2982
5810 Mineral Point Rd.
Madison, WI 53705
Tel. 608/231-7130
Fax 608/238-8020

Promotes the development of credit unions in developing countries. Maintains a full-time U.S. staff of 33 and a long-term staff abroad of 15. Also maintains a computerized Talent Bank for personnel to fill short-term consultancy requests. Operates in Africa, Asia, Latin America, and the Caribbean. Major funding sources include USAID, Canadian Co-operative Association, and Deutsche Gesellschaft fur Technische Zusammenarbeit. Previous projects included: "Development of the Togo National Credit Union Association" (Togo, USAID, $5.3 million), "Implement Small Farmer Organization Project" (Honduras, USAID, $3.4 million), and "Assist Private Sector Institutional Development" (Cameroon, USAID, $3.2 million)

## World Education
210 Lincoln Street
Boston, MA 02111
Tel. 617/482-9485
Fax 617/482-0617

U.S. staff of 9. Provides training and technical assistance in nonformal education for adults with emphasis on income generation, employment, refugee orientation, community development, small enterprise development, literacy, food production, and family life education. Sponsors programs in education, information dissemination, institutional development and training, refugee assistance, and women in development. Operates in Yeman, South Asia, China, Southeast Asia, and Sub-Saharan Africa. Operates with a $4.2 annual budget.

## World Neighbors, Inc.
4127 NW 122 Street
Oklahoma City, OK 73120-8869
Tel. 405/752-9700 or 800/242-6367
Fax 405/752-9393

This people-to-people organization focuses on eliminating hunger, disease, and poverty, Asia, Africa, and Latin America. Sponsors programs in community development, food production and agriculture, medicine and public health, reproductive health and family planning, communications, and development education. Operates in Haiti, Honduras, Mexico, South America, South and Southeast Asia, and Sub-Saharan Africa. Operates with a $4 million annual budget.

## World Rehabilitation Fund, Inc.
400 East 34th St.
New York, NY 10016
Tel. 212/340-6062
Fax 212/340-8218

U.S. staff of 13 and 5 abroad. Assists both government and voluntary agencies in improving rehabilitation health care services for the disabled.

## World Relief Corporation
450 Gundersen Drive
Carol Stream, IL 60188
Tel. 708/665-0235
Fax 708/653-8023

The official relief and development agency of the National Association of Evangelicals. Promotes rural development, agriculture, community development, health, nutrition, vocation training, refugee relief, and resettlement programs. Maintains a full-time staff in the U.S. of 200 and a long-term staff abroad of 40. Major funding sources include USAID and private donations. Previous projects included: "Support Child Mortality and Morbidity Programs" (Worldwide, USAID, $800,000 and "Support Development of Income Generation Projects in Poor Communities for Counterpart Organizations" (Worldwide, USAID, $365,000). Operates with a $20 million annual budget.

## World SHARE
6950 Friars Road
San Diego, CA 92108
Tel. 619/686-5818
Fax 619/686-5815

Promotes self supporting food and community development programs in 24 location serving over 400,000 families each month. Secures food commodities from the U.S. government (Title II) and sells them to support programs of NGO coordination, maternal/child health, infrastructure development, agroforestry, and income generation. Operates in Mexico and Guatemala. Operates with a $48 million annual budget.

## World Vision Relief and Development, Inc.

| | |
|---|---|
| 919 West Huntington Drive | 220 I Street, NE |
| Monrovia, CA 91016 | Washington, DC 20002 |
| Tel. 818/347-7979 | Tel. 202/547-3743 |
| Fax 818/303-7651 | Fax 202/547-4834 |

Provides disaster relief, primary health care and child survival, water development, natural resource management, microenterprise development, natural resource management, community leadership training, and development education. Maintains a full-time staff in the U.S. of 600, and a long-term staff abroad of over 3,000. Operates programs in the Caribbean, Central and South America, Greece, Egypt, the Middle East, the Pacific, Asia, and Sub-Saharan Africa. Graduate degrees in business, medicine, public, health or technical skills in related areas are most useful for employment. Knowledge of French or Spanish preferred; at least five years experience in development or related work usually required. Major funding sources include USAID, United Nations agencies, and numerous foundations, corporations, and individual donors. Previous projects included: "Support Management Information System and Use of Evaluation in Program Management/Planning" (Worldwide, USAID, $2.5 million), "Implement and Manage Water Development Programs" (Kenya, Senegal, Ghana, Malawi, USAID, $2 million), "Provide Drought Relief and Improve Health and Nutrition Status of Children and Families" (Mali and Sudan, USAID, $1.7 million). Operates with a $260 million annual budget.

## World Wildlife Fund—U.S.
1250 24th St., NW
Washington, DC 20002
Tel. 202/293-4800
Fax 202/293-9211

Recently merged with the Conservation Foundation. Promotes the protection of endangered wildlife and wildlands, with particular emphasis on the conservation of tropical forests. Maintains a full-time staff in the U.S. of 300 and long-term staff abroad. Operates programs in the Caribbean, Central and South America, Asia, the Pacific, and Sub-Saharan Africa. Major funding sources includes USAID and numerous foundations and corporations. Previous projects included: "Improve Management of Critical Wildland Areas to Insure That They can Be Used to Support Development Needs" (Worldwide, USAID, $1.2 million) and "Support Wildlife Conservation and Related Biological Diversity Activities" (Near East, USAID, $521,557). Operates with a $57 million annual budget.

## Y.M.C.A.—International Division
101 N. Wacker Drive
Chicago, IL 60606
Tel. 312/977-0031
Fax 312/977-9063

Provides assistance to local YMCAs for promoting social and economic development programs. Maintains a full-time U.S. staff of 14. Operates in Sub-Saharan Africa, Asia, the Pacific Islands, Central and South America, the Caribbean, the Middle East, Greece, and Egypt. Major funding provided by private donations and USAID. Previous projects included: "Strengthen International program for Development of Human Resources and Institutional Capacity" (Worldwide, USAID, $1.9 million). Operates with a $37 million annual budget.

## Y.W.C.A. of the U.S.A.
726 Broadway  
New York, NY 10003  
Tel. 212/614-2700  
Fax 212/677-9716

624 9th Street, NW, 2nd Fl.  
Washington, DC 20001  
Tel. 202/628-3636  
Fax 202/783-7123

Sponsors programs in community development, development education, enterprise development and management, public health, and social welfare. Operates in Jamaica, South America, Lebanon, India, Southeast Asia, the Pacific, and Sub-Saharan Africa. Operates with a $9 million annual budget.

## Zero Population Growth
1400 16th Street, NW, Suite 320
Washington, DC 20036
Tel. 202/332-2200
Fax 202/332-2302

Produces and disseminates population planning information throughout the world. Includes programs in development education, information dissemination, public policy and advocacy. Operates with a $2 million annual budget.

# 8

## NONPROFIT CORPORATIONS

$N$ot-for-profit corporations provide similar technical assistance services as private firms, private voluntary organizations (PVOs) or non-governmental organizations (NGOs), and many colleges and universities. Many of these corporations are closely linked to these other organizations in terms of mission, personnel, and funding sources. As nonprofit organizations, they have tax-exempt status.

### ORIENTATION

Most not-for-profit organizations conduct research or manage agricultural, rural development, health, population planning, energy, or educational projects in developing countries. Many work closely with counterpart PVOs and private contracting firms—often serving as either the prime contractor or subcontractor to these other organizations—and are largely indistinguishable from these organizations in all but corporate structure and tax exempt status. Several are university-based and thus provide many academic-relevant services, such as research, training, and educational development. Similar to private firms and PVOs, these nonprofit corporations compete alongside the other organizations for technical assistance contracts funded by USAID, World Bank, development banks, and private foundations.

While many of these organizations are large, receiving millions of dollars in contracts each year, none are involved in the design, construction, and implementation of large-scale infrastructure projects; few receive funding outside the network of public-oriented development agencies of government, international organizations, and private foundations.

## STRATEGIES

Nonprofit organizations offer numerous job opportunities for international specialists pursuing international careers rather than for individuals just looking for an international job. Many require higher education degrees, specialized training, exotic combinations of work skills, international experience, and foreign language capabilities. Operating similar to many private firms and PVOs, these organizations make up an intricate part of the job and career network of international specialists. They are especially appealing to individuals who wish to pursue development causes for alleviating the problems of Third World countries. Consequently, you may want to merge this list of organizations with the lists of private contractors and PVOs found in Chapters 4 and 5. Together, these organizations make up a major portion of organizations involved in spending billions of dollars in aid funds in the developing worlds of Asia, Africa, Middle East, Latin America, the Caribbean, Eastern Europe, and the former Soviet Union.

# THE ORGANIZATIONS

## Academy for Educational Development, Inc.
1255 23rd St., NW
Washington, DC 20037
Tel. 202/862-1900
Fax 202/862-1947

Provides technical assistance in the areas of education, health care, technical training, agriculture, communications, computer science, and student services. Maintains a full-time staff in the U.S. of 300 and a long-term staff abroad of 150. Operates in Africa, Asia, the Pacific Islands, Latin America, the Caribbean, Middle East, North Africa, Australia, New Zealand, and Western and Eastern Europe. Major clients include USAID, World Bank, United Nations agencies, several development banks, and private foundations. Previous projects included: "Develop/Demonstrate Effective Communication Methodology for Technical Transfer in Agriculture" (Worldwide, USAID, $6.9 million), "Presidential Training Initiative for the Caribbean Islands" (Barbados, USAID, $5.3 million), and "Complete Development of Methodology for Child Survival" (Worldwide, USAID, $5.4 million).

## Agricultural Co-op Development International
50 F St., NW, Suite 900
Washington, DC 20001
Tel. 202/638-4661
Fax 202/626-8726

Provides training, technical, and management assistance in the areas of agricultural cooperatives, farm credit, agribusiness, and marketing. Maintains a full-time staff in the U.S. of 28 and a long-term staff abroad of 24. Operates in Africa, Asia, Latin America, the Caribbean, Middle East, and North Africa. Major clients include USAID, World Bank, and host country governments and cooperatives. Previous projects included: "Cooperative Agriculture and Agribusiness Support Project" (Uganda, USAID, $5.2 million), "Cooperative Development Project" (West Bank & Gaza, USAID, $4.5 million), and "Small Farmer Organization Strengthening Project" (Honduras, USAID, $3.3 million).

## Air Serv International
1901 Orange Tree Lane, Suite 200
Redlands, CA 92373-0993
Tel. 714/793-2627
Fax 714/793-0226

Provides air transportation for relief agencies and PVOs in developing countries. U.S. staff of 13 and long-term staff abroad of 41. Operates with a $10 million annual budget.

## American Public Health Association
1015 15 St., NW, Suite 300
Washington, DC 20005
Tel. 202/789-5600
Fax 202/789-5661.

Membership organization providing health information and training services. U.S. staff of 60.

## Appropriate Technology International
1331 H St., NW, Suite 1200
Washington, DC 20005
Tel. 202/879-2900
Fax 202/628-4622

Specializes in providing appropriate technology services relating to agricultural production and wastes, local mineral resource development, and equipment and support for small farms. Maintains a full-time staff in the U.S. of 36 and a long-term staff abroad of 3. Operates in Sub-Saharan Africa, Asia, Central and South America, and the Caribbean. Major client is USAID. Previous project included: "Strengthen Capacity to Facilitate Development and Assessment of Technology Appropriate in Development Countries" (Worldwide, USAID, $25.6 million). Operates with a $4 million annual budget.

## Asia Foundation
465 California St., 14th Floor
San Francisco, CA 94104
Tel. 415/982-4640, Fax 415/392-8863

A major foundation providing assistance to Asian and Pacific government agencies, institutions, organizations, and individuals for promoting social and economic development in the areas of private and voluntary sector; representative government; public administration and government service; legal systems and human rights; education and national development; management, business, and economics; media, information, and communication; international relations; and regional cooperation. Maintains a full-time staff in the U.S. of 76 and a long-term staff abroad of 178. Operates throughout Asia and the Pacific Islands. Receives funding from private sources as well as the U.S. Congress and USAID. Major clients include government agencies, institutions, organizations, and individuals applying for assistance from the Asian Foundation. Previous projects included: "Participant Training for Asians and Pacific Islanders" (Asian/Pacific countries, Partners for International Education and Training, $10+ million), "Private Financial and Family Planning Advisory Support to Non-Government Organizations" (Bangladesh, USAID, $7.4 million), and "Population and Family Planning Services" (Bangladesh, USAID, $2.3 million).

## Association for Voluntary Surgical Contraception, Inc.

79 Madison Ave., 7th Floor
New York, NY 10016
Tel. 212/561-8000
Fax 212/779-9439

Provides technical assistance relating to voluntary sterilization, family planning, and maternal-child health care. Maintains a full-time staff in the U.S. of 90 and a long-term staff abroad of 30. Operates in Africa, Asia, Latin America, the Caribbean, Middle East, and North Africa. Major client is USAID. Previous projects included: "Support a Program to Increase High Quality Voluntary Sterilization services in LDC's" (Worldwide, USAID, $72.5 million), "Support a Delivery Program Through Satellite Clinics" (Bangladesh, USAID, $10.5 million), and "Support a Program of Technical Assistance to Voluntary Surgical Contraception Projects" (Worldwide, USAID, $10.2 million).

## Association of University Programs in Health Administration

1911 N. Fort Myer Drive, #503
Arlington, VA 22209
Tel. 703/524-5500
Fax 703/525-4791

Consortium of 96 colleges and universities in North America and 65 universities in 34 other countries. U.S. staff of 20. Recent project: "Support a Management Training Program for LAC Bureau/Missions to Train Health Services Administrators" (Latin American Region, USAID, $1.1 million).

## Battelle Memorial Institute

505 King Avenue
Columbus, OH 43201-2693
Tel. 614/424-6424
Fax 614/424-5263

This is the world's largest contract research firm specializing in the areas of biological and chemical sciences, engineering and manufacturing technology, electronic and engineering systems, biotechnology, advanced materials, and nuclear system. Maintains a full-time staff in the U.S. of 6,700 and a long-term staff abroad of 800. Operates worldwide. Major funding sources include USAID and numerous host country governments, and private firms. Previous projects included: "Provide for the Care and Breeding of Monkeys to be Used for AID Malaria Vaccine Research Projects" (Worldwide, USAID, $4.1) and "Technical and Management Advisory Services in Establishment of Energy Institute" (Indonesia, USAID, $2.9 million).

## Biomedical Research Institute
12111 Parklawn Drive
Rockville, MD 20852
Tel. 301/881-3300
Fax 301/881-7640

Focuses on developing malaria and schistosomiesis vaccines for developing countries. U.S. staff of 65. Recent project: "Support the Malaria Vaccine Research and Development Program" (US, USAID, $1.4 million).

## Board on Science and Technology For International Development
2101 Constitution Ave.
Milton Harris Bldg.
Room 476
Washington, DC 20418
Tel. 202/334-2639
Fax 202/334-2660

Provides technical assistance for strengthening local scientific and technological capabilities in agriculture, environmental planning, energy, forestry, health, industrial development, natural resource management and conservation, and nutrition. Functions as a unit within the Office of International Affairs of the National Research Council. Maintains a full-time staff in the U.S. of 30 and a long-term staff abroad of 1. Operates in Africa, Asia, Latin America, Middle East, North Africa, and Portugal. Major clients include USAID, National Science Foundation, and several foundations. Previous projects included: "Applying Science and Technology to Development" (Worldwide, USAID, $37 million), "Partnership for Research in Development" (Worldwide, USAID, $10 million), and "Government of Thailand Science and Technology Services to Thai Science and Technology Development Board" (Thailand, Department of Technology and Economic Cooperation, $3.3 million).

## Center for Applied Statistics
1118 22nd St., NW
Washington, DC 20037
Tel. 202/429-9292
Fax 202/659-5641

Provides language training, curriculum development, and training development services for U.S. Department of State, Department of Defense, USAID, Peace Corps, and multinational corporations. U.S. staff of 65.

## Consortium for International Development (CID)
6367 East Tanque Verde
Suite 200
Tucson, AZ 85715
Tel. 602/885-0055
Fax 602/886-3244

A consortium of universities located in the west and southwest, such as Utah State, Oregon State, Washington State, California State Polytechnic, University of Arizona, and the University of New Mexico. Maintains a full-time staff in the U.S. of 17 and a long-term staff abroad of 61. Operates in Africa, Asia, Latin America, Middle East, and North Africa. Major clients include USAID, World Bank, and the Government of the Arab Republic of Egypt. Previous projects included: "Agriculture Development Support" (Yemen Arab Republic, USAID, $48.7 million), "Irrigation Improvement Project" (Egypt, USAID, $17.1 million), and "Cameroon Agricultural Policy and Planning Project" (USAID, $11 million).

## Educational Development Center, Inc.
| | |
|---|---|
| 55 Chapel St. | 1250 24th St., NW, Suite 875 |
| Newton, MA 02160 | Washington, DC 20037 |
| Tel. 617/969-7100 | Tel. 202/466-0540 |
| Fax 617/224-3436 | |

Provides technical assistance in the areas of education, communications, social marketing, management training, private sector development, health, nutrition, agriculture, institution building, and technology transfer. Maintains a full-time staff in the U.S. of 140 and a long-term staff abroad of 3. Operates in Africa, Asia, the Pacific Islands, Latin America, the Caribbean, Middle East, North Africa, and Western Europe. Major clients include USAID, World Bank, USIA, and United Nations agencies. Previous projects included: "Radio Learning Project" (Worldwide, USAID, $7.5 million), "Yemen Educational Development Support Project" (USAID, $4.1 million), and "Develop Tested Model for Using Radio to Provide Effective Primary Science Instruction at Low Cost" (Lesotho, USAID, $3.1 million).

## Environmental Research Institute of Michigan
1975 Green Road
Ann Arbor, MI 48105
Tel. 313/994-1200
Fax 313/994-1575

Designs, establishes, and operates remote sensing centers and provides assistance in agriculture, forestry, water resources, and geology. U.S. staff of 600.

## Family Health International
P.O. Box 13950
Research Triangle Park, NC 27709
Tel. 919/544-7040
Fax 919/544-7261

Provides technical assistance relating to family planning and health care issues. Maintains a full-time staff in the U.S. of 173. Operates in Africa, Asia, Latin America, the Caribbean, Middle East, North Africa, Canada, Australia, and Western and Eastern Europe. Major clients include USAID, National Institutes for Health, and several foundations. Previous projects included: "Support a Program Fostering Development, Introduction, Assessment, and Evaluation of Fertility Control Technology" (Worldwide, USAID, $63 million), "AIDS Technical Support Project" (Worldwide, USAID, $28 million), and "Development of New Contraceptive Technology" (Worldwide, Andrew W. Mellon Foundation, $900,000).

## Industry Council for Development
50 West 29th St., Suite 114
New York, NY 10001
Tel. 212/684-2920
Fax 212/684-2017

Provides agribusiness development, information management, health education, and marketing systems assistance to industries. U.S. staff of 2.

## Institute for Contemporary Studies
243 Kearny Street
San Francisco, CA 94108
Tel. 415/981-5353
Fax 415/986-4878

Serves as a forum for discussions between scholars and policymakers on key economic and development issues. U.S. staff of 10 and long-term staff abroad of 5.

## Institute for Development Anthropology
99 Collier Street
Binghamton, NY 13902
Tel. 607/772-6244
Fax 607/773-8993

Conducts studies on rural development, river basin development, natural resources, regional planning, social analysis, remote sensing, and cartography. U.S. staff of 14 and long-term staff abroad of 7.

## Institute of Gas Technology
3424 South State Street
Chicago, IL 60616
Tel. 312/576-3650
Fax 312/567-3903

Provides technical assistance relating to energy planning, pricing, utilization, transmission, distribution, storage, and development. Maintains a full-time staff in the U.S. of 260 and a long-term staff abroad of 10. Operates in Africa, Asia, Latin America, Middle East, Africa, and Europe. Major clients include: World Bank, Asian Development Bank, USAID, and numerous national petroleum companies. Previous projects included: "Establish a Career Development Center" (United Arab Emirates, Abu Dabai National Oil Co., $28.7 million), "Molten Carbonate Fuel Cell Development Program" (Japan, $6.8 million), and "Fuel Cell Technology Transfer Program" (Netherlands, E.C.N., $3.5 million).

## Latin American Scholarship Program of American Universities
25 Mount Auburn St.
Cambridge, MA 02138
Tel. 617/495-5255
Fax 617/495-8990

A consortium of more than 300 universities and public/private institutions affiliated with Harvard University involved in administering scholarship programs for several sponsors, especially in Latin America and the Caribbean. Provides technical assistance relating to human resource development for educational institutions, designing offshore degree training programs, recruiting U.S. professors for overseas assignments, and assessing degree training needs. Maintains a full-time U.S. staff of 65. Operates primarily in Latin America and the Caribbean but also in a few countries in Africa and Asia as well as Egypt and Italy. Major clients include USIA (Fulbright Academic Exchange Program), USAID, World Bank, Inter-American Development Bank and several Latin American and Caribbean organizations. Previous projects included: "Fulbright-LASPAU Scholarship Program" (Latin America/Caribbean, USIA, $5 million yearly), "ONAPLAN Agricultural Sector Training Project" (Dominican Republic, USAID, $5 million), and "ESPOL/BID Faculty Training" (Ecuador, Inter-American Development Bank, $2.8 million).

## Management Sciences for Health
165 Allandale Rd.
Boston, MA 02130
Tel. 617/524-7799
Fax 617/524-2825

Provides technical assistance in several public health areas—human resource management, drug management, maternal and child health, health services, health financing, and management information systems. Maintains a full-time U.S. staff of 80 and a long-term staff abroad of 30. Operates in Africa, Asia, the Pacific Islands, Latin America, the Caribbean, Middle East, North Africa, and Portugal. Major client is USAID. Previous projects included: "Assist USAID Missions and Host Countries to Improve Primary Health Care Services" (Worldwide, USAID, $18.9 million), "Recipient Shall Coordinate Program to Expand and Strengthen Health Sciences" (Pakistan, USAID, $17.1 million), and "Assist Child Survival, Diarrheal Disease Control and ORT Programs" (Worldwide, USAID, $11.1 million).

## Medical Care Development, Inc.
1742 R Street, NW
Washington, DC 20009
Tel. 202/462-1920
Fax 202/265-4078

Provides technical services in a variety of health care areas. U.S. staff of 85 and long-term staff abroad of 20.

## MidAmerica International Agricultural Consortium
14 Varner Hall
University of Nebraska
3835 Holdredge
Lincoln, NE 68583-0744
Tel. 402/472-3900
Fax 402/472-3901

A consortium of five major Midwest universities—Kansas State, Iowa State, Missouri, Nebraska, and Oklahoma State—providing agricultural development assistance to Third World countries. Maintains a full-time staff in the U.S. of 3 and a long-term staff abroad of 30. Operates in a few countries of Africa, Asia, Latin America, and North Africa. Major client is USAID. Previous projects included: "Dryland Agriculture Applied Research Project" (Morocco, USAID, $23.1 million), "National Agricultural Research Project" (Kenya, USAID, $12.3 million), and "Agricultural Technology Transfer Project" (Tunisia, Host Country & USAID, $8.8 million).

## Midwest Universities Consortium
## for International Activities
66 East 15th Avenue
Columbus, OH 43201
Tel. 614/291-9646
Fax 614/291-9717

Consortium of eight midwest universities provides a wide range of educational, training, and technical assistance programs involving everything from architecture, law, and nursing to public affairs and agricultural development. Maintains a full-time staff in the U.S. of 15 and a long-term staff abroad of 78. Operates in

Africa, Asia, Latin America, the Caribbean, Middle East, and the USSR. Major clients include USAID, World Bank, Asian Development Bank, and host country governments. Previous projects included: "Coordinate Implementation of Second University Development Project" (Indonesia, World Bank, $65 million), "Strengthen the Institut Teknologi MARA Through Technical Assistance and Training" (Malaysia, Government of Malaysia, $55.8 million), and "Provide Technical Assistance and Training to Increase Production of Oilseed Crops" (Burma, USAID, $6.8 million).

## National Association of Schools of Public Affairs and Administration (NASPAA)
1120 G St., NW #730
Washington, DC 20005
Tel. 202/628-8965
Fax 202/626-4978

An accrediting organization for schools of public affairs and public administration that also sponsors research on institutional development. U.S. staff of 10 and long-term staff abroad of 1.

## New Transcentury Foundation
1901 North Fort Myer Drive, Suite 1017
Arlington, VA 22209
Tel. 703/351-5500
Fax 703/351-5507

Provides technical assistance and management consulting services relating to human resource development, small enterprise development, rural infrastructure, agriculture, public administration, recruitment, and program design and evaluation. Maintains a full-time staff in the U.S. of 15 and a long-term staff abroad of 25. Operates in Africa, Asia, the Pacific Islands, Latin America, the Caribbean, Middle East, North Africa, Australia, and New Zealand. Major clients include USAID and the United Nations Development Programme. Previous projects included: "Swaziland Manpower Development Project" (USAID, $15 million), "Strengthen Management, Technical and Financial Analytical Capabilities of Rural Water Supply Department" (Yemen Arab Republic, USAID, $12.4 million), and "Somalia Refugee Assistance" (Somalia, USAID/UNDP, $2.5 million).

## Partners in International Education and Training
2000 M St., NW, Suite 480
Washington, DC 20036
Tel. 202/429-0810
Fax 202/429-8764

Provides education and training services for USAID-sponsored participants. Maintains a full-time staff in the U.S. of 80 where all education and training programs take place. Incorporates all USAID missions in Africa, Asia, Pacific Islands, Latin America, the Caribbean, Middle East, North Africa, and Portugal. Previous program: "Provide Placement, Programming, Implementation, Evaluation, and Monitoring for AID's Participant Training Program" ($90.2 million).

## Population Reference Bureau
1875 Connecticut Ave., NW, Suite 520
Washington, DC 20009
Tel. 202/483-1100
Fax 202/3328-3937

Provides publications to communicate research findings on population issues relating to developing countries. U.S. staff of 40.

## Population Services International
1120 19th St., NW, Suite 600
Washington, DC 20036
Tel. 202/785-0072
Fax 202/785-0120

Provides social marketing, information, education, and communication services relating to family planning, oral rehydration therapy, and AIDS prevention. Maintains a full-time staff in the U.S. of 30 and a long-term staff abroad of 500. Operates in a few countries of Africa and Asia as well as in Haiti, Mexico, and Jordan. Major client is USAID. Previous projects included: "Advisory Services to the Family Planning Social Marketing Project" (Bangladesh, USAID, $16.3 million), "Implement a Program to Extend Availability of Family Planning Services" (Bangladesh, USAID, $8.8 million), and "Advisory Services in Oral Rehydration Therapy" (Bangladesh, USAID, $5.5 million).

## Research Triangle Institute
P.O. Box 12194
Research Triangle Park, NC 27709
Tel. 919/541-6000
Fax 919/541-5945

A contract research organization providing a wide range of technical capabilities in the areas of economic policy, development planning, urban finance, agriculture, women in development, regional planning, health, nutrition, family planning, and water sanitation. Maintains a full-time staff in the U.S. of 1,400 and a long-term staff abroad of 12. Operates in Africa, Asia, Latin America, the Caribbean, Middle East, North Africa, and the United Kingdom. Major clients include USAID, World Bank, UN agencies, Asian Development Bank and the Inter-American Development Bank. Previous projects included: "Integrated Population and Development Planning II" (Worldwide, USAID, $6.3 million), "Water and Sanitation for Health" (Worldwide, USAID, $5.5), and "Resources for the Awareness of Population Impacts on Development" (Worldwide, USAID, $5.3 million).

## SRI International
333 Ravenswood Avenue
1611 North Kent St.
Menlo Park, CA 94025-3493
Tel. 415/326-6200
Fax 415/326-5512

7th Floor
Arlington, VA 22209
Tel. 703/524-2053

A major consulting and development firm involved in providing technical assistance in numerous areas—economic analysis, engineering, energy research, environmental management, health sciences, information sciences, management consulting, national security, physical sciences, and social sciences. Maintains a full-time staff in the U.S. of 2,700 and a long-term staff abroad of 900. Operates in Africa, Asia, the Pacific Islands, Latin America, the Caribbean, Middle East, North Africa, Western Europe, and Australia with branch offices in France, Italy, Japan, Philippines, Saudi Arabia, Singapore, Sweden, Switzerland, United Kingdom, West Germany, and Arlington, Virginia. Major clients include USAID and numerous government agencies and private firms. Recent projects include: "Private Enterprise Development Support" (Worldwide, USAID), "Africa-wide Private Sector Development" (Africa, USAID), and "Evaluate Alternatives for Exploration of Oil and Gas Reserves" (Norway, Statoil).

## Urban Institute
2100 M St., NW
5th Floor
Washington, DC 20037
Tel. 202/833-7200
Fax 202/223-3043

A policy and research organization providing assistance with health policy, public finance, housing, human resources, population, and income policy. U.S. staff of 130.

## Wellstart/The San Diego Lactation Program
P.O. Box 87549
San Diego, CA 92138
Tel. 619/295-5192
Fax 619/454-1799

Provides lactation management education and training for health professionals in developing countries. U.S. staff of 11.

## Western Consortium for Public Health
2001 Addison St., Suite 200
Berkeley, CA 94704
Tel. 510/644-9300
Fax 510/644-9319

A consortium of six universities providing a broad range of health services to developing countries. U.S. staff of 200.

## World Learning, Inc.
Kipling Road
P.O. Box 676
Brattleboro, VT 05302-0676
Tel. 802/257-7751
Fax 802/258-3248

Founded in 1932, this is one of the oldest private international industrial services in the world. It operates international exchange programs, conducts training programs, and provides technical assistance in the areas of agricultural and rural development, refugees, family planning, and water resources. A major force for cross-cultural training and ESL programs, it operates 260 programs in 70 countries. Operates the highly respected School for International Training. Maintains a full-time staff in the U.S. of 350 and a long-term staff abroad of 750. Operates in Africa, Asia, Latin America, the Caribbean, and the Middle East. Major clients include USAID, USIA, U.S. Department of State, United Nations agencies, CIDA, and host country governments. Previous projects included: "Intensive ESL, CO, WO, and Pass Training for Indochinese Refugees" (Thailand, U.S. Department of State, $42.7 million), "Partners for International Education and Training" (Latin America and Caribbean, USAID, $29.95 million), and "Pakistan Participant Training Program" (USAID, $4 million). Operates with a $52 million annual budget.

## World Resources Institute
1709 New York Ave., NW, Suite 700
Washington, DC 20006
Tel. 202/638-6300
Fax 202/638-0036

A policy research center providing assistance with major policy questions relating to development issues. U.S. staff of 90.

# 9

# COLLEGES AND UNIVERSITIES

*C*olleges and universities play a significant role in developing countries. While these institutions are especially well organized to offer traditional education and training programs, many also operate similarly to consulting firms, nonprofit corporations, and private voluntary organizations—they conduct research, provide technical assistance, and manage projects. Indeed, colleges and universities compete alongside these other organizations for contracts, grants, and cooperative agreements dispensed by USAID, the World Bank, foundations, and other funding institutions involved in promoting development in Third World countries.

## MAJOR STRENGTHS

Colleges and universities are especially strong competitors in five major research and technical assistance areas—agriculture, aquaculture, forestry, public health, and family planning. They are uniquely equipped to offer education and training services such as providing degree programs for foreign students, developing institutional linkages for developing programs in foreign universities, and exchanging faculty with counterpart institutions. Many operate interdisciplinary area studies programs which focus on conducting research on Europe, Asia, Africa, Latin America, and the Middle East.

## FUNDING SOURCES

International contracts and grants acquired through government agencies and private foundations play an important role in the overall funding of many colleges and universities. Such funds also affect the allocation of faculty positions and determine workloads of faculty members. In some institutions, research "institutes", "centers", "programs", or "international offices"—especially those in agriculture and public health—operate like independent contractors. Organized to compete for outside contracts, most of their funding is dependent on receiving such contracts and grants; the college or university may provide little or no financial support since such operations are designed to be both self-supporting and income-generating for the college or university.

Full-time faculty may be directly hired by the institute/center/ program/office, or they are assigned to it by a department where they primarily engage in research and technical assistance activities. In other cases, a particular school, center, or institute, such as agriculture, health, population, marine science, engineering, health, or area studies, operate international programs independent of other international programs within the university or in cooperation with one another; a committee of deans or program administrators may more or less coordinate these diverse institutional efforts. In other cases, faculty members may receive part-time appointments and "release time" in order to work with such an in-stitute/center/program or engage in research projects; their teaching loads are normally reduced in order to participate in such programs. This often leads to resentment and petty politics amongst other faculty members who usually take on additional teaching loads in order to make up for the "teaching slack" created by their "research" colleagues who are off engaging in more financially rewarding and professionally enhancing activities. And in still other cases, a college or university may provide little organizational support for such activities other than operate a small research and development office that helps procure and administer contracts acquired by enterprising faculty members.

However, the **academic department** remains the basic organizational unit from which all international programs and activities are developed. In this sense, international activities tend to be decentralized and fragmented within most higher educational institutions.

## THE BENEFICIARIES

Each year hundreds of colleges and universities receive billions of dollars in contracts and grants to conduct research, provide technical assistance, and operate university-based educational programs aimed at developing countries and foreign students. Agriculture, population, health, and education programs are the four major beneficiaries of contracts, grants, and cooperative agreements dispensed to colleges and universities by government agencies, international organizations, and private foundations. During the past 13 years, the major recipients of such largess have been:

- Colorado State University
- Florida State University
- Georgetown University
- Harvard University
- Indiana University
- Johns Hopkins University
- Michigan State University
- North Carolina State University
- Ohio State University
- Oregon State University
- Purdue University
- State University of New York—System
- Texas A&M University
- University of Florida
- University of Hawaii
- University of Illinois
- University of Kentucky
- University of Minnesota
- University of Missouri
- University of Nebraska

As noted in Chapter 8, many colleges and universities also belong to consortia (Consortium for International Development, Midwest Universities Consortium for International Activities, MidAmerican International Agricultural Consortium, South-East Consortium for International Development) or are closely linked to other nonprofit corporations

(Research Triangle Institute) and private firms (Development Alternatives, Inc.). The consortium are able to better mobilize the diverse resources of member institutions in organizing for large technical assistance projects. If you are primarily interested in pursuing international opportunities with the colleges and universities listed in this chapter, do keep in mind the consortia in Chapter 8 which also have their own full-time staffs in the U.S. and abroad.

## OPPORTUNITIES

Finding positions in colleges and universities to engage in international work takes two major paths. Entry into most institutions is still via the basic organizational unit—the academic department. You must possess the necessary academic credentials and professional experience to qualify for an academic position. The basic requirement is a Ph.D. although Masters' degrees are acceptable in some institutions. Opportunities to do international contract and grant work may arise from your own efforts to acquire a contract or grant or in conjunction with the activities of fellow faculty members, including an institute or center specifically organized for contract and grant work. In many institutions, you must first acquire an academic appointment in a department *before* you can participate in the activities of such an institute or center; you may also receive a joint appointment involving both an academic department and an institute or center. Your workload within the department versus the institute or center will be a matter of negotiation between you, your department chair, the dean, and institute/center personnel. In other colleges and universities, the institute or center operates like an independent contractor by directly hiring its own personnel. Positions may be strictly research or administrative in nature with no teaching or other academic responsibilities involved. Entry into these positions also requires advanced educational degrees (Masters' or Ph.D.). These positions place greater emphasis on contracting and grantsmanship skills as well as practical field and research experience than on scholarly credentials normally associated with academic departments.

The following list of academic institutions includes the major recipients of international contracts, grants, and cooperative agreements funded primarily by USAID, the World Bank, and private foundations. Many other educational institutions also have international programs, engage in international research, and provide technical assistance but on a smaller scale than the institutions listed here. While faculty in many departments may possess international expertise, engage in international research, or provide technical assistance, each institution tends to take on a particular international orientation, be it agriculture, health, public policy, area studies, or education and training.

## MAJOR RECIPIENTS

### Alabama A&M University
P.O. Box 1177
Normal, AL 35762-0030
Tel. 205/851-5418
Fax 205/851-9157
Organization: Office of International Programs
Focus: agriculture

### University of Alabama—Birmingham
University Station, 315 Tim Howell
720 20th Street
Birmingham, AL 35294-0098
Tel. 205/934-8647
Fax 205/975-3329
Organizations: Office of International Programs, John Sparkman Center for International Public Health Education
Focus: public health

### University of Alaska—Fairbanks
172 Arctic Health Research Bldg.
Fairbanks, AK 99775-0100
Tel. 907/474-7083
Fax 907/474-6567
Organization: School of Agriculture and Land Resources Management
Focus: agriculture and land use

### Alcorn State University
Rural Station, P.O. Box 690
Lorman, MS 39096
Tel. 601/877-6136
Fax 601/877-6219
Organization: Agricultural Research and Applied Science
Focus: agriculture, animal science, nursing

## American University
4400 Massachusetts Ave., NW
Washington, DC 20016-8071
Tel. 202/885-1600
Fax 202/885-2494
Organization: School of International Service
Focus: politics and public policy

## Arizona State University
Box 874105
Tempe, AZ 85287-4105
Tel. 602/965-5965
Fax 602/965-4026
Organizations: Office of International Programs, Center for Asian Studies, Center for Latin American Studies
Focus: Asian and Latin American studies, rural credit, engineering, training

## University of Arizona
Harville 151
Tucson, AZ 85721
Tel. 602/621-1900
Fax 602/621-7257
Organizations: Office of International Agricultural Programs, Middle East Center
Focus: agriculture, natural resources, environment, socio-economic analysis

## University of Arkansas—Fayetteville
300 Hotz Hall
Fayetteville, AR 72701
Tel. 501/575-6857
Fax 501/575-5055
Organization: School of Agriculture
Focus: agriculture, aquaculture

## University of Arkansas—Pine Bluff
Box 4005, 1200 North University
Pine Bluff, AR 71601
Tel. 501/543-8131
Fax 501/543-8033
Organization: School of Agriculture
Focus: agriculture, aquaculture, health/nutrition

## Auburn University

International Programs
146 College of Business Bldg., Box P
Auburn, AL 36849-5159
Tel. 205/844-5766
Fax 205/844-4983
Organizations: Office of International Programs, International Center for Aquaculture, International Agricultural Programs.
Focus: agriculture, fisheries, education training.

## Boston University

19 Deerfield St.
Second Floor
Boston, MA 02215
Tel. 617/353-3565
Fax 617/353-5891
Organizations: International Student Services Office, College of Communication, School of Education, Medical School, and Centers for African Studies, Asian Development, and Latin American Development.
Focus: training, education, health, and area studies.

## Brigham Young University

Benson Institute 110 B-49
Provo, UT 84602
Tel. 801/378-2607
Organizations: Ezra Taft Benson Agriculture and Food Institute; David M. Kennedy Center for International Studies
Focus: agriculture, nutrition, rural development, archaeology, pharmacology, education and training.

## California State University—Fresno

School of Agricultural Sciences & Technology
Fresno, CA 93740-0079
Tel. 209/278-5118
Fax 209/278-4496
Organizations: Office of International Agricultural Programs, International Business Programs, and Office of International Student Services and Programs
Focus: agriculture, business, education and training

## University of California—Berkeley
College of Natural Resources
101 Gianinni Hall
Berkeley, CA 94720
Tel. 510/642-0542
Fax 510/642-4612
Organizations: College of Natural Resources; African Studies Center; South Asian
Center; East Asian Center; Middle East Studies Center; Collaborative Research
Support Program in Nutrition Sciences.
Focus: natural resource management, water and sanitary management, nutrition,
agriculture, area studies, education and training.

## University of California—Davis
424 2nd Street
Suite B
Davis, CA 95616
Tel. 916/752-7071
Fax 916/752-7523
Organizations: International Programs; Graduate Studies and Research
Focus: agriculture, engineering, management, and law

## University of California—Los Angeles
10833 Le Conte
Los Angeles, CA 90024-1772
Tel. 310/825-4321
Organizations: School of Public Health, Office of International Students and
Scholars, East Asia Center, Russian and East European Center, Latin American
Center, Near Eastern Center, African Studies Center, Chinese Studies Center,
Japanese Research and Exchange Program, Mexican Studies Center, Pacific Rim
Studies Center
Focus: health, education, and training

## Case Western Reserve University
10900 Euclid Ave.
Cleveland, OH 44106
Tel. 216/368-2000
Fax 216/368-3013
Organizations: Office of International Student Services, Medical School,
International Health Center University Hospital
Focus: health, applied social sciences, and management

## Clark Atlanta University
223 James P. Brawley Dr., SW
Atlanta, GA 30314
Tel. 404/880-6662
Fax 404/880-8654
Organizations: Research and Sponsored Programs; Institute for International Affairs
Focus: health, child survival, human resource development, rural sanitation, education and training

## Clark University
Program for International Development
950 Main Street
Worcester, MA 01610-1477
Tel 508/793-7201
Fax 508/793-8820
Organization: International Development Program
Focus: resource management, population, rural development, energy

## Clemson University
101 Barre Hall
Clemson, SC 29634-5201
Tel. 803/656-3642
Fax 803/656-3608
Organization: International Programs
Focus: agriculture, resource management, education and training

## Colorado State University
Office of International Programs
Fort Collins, CO 80523
Tel. 303/491-7223
Fax 303/491-2293
Organization: International Programs
Focus: agriculture, water resource development, education and training

## Columbia University
600 West 168th St., 7th Floor
New York, NY 10032
Tel. 212/305-3927
Fax 212/305-1460
Organizations: School of Public Health and Administration Medicine, Center for Population and Family Health, School of International and Public Affairs, South Asian Institute, East Asian Institute, Latin American Institute, Middle East Institute
Focus: family planning, health, education and training

## University of Connecticut
1376 Storrs Road
Box U66
Storrs, CT 06269-4066
Tel. 203/486-2917
Fax 203/486-5113
Organizations: College of Agriculture and Natural Resources, Latin American Center, Institute of Public Service International
Focus: agriculture, nutrition, natural resources, human resource management, computer systems, education and training

## Cornell University
170 Uris Hall
Ithaca, NY 14853
Tel. 607/255-6370
Fax 607/254-5000
Organizations: Center for International Studies, International Agricultural Programs, Institute for African Development, Rural Development Committee, South Asia Program, Population and Development Program, International Nutrition Program
Focus: agriculture, nutrition, rural development, law, population, education and training

## Delaware State College
1200 N. Dupont Hwy.
Dover, DE 19901
Tel. 302/739-4924
Organization: International Programs
Focus: agriculture, nutrition, family health education

## University of Delaware
Office of International Programs
4 Kent Way
Newark, DE 19716
Tel. 302/831-2852
Fax 302/831-6042
Organizations: Office of International Programs, College of Agricultural Sciences
Focus: agriculture, engineering, marine resources, development administration, education and training

## Duke University
2122 Campus Drive, Box 90404
Durham, NC 27708-0404
Tel. 919/684-2765
Fax 919/684-8749
Organizations: Center for International Studies, Center for International Development Research (Institute of Policy Science), School of Forestry and Environmental Studies
Focus: natural resources, ecology, area studies, education, training

## East Michigan University
The World College
307 Goodison Hall
Ypsilanti, MI 48197
Organization: The World College
Focus: education and training

## East-West Center
1777 East West Road
Honolulu, HI 96848
Tel. 808/944-7111
Fax 808/944-7970
Organizations: Resource Systems Institute, Environment and Policy Institute, Population Institute, Institute of Culture and Communication, Pacific Islands Development Program, Student Affairs and Open Grants Program Focus: environment, population, economic development, natural resources

## Eastern Virginia Medical School
601 Colley Avenue
Norfolk, VA 23507
Tel. 804/446-5899
Fax 804/446-5905
Organization: Contraceptive Research and Development Program
Focus: fertility and population planning

## Florida A&M University
P.O. Box 338
Tallahassee, FL 32307
Tel. 904/599-3562
Fax 904/561-2587
Organization: College of Engineering, Sciences, Technology, and Agriculture
Focus: engineering, pharmacy, architecture, agriculture, and institutional development

## Florida International University
Latin America and Caribbean Center
University Park—DM363
Miami, FL 33199
Tel. 305/348-2894
Fax 305/348-3593
Organization: Latin America and Caribbean Center
Focus: journalism, communication, business, education and training

## Florida State University
Learning Systems Institute
205 Dodd Hall
Tallahassee, FL 32306-4041
Tel. 904/644-2570
Fax 904/644-3783
Organization: Learning Systems Institute
Focus: education and training

## University of Florida
3028 McCarty Hall
Gainesville, FL 32611
Tel. 904/392-1965
Fax 904/392-7127
Organizations: Institute of Food and Agricultural Sciences, Center for Tropical
Agriculture, Center for African Studies, Center for Latin American Studies,
Farming Systems and Small Farms Program, Agroforestry Program
Focus: agriculture, education and training

## Fort Valley State College
1005 State College Drive
Fort Valley, GA 31030-3298
Tel. 912/825-6320
Fax 912/825-6376
Organization: International Programs
Focus: agriculture, nutrition, health, rural development, communication, education
and training

## Georgia Institute of Technology
Centennial Research Building
Atlanta, GA 30332
Tel. 404/894-2375
Fax 404/894-7339
Organizations: Office of Interdisciplinary Programs, Research Institute,
Continuing Education, Advanced Technology Development Center
Focus: institutional development, education and training

## University of Georgia
111 Candler Hall
Athens, GA 30602-1773
Tel. 706/542-7889
Fax 706/542-7891
Organization: International Development
Focus: agriculture, forestry, veterinary medicine, home economics, education and training

## Harvard University
Harvard Institute for International Development
One Eliot St.
Cambridge, MA 02138
Tel. 617/495-2161
Fax 617/495-0527
Organizations: Harvard Institute for International Development, Harvard School of Public Health, Population Sciences and International Health Programs, John F. Kennedy School of Government, Center for Middle Eastern Studies
Focus: health, agriculture, food, public policy, education and training

## University of Hawaii
2565 The Mall
PSB 103
Honolulu, HI 96822
Tel. 808/956-6940
Fax 808/956-5030
Organizations: College of Tropical Agriculture and Human Resources, International Programs, School of Public Health, School of Medicine
Focus: agriculture, health, engineering, management, education and training

## University of Houston
One Main Street
Houston, TX 77002
Tel. 713/221-8048
Fax 713/221-8157
Organizations: International Business Programs, Madrid Business School Project, Office of Overseas International Education, Office of International Student Office, Language and Culture Center
Focus: business, education and training

## Howard University
520 W St., NW
Washington, DC 20059
Tel. 202/806-6270
Fax 202/806-7934
Organizations: College of Medicine, School of Education, School of Engineering,
Office of International Student Services, African Studies and Research
Focus: education and training

## University of Idaho
216 Morrill Hall
Moscow, ID 83843
Tel. 208/885-8984
Fax 208/885-6198
Organization: International Trade and Development Office, College of Agriculture
and Forestry
Focus: agriculture, forestry, education and training

## University of Illinois
109 Mumford Hall
1301 West Gregory Dr.
Urbana, IL 61801
Tel. 217/333-6420
Fax 217/244-6537
Organization: Office of International Agriculture
Focus: agriculture, health, education and training

## University of Illinois—Chicago
1033 West Van Buren
Chicago, IL 60607
Tel. 312/413-7857, Fax 312/996-9391
Organization: Office of International Affairs, College of Pharmacy, College
Nursing, Center for Research in Law and Justice, College of Business Adminis-
tration
Focus: business, health, education and training

## Indiana University
International Programs
Bryan Hall, Room 205
Bloomington, IN 47405
Tel. 812/855-7557
Fax 812/855-6884
Organizations: International Development Institute, International Programs, Center
for African Studies
Focus: management, education and training

## Iowa State University
117 Curtiss Hall
Ames, IA 50011
Tel. 515/294-1851
Fax 515/294-9477
Organizations: International Agricultural Programs
Focus: agriculture, education and training

## University of Iowa
120 International Center
Iowa City, IA 52242
Tel. 319/335-0335
Fax 319/335-2021
Organization: Office of International Education and Services, Center for International and Comparative Studies, Center for Asian and Pacific Studies
Focus: economics, social sciences, education and training

## Johns Hopkins University
103 E. Mount Royal Ave.
Baltimore, MD 21202
Tel. 410/659-4108
Fax 410/659-4118
Organization: School of Hygiene and Public Health, Department of Population Dynamics, Department of International Health, Institute for International Programs, Center for Communications Programs, School of Advanced International Studies, School of Medicine, JHPIEGO, International·Center for Epidemiology and Preventive Ophthalmology
Focus: health, population, area studies, education and training

## Kansas State University
Manhattan, KS 66506
Tel. 913/532-5932
Fax 913/532-6035
Organization: International Programs
Focus: agriculture, business, education and training

## University of Kansas
International Studies & Programs
108 Lippincott Hall
Lawrence, KS 66045
Tel. 913/864-4141
Fax 913/864-4555
Organization: International Studies and Programs
Focus: nutrition, area studies, education and training

## Kentucky State University
Atwood Research Facility
Frankfurt, KY 40601
Tel. 502/227-6000
Fax 502/227-5933
Organization: Cooperative Extension and Community Research
Focus: aquaculture, rural development, nutrition, education and training

## University of Kentucky
Office of International Affairs
212 Bradley Hall
Lexington, KY 40506
Tel. 606/257-4067
Fax 606/323-1026
Organization: International Agricultural Programs
Focus: agriculture, engineering, medicine, nutrition, business, education and training

## Langston University
P.O. Box 730
Research Building
Langston, OK 73050
Tel. 405/466-3836
Fax 405/466-3138
Organization: American Institute of Dairy Goat Research
Focus: agriculture and animal health

## Lincoln University
202 Soldiers Hall
Jefferson City, MO 65101
Tel. 314/681-5360
Fax 314/681-5596
Organization: International Programs
Focus: agriculture, animal science, nutrition

## Louisiana State University
P.O. Box 16090
Baton Rouge, LA 70893
Tel. 504/388-6963
Fax 504/388-6775
Organization: International Programs, LSU Agricultural Center
Focus: agriculture, aquaculture, forestry, home economics, food and nutrition, business

## University of Maine—Orono
Office of International Research and Education Programs
204 Roger Clapp
Orono, ME 04469-0102
Organization: International Programs
Focus: agroforestry and wildlife management, education and training

## University of Maryland—College Park
0145 Tydings Hall
College Park, MD 20742
Tel. 301/314-7703
Fax 301/314-9256
Organization: College of Agriculture, College of Life Science, Consortium for International Crop Protection, Center for International Development and Conflict Management
Focus: agriculture, aquaculture, economics, water resources, management, education and training

## University of Maryland—Eastern Shore
Early Childhood Research Center
Princess Anne, MD 21853
Tel. 410/651-6080
Fax 410/651-6085
Organization: International Programs
Focus: agriculture, aquaculture, education and training

## Massachusetts Institute of Technology
Center for International Studies, MIT E38-648
Cambridge, MA 02139-8093
Tel. 617/253-8093
Fax 617/253-9330
Organizations: Center for International Studies, MIT-Japan Science and Technology Program, Technology and Development Program
Focus: engineering, technology, economics, politics, education and training

## University of Massachusetts
Center for International Education
285 Hills House South
Amherst, MA 01003
Tel. 413/545-0465
Fax 413/545-1263
Organizations: International Programs Office, Center for International Education, Center for International Agriculture, African Studies Program, Japanese Work Experience Program
Focus: education and training, agriculture

## Meharry Medical College
1005 D.B. Todd, Jr. Blvd.
Nashville, TN 37208
Tel. 615/327-6565
Fax 615/327-6948
Organization: International Center
Focus: health

## University of Miami
P.O. Box 248123
Coral Gables, FL 33124
Tel. 305/284-4303
Fax 305/284-4406
Organizations: Graduate School of International Studies, North-South Center, Rosenstiel School of Marine and Atmospheric Sciences, International Business and Banking Institute, School of Business Administration, International Student and Scholar Services
Focus: marine sciences, fisheries, oceanography, business, law, medicine, education and training

## Michigan State University
207 Center for International Programs
East Lansing, MI 48824-1035
Tel. 517/355-2350
Fax 517/353-7254
Organization: International Studies and Programs
Focus: agriculture, health, business, communication, education and training

## University of Michigan
Division of Research Development
   and Administration
475 East Jefferson St.
Ann Arbor, MI 48109
Tel. 313/764-5500
Fax 313/936-3231
Organizations: Center for Research on Economic Development, Institute for Public Policy Studies, School of Natural Resources, Department of Population Planning and International Health
Focus: economics, agriculture, natural resources, health, population planning, education and training

## University of Minnesota
43 Class Room Office Building
1994 Buford Avenue
St. Paul, MN 55108
Tel. 612/624-3221
Fax 612/625-3111
Organization; International Agricultural Programs
Focus: agriculture

## Mississippi State University
P.O. Box 9733
Mississippi State, MS 39762
Tel. 601/325-3204
Fax 601/325-4561
Organizations: Office of International Programs, Seed Technology Laboratory
Focus: agriculture, education and training

## University of Missouri
2-69 Agriculture Building
Columbia, MO 65211
Tel. 314/882-7740
Fax 314/882-0388
Organization: College of Agriculture
Focus: agriculture, education and training

## Montana State University
14 Hamilton Hall
Bozeman, MT 59717
Tel. 406/994-4031
Fax 406/994-2893
Organization: Office of International Education
Focus: agriculture, education and training

## Morehouse School of Medicine
720 Westview Drive, SW
Atlanta, GA 30310-1495
Tel. 404/752-1500
Fax 404/755-7505
Organization: Sponsored Programs
Focus: health, nutrition

## Morgan State University
Cold Spring Lane and Hillen Road
Baltimore, MD 21239
Tel. 410/319-3078
Fax 410/444-3698
Organizations: International Studies Program, Institute for Urban Research, Office
of International Student Affairs
Focus: education and training

## Murray State University
Center for International Programs, Box 9
Murray, KY 42071-0009
Tel. 502/762-4152
Fax 502/762-3237
Organization: Center for International Programs
Focus: education and training

## University of Nebraska
110 Agriculture Hall
Lincoln, NE 68583-0706
Tel. 402/472-2758
Fax 402/472-2759
Organizations: International Program Division, Institute of Agriculture and
Natural Resources
Focus: agriculture, animal science, education and training

## University of Nevada
4505 Maryland Parkway
Las Vegas, NV 89154
Tel. 702/739-3011
Fax 702/739-3850
Organizations: Office of International Programs, International Student Services
Focus: hotel administration, area studies, education and training

## University of New Hampshire
316 James Hall
Durham, NH 03824
Tel. 603/862-1234
Fax 603/862-2030
Organization: Center for International Perspectives
Focus: agriculture, education and training

## New Mexico State University

Box 30001, Dept. 3567
Las Cruces, NM 88003-0001
Tel. 505/646/3199
Fax 505/646-1517
Organization: Center for International Programs
Focus: agriculture, rural development, education and training

## University of New Mexico

Earth Data Analysis Center
2500 Yale Center Southeast, Suite 100
Albuquerque, NM 87131-6031
Tel. 505/277-3622
Fax 505/277-3614
Organization: International Programs
Focus: remote sensing, education and training

## State University of New York—System

SUNY Plaza
Office of International Programs
Albany, NY 12246
Tel. 518/443-5124
Fax 518/443-5126
Organization: Office of International Programs
Focus: education and training, agriculture, management and public administration, natural resources, health care financing

## North Carolina State University

Box 7112
Raleigh, NC 27695-7112
Tel. 919/515-3201
Fax 919/515-6835
Organization: International Programs
Focus: agriculture, forestry, veterinary medicine

## University of North Carolina—Chapel Hill

207 Caldwell Hall
Chapel Hill, NC 27519-3130
Organizations: Office of International Programs, School of Medicine, School of Public Health, Population Center
Focus: medicine, health, family planning, education and training

## North Dakota State University
State University Station, Box 5636
Fargo, ND 58105
Tel. 701/237-7441
Fax 701/237-7400
Organizations: Department of Agricultural Economics, Northern Crops Institute
Focus: agriculture

## Northwestern University
633 Clark Street
Evanston, IL 60208
Tel. 312/491-7264
Fax 312/491-7973
Organizations: Medical School, Program of African Studies, Transportation Center, International Office
Focus: medicine, area studies, education and training

## Ohio State University
2120 Fyffe Road
Columbus, OH 43210
Organization: International Programs in Agriculture, Research Foundation
Focus: agriculture, rural development, education and training

## Ohio University
Center for International Studies
56 E. Union St.
Athens, OH 45701
Tel. 614/593-1840
Fax 614/593-1837
Organizations: Center for International Studies, College of Education, ITM/BBA Program
Focus: education and training

## Oklahoma State University
Office of International Programs
307 Center for International Trade Development
Stillwater, OK 74078-0437
Tel. 405/744-6535
Fax: 405/744-7529
Organization: International Programs, English Language Institute
Focus: agriculture, engineering, education and training

## Oregon State University
Office of International Research and Development
Snell 400
Corvallis, OR 97331-1641
Tel. 503/737-2228
Fax 503/737-3447
Organization: Office of International Research and Development
Focus: natural resources, agriculture, human resources, fisheries, education, and training

## Pennsylvania State University
222 Boucke Building
University Park, PA 16802
Tel. 814/865-7681
Fax 814/865-3336
Organizations: Office of International Programs, International Agricultural Programs
Focus: agriculture, business, health, engineering, education and training

## University of Pennsylvania
International Programs, 133 Bennett Hall
Philadelphia, PA 19104-6275
Tel. 215/898-4661
Fax 215/898-2622
Organizations: Office of International Programs, Joseph H. Lauder Institute of Management and International Studies, PENN/PACIE Institute, South Asian Studies Center, Near East Studies Center, Center for International Management
Focus: business, management, area studies, education and training

## University of Pittsburgh
4040 Forbes Quadrangle
230 South Bouquet St.
Pittsburgh, PA 15260
Tel. 412/648-7390
Fax 412/648-2199
Organization: Center for International Studies
Focus: health, rural development, area studies, education and training

## Prairie View A&M University
P.O. Box 4079
Prairie View, TX 77446-0608
Tel. 409/857-3311
Fax 409/857-3225
Organization: Institute for International Agribusiness Studies
Focus: agriculture, animal science, education and training

## Princeton University
Woodrow Wilson School
Robertson Hall
Princeton, NJ 08544-1013
Tel. 609/258-4831
Fax 609/258-2809
Organizations: Woodrow Wilson School of Public and International Affairs, Center of International Studies, Middle East Center
Focus: international relations, economic development, biomass conversion techniques, forestry, education and training

## University of Puerto Rico
Box 5000
Mayaguez, PR 00708
Tel. 809/832-4142
Fax 809/832-3413
Organization: College of Agricultural Sciences
Focus: agriculture

## Purdue University
Agricultural Administration Building
West Lafayette, IN 47907
Tel. 317/494-8459
Fax 317/494-9613
Organization: International Programs in Agriculture
Focus: agriculture, education and training

## University of Rhode Island
128 Woodward Hall
Kingston, RI 02818
Tel. 401/792-2479
Fax 401/789-3342
Organization: International Center for Marine Resource Development
Focus: marine sciences

## Rutgers University
Cook College
109 Martin Hall
New Brunswick, NJ 08903
Tel. 908/932-8954
Fax 908/932-6769
Organizations: University International Programs, Remote Sensing Center, Center for Advanced Food Technology, Center for Agricultural Molecular Biology
Focus: agriculture, food technology, remote sensing

## Sam Houston State University
Box 2088
Huntsville, TX 77341
Tel. 409/294-1111
Fax 409/294-1597
Organization: International Programs
Focus: education and training

## San Diego State University
Career Services
San Diego, CA 92182-0578
Tel. 619/594-5200
Fax 619/594-5642
Organizations: Office of International Programs, SDSU Foundation, Office for International Student Services
Focus: agriculture, education and training

## South Carolina State College
300 College St., NE
Orangeburg, SC 29117
Tel. 803/536-7000
Fax 803/536-8429
Organizations: International Programs, School of Business
Focus: agribusiness, nutrition, home economics, education and training

## University of South Carolina
Byrnes International Center, Suite 100
Columbia, SC 29208
Tel. 803/777-7461
Fax 803/777-0462
Organizations: James F. Byrnes International Center, Belle W. Baruch Institute for Marine Biology and Coastal Research, International Business Programs, Earth Sciences and Resources Institute, School of Public Health, Institute of International Studies
Focus: education and training

## South Dakota State University
Office of International Programs
Administration Building
Brookings, SD 57007
Tel. 605/688-4173
Fax 605/688-4443
Organizations: International Programs, College of Agriculture and Biological Science, College of Engineering, Office of Remote Sensing, Student Affairs
Focus: agriculture, remote sensing, area studies, education, training

## University of Southern California
University Park, VKC #362
Los Angeles, CA 90089
Tel. 213/740-6278
Fax 213/747-4176
Organizations: International Public Administration Center, School of International Relations, Center for International Studies, Office of International Students and Scholars
Focus: administration, management, health, education and training

## Southern Illinois University
910 S. Forest
Carbondale, IL 62901-4418
Tel. 618/453-5774
Fax 618/453-7660
Organization: Office of International Programs and Services, Office of International Agriculture, Center for English as a Second Language
Focus: agriculture, applied technologies, business, education and training

## Southern University A&M College
P.O. Box 10596
Baton Rouge, LA 70813-2004
Tel. 504/771-2004
Fax 504/771-2026
Organizations: International Development Programs, Small Farm Research Center
Focus: agriculture, education and training

## Stanford University
Encina Hall, Room 200
Stanford, CA 94305-5013
Tel. 415/723-4581
Fax 415/725-7007
Organizations: Institute for International Studies, Stanford Project on International and Cross Cultural Education, Latin American Center, Center for East Asian Studies, African Studies Center, Food Research Institute
Focus: area studies, education and training

## Syracuse University
310 Walnut Place
Syracuse, NY 13244-5040
Tel. 315/443-2457
Fax 315/443-3091
Organizations: Maxwell School of Citizenship and Public Affairs, Office of International Services, Foreign and Comparative Studies, South Asia Center
Focus: public administration, management, education and training

## University of Tennessee
404 Andy Holt Tower
Knoxville, TN 37996-0140
Tel. 615/974-2475
Fax 615/974-2708
Organizations: Agricultural Experiment Station, International Agricultural
Programs
Focus: agriculture, education and training

## Texas A&M University at Kingsville
Campus Box 156
Kingsville, TX 78363
Tel. 512/595-3712
Fax 512/595-3113
Organizations: College of Agriculture and Human Sciences, Office of International Programs
Focus: agriculture, home economics

## Texas A&M University
International Agricultural Programs
College Station, TX 77843-2477
Tel. 409/845-4164
Fax 409/845-5663
Organization: International Agricultural Programs
Focus: agriculture, education and training

## Texas Southern University
3100 Cleburne St.
Houston, TX 77004
Tel. 713/527-7011
Fax 713/527-7842
Organization: Office of International Affairs, Office of International Student
Affairs
Focus: education and training

## Texas Tech University
ICASALS, P.O. Box 41036
Lubbock, TX 79409-1036
Tel. 806/742-2218
Fax 806/742-1954
Organization: International Center for Arid and Semiarid Land Studies
Focus: agriculture, natural resources, education and training

## University of Texas
International Office, 100 West 26th St.
Austin, TX 78712
Tel. 512/471-3434
Fax 512/471-8848
Organizations: International Office, East European Studies Center, Center for Latin American Studies, Middle East Studies Center, Center for South Asian Studies
Focus: area studies, education and training

## Tufts University
Packard Hall
Medford, MA 02155
Tel. 617/627-3484
Fax 617/666-1008
Organizations: International Programs Development, Fletcher Program in International Resources and Development, School of Veterinary Medicine, School of Dental Medicine, School of Medicine
Focus: medicine, health, dentistry, education and training

## Tulane University
1501 Canal St., Suite 1300
New Orleans, LA 70112
Tel. 504/584-3655
Fax 504/584-3653
Organizations: International Communication Center, Center of Resource Development and Department of International Health and Development
Focus: family planning, public health, education and training

## Tuskegee University
219 Kresge Center
Tuskegee, AL 36088
Tel. 205/727-8927
Fax 205/727-8451
Organizations: International Programs, Carver Research Foundation, School of Agriculture and Home Economics
Focus: agriculture, veterinary medicine, health, education and training

## Utah State University
UMC 9500
Logan, UT 84322
Tel. 801/750-1840
Fax 801/797-3769
Organization: International Programs and Studies
Focus: agriculture, education and training

## University of Vermont
International Studies Program/Nolin House
Burlington, VT 05405
Tel. 802/656-1096
Organizations: International Studies Program, Office of International Education Services
Focus: agriculture, health, education and training

## Virginia Polytechnic Institute and State University
1060 Reaves
Litton Hall
Blacksburg, VA 24061
Tel. 703/231-6338
Fax 703/231-6741
Organization: Office of International Development
Focus: agriculture, education and training

## Virginia State University
Box 9416
Petersburg, VA 23803
Tel. 804/524-5613
Fax 804/524-5638
Organization: International Agriculture Programs
Focus: agriculture

## Washington State University
French Administration Building No. 328
Pullman, WA 99164-1034
Tel. 509/335-2541
Fax 509/335-1060
Organization: International Program Development
Focus: agriculture, rural development

## University of Washington
Office of International Programs, PA-10
Seattle, WA 98195
Tel. 206/543-9272
Fax 206/685-3511
Organizations: International Programs, Institute of Marine Studies, College of Forest Resources, School of Public Health, Institute of Food Science and Technology, Jackson School of International Studies, East Asian Studies Center, Middle East Studies Center, International Studies Center, South Asia Center, Southeast Asian Center
Focus: forestry, marine sciences, health, area studies, education and training

## West Virginia University
Box 6108
2112 Agricultural Sciences Bldg.
Morgantown, WV 26506-6957
Tel. 304/293-2041
Fax 304/293-3740
Organization: College of Agriculture and Forestry
Focus: agriculture, forestry, education and training

## West Carolina University
Center for Technical Assistance Programs
Cullowee, NC 28723
Tel. 704/227-7492
Fax 704/227-7422
Organizations: International Economic Development Programs, International
Programs, Center for Improving Mountain Living
Focus: rural development, agriculture

## University of Wisconsin—Madison
International Agriculture Programs
240 Agriculture Hall
1450 Linden Dr.
Madison, WI 53606-1562
Tel. 608/262-1271
Fax 608/262-8852
Organization: International Agriculture Programs
Focus: agriculture, rural development, area studies

## University of Wyoming
P.O. Box 3228 University Station
Laramie, WY 82071
Tel. 307/766-5193
Fax 307/766-4053
Organizations: International Programs, International Agriculture
Focus: agriculture, education and training

## Yale University
Yale Station
New Haven, CT 06520
Tel. 203/432-4771
Fax 203/432-1323
Organizations: Tropical Resources Institute, Economic Growth Center, Center for
International and Area Studies, African Studies Center
Focus: forestry, natural resources, public policy, area studies

# 10

# TEACHING ABROAD

*O*ne of the quickest ways to break into the international employment arena is to teach abroad. Numerous teaching opportunities exist in schools throughout the world. Many of these jobs are for certified teachers who teach in the U.S. Department of State schools, U.S. Department of Defense schools, or international schools. Teaching jobs with these schools include all subject matters as well as administrative positions. These teaching positions pay comparable to teaching positions in the United States. Moving from one country to another every three to six years, many teachers make a career of teaching in these overseas schools.

However, the largest number of overseas teaching positions are for teachers of English who work in local schools, institutes, or universities on either a short- or long-term basis. While few of these positions require teaching experience or teacher certification, some type of teacher training will be helpful for landing such teaching positions. Several universities in the United States, for example, offer special training as well as overseas placements for individuals interested in teaching English as a foreign language. Earnings for these types of teaching positions vary greatly. Most such positions are low paying or volunteer positions, but earnings can be very good in such countries as Japan, Korea, or Taiwan.

# TEACHING ENGLISH AS A FOREIGN LANGUAGE

If you are willing to teach English as a foreign language, you can easily find a job abroad. Indeed, the worldwide demand for English language teachers remains high and the jobs are plentiful. Most recently, the demand for English teachers has increased substantially in Eastern Europe, Russia, and the former Soviet republics.

The first thing you need to do is to understand the language of this occupational group. Teachers of English language usually refer to themselves and their training programs in the following abbreviated forms:

> **TEFL or TFL:** teaching English as a foreign language
> **TESL or TSL:** teaching English as a second language
> **TESOL:** teaching English to speakers of other languages

Several universities in the United States and abroad provide degree programs in TEFL or TESOL, and many others offer teacher training courses in TEFL or TESOL. You are well advised to participate in such a program. After all, teaching English as a foreign language involves specific methodologies you should be familiar with before venturing into this field. Fortunately you can participate in several short intensive TEFL or TESOL training programs which will get you up and running quickly for English language teaching.

You basically have two approaches to landing an English language teaching position abroad—either apply through a U.S.-based organization specializing in the training and placement of English language teachers or apply directly to an overseas school, institute, or university. It is probably easiest to work through a U.S.-based organization since most handle placements and arrange other details such as visas, work permits, housing, and transportation. A third option is to become a freelance teacher of English, offering your services to individuals and groups at an hourly rate.

During the past 30 years the U.S. Peace Corps has trained thousands of volunteers to teach English in many Third and Fourth World countries throughout the world. While today's Peace Corps places volunteers in many technical and business fields, it still recruits volunteers to teach English and other subjects in nearly 100 countries, including most recently the Peoples' Republic of China. In fact, nearly 40 percent of the 6,529 volunteers serving in 1994 were in the field of education; most were English teachers. Volunteer assignments are for two years. For more information on the Peace Corps program, contact:

> **Peace Corps**
> Box 941
> Washington, DC 20526
> Tel. 800/424-8580, Ext. 2293

Several private, nonprofit, and educational organizations also recruit, train, and place college graduates who are interested in teaching English and other subjects abroad. Many are volunteer positions similar to internships while others are salaried positions. Contact the following organizations for information on their placement programs:

### AEON
9301 Wilshire Blvd., #202, Beverly Hills, CA 90210, Tel. 310/550-0940 or 2 Mid-America Plaza, Suite 800, Oakbrook Terrace, IL 60181, Tel. 718/954-2323. This is a private language school which places English teachers in 190 schools in Japan. Applicants need a bachelor's degree and are required to pay one-way airfare. Teachers earn around 250,000 yen ($2,300) per month.

### AMITY TWO PROGRAM
Amity Institute, P.O. Box 118, Del Mar, CA 92014, Tel. 619/755-3582. Places TEFL teachers in K-12 schools in Latin America and Martinique. Room and board provided, but participants are responsible for their own living expenses. Applications should be submitted six to nine months prior to anticipated starting date.

### AASSA
The Association of American Schools in South America Teacher Service (AASSA), 14750 NW 77th St., Suite 210, Miami Lakes, FL 33016, Tel. 305/821-0345 or Fax 305/821-4244. Contact the Placement Coordinator. Sponsors a yearly job fair in Orlando, Florida during the last week of November or the first week of December. At present there is a $40 registration fee to attend this job fair. Call or write for details, including an application/job fair package.

### BRETHREN VOLUNTEER SERVICES
1451 Dundee Ave., Elgin, IL 60120, Tel. 708/742-5100. Fields English teachers for two-year assignments in the Czech and Slovak Republics, Poland, Israel, Nigeria, South Korean, and the People's Republic of China. Provides expenses.

### CHARTER 77 FOUNDATION
Masaryk Fellowship Program, 1270 Avenue of the Americas, Suite 609, New York, NY 10020, Tel. 212/332-2890. Places TEFL-trained English teachers in the Czech and Slovak Republics for one month during the summer as well as offers one-year teaching positions for TEFL professionals. Provides homestay and stipend. Application deadline is March.

### ELS INTERNATIONAL INC.
5761 Buckingham Parkway, Culver City, CA 90230-6583, Tel. 213/642-0982 or Fax 213/410-4688. This private firm operates a network of 40 language schools in Asia, Latin America, and Europe. They recruit individuals with bachelor's degrees and one to two years of ESL/EFL experience.

### EDUCATION FOR DEMOCRACY
P.O. Box 40514, Mobile, AL 36640-0514, Tel. 205/434-3889. Places TEFL trained teachers in the Czech and Slovak Republics for periods of five months to one year. Provides accommodations and stipend. Requires a $50 processing fee.

### FANDANGO OVERSEAS PLACEMENT
1613 Escalero Road, Santa Rose, CA 95409, phone or fax 707/539-2722. Arranges teacher placements in client schools of the Czech Republic, Hungary, France, Baltic States, Russia, Poland, and Japan. Charges a $375 placement fee for graduates of Transworld Teachers, Inc. (San Francisco) or $450 for graduates of a comparable 100-hour teacher training program.

### GEORGETOWN UNIVERSITY
Internship Program, CIPRA-AIR, P.O. Box 2298, Washington, DC 20057-1011, Tel. 202/298-0200. Students earn six academic credit hours for completing a two-week TEFL training course and teaching abroad for one-year. Current placements are in the Czech and Slovak Republics, Bulgaria, Poland, Hungary, Russia, Lithuania, Estonia, Vietnam, Indonesia, and the People's Republic of China. Participants pay a $1,500 tuition fee as well as receive room, board, and a small stipend while in-country. Application deadline is March 1.

### GLOBAL ROUTES
5554 Broadway, Oakland, CA 94618, Tel. 510/655-0321 or Fax 510/655-0371. Offers volunteer English teaching internships for 10-week periods. Interns are assigned to village schools in Ecuador, Kenya, and Thailand. Requires a program fee of $3,200 for the summer and $3,400 for the spring and fall semesters. Airfare is extra.

### INTERCRISTO
P.O. Box 33487, 19303 Fremont Ave. N., Seattle, WA 98133, Tel. 206/546-7330. This is a Christian ministry group which operates a computerized job network and placement service for nonprofit Christian organizations.

## INTERNATIONAL SCHOOLS INTERNSHIPS PROGRAM
P.O. Box 103, W. Bridgewater, MA 02379, Tel. 508/580-1880. Places interns in the network the international schools found throughout the world. K-12 certification is not required. Application deadline is December. Requires two $75 application fees.

## INTERNATIONAL SCHOOLS SERVICES
P.O. Box 5910, 15 Roszel Road, Princeton, NJ 08543, Tel. 609/452-0990. The New Perspectives program places teachers without previous teaching experience but who have teacher certification. Places over 500 teachers and administrators in international and American schools around the world each year. Requires as $50 application fee. Its regular staffing program places teachers in international schools for a placement fee of $600. Individuals must have two years of current teaching experience (no certification required). Math and science teachers with certification but no experience are eligible for consideration. Holds recruitment meetings in February and June.

## JET PROGRAM
Embassy of Japan, 2520 Massachusetts Ave., NW, Washington, DC 20008, Tel. 202/939-6700. This Japanese government-sponsored program places English teachers in Japanese schools for one-year assignments. Application deadline is December 15.

## KOREA SERVICES GROUP
147-7 Bum Jeon Dong Jin-Ku, Pusan 614-064, Korea, Tel. 011-82-51-817-3611 or Fax 011-82-51-817-3612. Provides native speaking instructors for more than 50 Korean foreign language institutes. Hires a large number of foreign instructors each year. Some hirees can expect to start within 60 days. Recruits extensively amongst former U.S. Peace Corps Volunteers. Expects to place over 150 American instructors in 1994.

## OHIO STATE UNIVERSITY JOB FAIR
Educational Career Services, 110 Arps Hall, 19435 N. High St., Columbus, OH 43201-1172, Tel. 614/292-2741. In February of each year this program sponsors a job placement fair for international elementary and secondary teachers.

## OVERSEAS PLACEMENT SERVICE FOR EDUCATORS
University of Northern Iowa, Student Services Center #19, Cedar Falls, IA 50614-0390, Tel. 319/273-2061 or Fax 319/273-6998. Conducts an annual recruiting fair and publishes a newsletter which includes overseas teaching vacancies.

## PRINCETON-IN-ASIA
224 Palmer Hall, Princeton, NJ 08544, Tel. 609/458-3657. Operates one- and two-year teaching programs in the People's Republic of China, Taiwan, Korea, Hong Kong, Japan, Thailand, Singapore, and Indonesia. Application deadline is December 15. Requires a $30 application fee and a $250 participant fee.

## QUEEN'S UNIVERSITY
Overseas Recruiting Fair Placement Office, Faculty of Education, Kingston, Ontario K7L1 3N6, Tel. 613/545-6222. Hosts an annual overseas teaching job fair.

## SEARCH ASSOCIATES
P.O. Box 100, Mountaintop, PA 18707, Tel. 717/474-0370 or Fax 717/474-0380. Recruits experienced elementary and secondary teachers for schools throughout the world. Holds recruiting fairs in Massachusetts, California, Indonesia, and New Zealand. Charges a $600 placement fee.

## TEACHERS OVERSEAS RECRUITMENT CENTER
National Teacher Placement Bureau, P.O. Box 609027, Cleveland, OH 44109, Tel. 216/741-3771. Sponsors a job placement fair for international teachers.

## TESOL INC.
Teachers of English to Speakers of Other Languages, 1600 Cameron St., Suite 300, Alexandria, VA 22314, Tel. 703/836-0774. This 23,000 member nonprofit organization includes a placement service for its members. Membership dues are $69 for regular members or $48.50 for students. A basic membership also is available for $38. The placement service costs an additional $20 in North American and $30 abroad.

## UNIVERSITY OF NORTHERN IOWA JOB FAIR
Overseas Placement Services for Educators, Cedar Falls, IA 50614-0390, Tel. 319/273-2311 or Fax 319/273-6998. Sponsors an annual job fair for international teachers and administrators attended by more than 60 overseas schools.

## YMCA OVERSEAS SERVICE CORPS
909 4th Avenue, Seattle, WA 98104, Tel. 206/382-5008. Sponsors teaching programs in Taiwan and Japan for one- and two-year assignments respectively. Application deadlines are February and September for fall and spring placements. Requires a $25 application fee.

## WORLDTEACH
Harvard Institute for International Development, One Eliot Street, Cambridge, MA 02138-5705, Tel. 617/495-5527 or Fax 617/495-1239. Each year places nearly 200 volunteer teachers in the local schools of Costa Rica, Ecuador, Namibia, Poland, Thailand, Russia, and South Africa. Positions are for one year. Participants pay a fee of $3,300-$4,300 which covers the cost of airfare, health insurance, training, and administration. Local employers provide room and board and provide a small stipend.

# TRAINING PROGRAMS TO GET YOU UP AND RUNNING

The best qualified candidates possess teacher certification and are skilled in teaching English as a foreign language. Ideally, you should have a bachelor's or master's degree in TEFL or in a substantive academic field. If you lack such qualifications, don't worry. You can easily establish your teaching credentials and land an overseas teaching job by enrolling in a TEFL program that also has a good placement record. In fact, we do not recommend looking for an English language teaching position unless you have completed a TEFL program. You will quickly discover these programs have several advantages. Many use the highly respected RSA/University of Cambridge and Trinity College London teaching methods for qualifying participants.

In the United States most TEFL programs are integrated into regular university academic programs which are usually part of an undergraduate or graduate Applied Linguistics program. A few universities and private institutes now offer intensive four-week TEFL programs modelled after the British 100-hour intensive TEFL teacher certification programs. These intensive four-week programs quickly prepare you for overseas teaching positions and thus save you time and money in the process of getting ready for an overseas job. Many of these programs also provide job assistance through their employment contacts with schools, institutes, and universities abroad.

Within the United States, the following public and private organizations provide training for teachers of English as a foreign language. While most are traditional university-based applied linguistics degree programs requiring two to four years preparation, many are private institutes offering certification through intensive four- to eight-week training programs. We've assigned asterisks (*) to quickly identify the intensive four to six-week programs. Others are degree programs.

### BALL STATE UNIVERSITY
Director of Graduate Programs, Department of English, Muncie, IN 47306-0460, Tel. 317/285-8415 or Fax 317/285-3766. Offers an M.A. in TESOL. Out-of-state tuition is $2,488 per semester.

### BRIGHAM YOUNG UNIVERSITY—Hawaii Campus
Director, TESOL Studies, LLC Division, Laie, HI 96762. Offers a bachelor's degree in TESOL. Tuition is $1,335 per semester for non-LDS church members or $890 per semester for LDS members.

### *CENTER FOR ENGLISH STUDIES

330 Seventh Avenue, New York, NY 10001, Tel. 212/620-0760 or Fax 212/594-7415. Offers a four-week intensive TEFL course four times a year, from June to September. Costs $1,475.

### *COAST LANGUAGE ACADEMY

20720 Ventura Blvd., Suite 300, Woodland Hills, CA 91364, Tel. 818/346-5113 or Fax 818/346-6619. Offers an intensive four-week or a part time eight-week, TEFL course four times a year. Cost $1,675. Homestay accommodations available for $500 a month.

### *ENGLISH INTERNATIONAL

655 Sutter St., Suite 500, San Francisco, CA 94102, Tel. 415/749-5633 or Fax 415/749-5629. Excepting December, each month this organization offers an intensive four-week TEFL course. Participants become RSA/University of Cambridge certified TEFL teachers. Tuition is $1785.00.

### FAIRLEIGH DICKINSON UNIVERSITY

Director of M.A.T., School of Education, 1000 River Rd., Bancroft Hall Rm. 208, Teaneck, NJ 07666, Tel. 201/692-2838. Offers a Multilingual M.A. and a M.A.T. in ESL which takes from one and one-half to five years to complete. Requires 36-credit hours which cost $400 per credit.

### *GEORGETOWN UNIVERSITY

Center for Language Education and Development, 3607 O Street, NW, Washington, DC 20007, Tel. 202/687-4400 or Fax 202/337-1559. Offers an intensive 150-hour RSA/Cambridge Certificate in Teaching English as a Foreign Language to Adults (CTEFLA) course. Successful participants receive the RSA/CTEFLA and a Georgetown certificate. Tuition is $3,000 for this five-week course.

### HAWAII PACIFIC UNIVERSITY

TESL Coordinator, 1188 Fort St. Mall, Honolulu, HI 96813. Offers a four-year B.A. and a one-year post-bachelor's certificate in TESL. Tuition costs $7,030 per academic year.

### PORTLAND STATE UNIVERSITY

Chair, Department of Applied Linguistics, P.O. Box 751, Portland, OR 97207-0751, Tel. 503/725-4088. Offers a post-bachelor's TESL Certificate and an M.A. in TESOL. Costs $2,641 per term for post-bachelor program and $2,204 per term for graduate program.

### *THE SCHOOL OF TEACHING ENGLISH AS A SECOND LANGUAGE

2601 NW 56th, Seattle, WA 98107, Tel. 206/781-8607 or Fax 206/781-8922. Offers an intensive four-week ESL/EFL teacher training program. Participants can earn 12 academic credits (graduate or post-baccalaureate) and a Certificate in TESL from the Seattle University School of Education. Costs $145 per credit or $1,740 for the intensive 12-credit program.

### *ST. GILES LANGUAGE TEACHING CENTER
One Hallidie Plaza, Suite 350, San Francisco, CA 94102, Tel. 415/788-3552. Offers a four-week intensive RSA/University of Cambridge teacher training certificate course. Requires a $35 application fee. Tuition is $1,690.

### *TRANSWORLD TEACHERS, INC.
683 Sutter Street, San Francisco, CA 94102, Tel. 800/241-8071. Offers a one-month intensive or three-month part time TEFL Certificate Course involving 100+ hours of instruction. Tuition is $1,675. Guest house accommodations cost $460 per month.

### *UNIVERSITY OF CALIFORNIA
P.O. Box 6050, Irvine, CA 92716-6050, Tel. 714/856-2033. Offers an accelerated certificate program in TEFL. Costs $3,900 (includes tuition, materials, accommodations, and student services).

### UNIVERSITY OF DELAWARE
ESL/Bilingual Coordinator, Department of Educational Studies, Newark, DE 19716. Offers an M.S. with a specialization in TESOL. Tuition for in-state students is $3,500 per year; out-of-state students pay $9,500 per year.

### UNIVERSITY OF ILLINOIS
Division of English as an International Language, 3070 FLB, 707 S. Mathews Ave., Urbana, IL 61801. Offers an M.A. in the Teaching of English as a Second Language. Costs $2,023 per semester for in-state students and $4,219 for out-of-state students.

### UNIVERSITY OF NEW HAMPSHIRE
Graduate Director, Department of Education, Durham, NH 03824. Offers an M.A. in English Language and Linguistics with a specialization in ESL. Costs $2,142.50 per semester for in-state students and $5,967.50 for out-of-state students.

### UNIVERSITY OF GEORGIA
Graduate Coordinator, Language Education Department, 125 Aderhold Hall, Athens, GA 30602-7123. Offers M.Ed. and Ph.D. programs in TESOL. Costs $1,980 per quarter (out-of-state).

### WRIGHT STATE UNIVERSITY
Department of English Language and Literatures, 441 Millett Hall, Dayton, OH 45435. Offers undergraduate and graduate certificates (22 quarter hours) and an M.A. (50-52 quarter hours) in TESOL. Costs $122 per credit hour for in-state students and $218 per credit hour for out-of-state students.

Numerous other teacher training programs are offered by universities and private institutes in Canada, England, Ireland, France, Germany, Greece, Hong Kong, Malaysia, Spain, Turkey, and Australia. The oldest, largest, and most highly respected TEFL training program awarding the

RSA/University of Cambridge Certificate is in England. For detailed information on their programs, contact:

**INTERNATIONAL HOUSE TEACHER TRAINING**
International House, 106 Piccadilly, London W1V 9FL,
Tel. 44 71 491 2598 or Fax 44 71 499 0174.

This four-week (110 hour) program costs about $2,000. International House offers courses at Teacher Training Centers in its affiliated schools in Barcelona, Budapest, Cairo, Krakow, Lisbon, Madrid, New York, Paris, Poznan, Rome, San Sebastian, and Vienna. It also recruits nearly 200 teachers each year for its network of over 100 schools in 23 countries. If you want premier training in TEFL, enroll in this well established program. For more information on TEFL training programs in these and other countries, consult Susan Griffith's latest edition of *Teaching English Abroad.*

# JOB LISTING SERVICES FOR TEACHERS

Several organizations offer current job vacancy listings for teachers interested in overseas positions. The most popular such publications include:

**Bulletin of Overseas Teaching Opportunities:** 72 Franklin Avenue, Ocean Grove, NJ 07756, $38 per year.

**Instant Alert:** Education Information Service, 15 Orchard St., Wellesley Hills, MA 02181, Tel. 617/237-0887 or 4523 Andes Drive, Fairfax, VA 22030. Every six weeks this organization publishes a listing of nearly 150 vacancies in international and American schools.

**International Education Placement Hotline:** World Learning, Box 676, Kipling Road, Brattleboro, VA 053-02-676, Tel. 802/258-3397 or Fax 802/258-3248; $15 for 6 months of $25 for 1 year. Publishes a monthly newsletter which includes job vacancies for international education administrators and teachers of TESOL.

**International Educator:** International Educator's Institute, P.O. Box 513, Cummaquid, MA 02637, Tel. 508/362-1414. $25. Published quarterly. July issue includes a "Jobs Only" supplement.

**Options Newsletter:** 20533 Biscayne Boulevard, Suite 4/467, Miami, FL 33180.

**Overseas Academic Opportunities:** 949 E. 29th Street, Brooklyn, NY 11210. $38 per year.

**TESOL Placement Bulletin:** TESOL Inc., 1600 Cameron St., Suite 300, Alexandria, VA 22314, Tel. 703/836-0774. Must be a member of TESOL Inc. ($38-$60) in order to subscribe to this publication. $20 per year if mailed to addresses in the U.S., Canada, Mexico; $30 per year for all other countries.

Several enterprising companies sell country-by-country listings of schools for $10 to $20 per country. One of the most popular such publications is *Overseas Teaching Opportunities* which is available through Friends of World Teaching (P.O. Box 1049, San Diego, CA 92112-1049 or 619/275-4066, $20 for first three countries and $4 for additional countries). This publication includes over 1,000 schools in 100+ countries of interest to Americans and Canadians. However, much of this same information is readily available through several other less expensive resources such as Susan Griffith's *Teaching English Abroad*, Transition Abroad's *Teaching English Abroad, The ISS Directory of Overseas Schools,* and the free directories available through the U.S. Department of Defense and the U.S. State Department. You may want to consult these directories before purchasing similar lists.

## OTHER TEACHING OPPORTUNITIES

If you teach at the university level, you may find opportunities to teach and conduct research abroad through your present institution, through a regional international consortium or through special programs such as the Fulbright Program (Council for International Exchange of Scholars). You should also monitor the job vacancy announcements appearing in The *Chronicle of Higher Education* as well as in professional journals and newsletters of your academic discipline. Occasionally overseas university vacancy announcements appear in *The New York Times, Washington Post, Wall Street Journal, National Business Employment Weekly,* and a few other major newspapers. Major international magazines, such as *The Far Eastern Economic Review* and *The Economist,* regularly list university vacancy announcements.

Enterprising job seekers don't limit their search to established teaching programs, training institutes, and placement and job listing services. Numerous other teaching opportunities are available by directly applying to local schools in each country without the assistance of a U.S.-based organization or with a U.S.-sponsored school. While salaries may appear low in many of these schools, such teaching positions often come with free housing and they do offer an opportunity to gain experience in living and working abroad. They enable you to work in a truly international environment where you get to know faculty members and become a member of the local community—important international experiences which are sometimes best acquired by living off the local economy at the level of fellow faculty members.

Take, for example, one of our favorite colleges abroad in which we have been involved for years as both advisory board members and donors. If you are interested in teaching English in Thailand, you might consider applying directly to Yonok College in Northern Thailand. We know this college very well since we have been closely involved with its evolution since 1973. One of Thailand's newest and most rapidly expanding and beautiful private colleges located in a delightful provincial town near the famous city of Chiengmai, Yonok College offers an excellent English language program for its nearly 2,000 students who are studying for bachelor's degrees in business, arts, and the sciences. Actively promoting a diverse international faculty, Yonok College has an on-going exchange program with the faculty and students of Baylor University in Waco, Texas as well as welcomes applicants from other education institutions around the world. Numerous Americans have taught English here for periods of one to five years, and they love their work.

If you are interested in working at Yonok College, contact the president directly. Send him a cover letter and a copy of your resume:

> Dr. Nirund Jivasantikarn, President
> YONOK COLLEGE
> Lampang-Denchai Road
> Lampang 52000, Thailand

Indicate in your letter what you would like to do and when you are available. Yonok College also welcomes resumes and applications from individuals who have experience in educational administration at the university level.

## KEY RESOURCES ON TEACHING

The following books and directories provide useful information on teaching abroad:

**Directory of English Schools in Spain**. Robert Kloer, 3 Sunset Avenue, Suncook, NH 03275. $9.95 plus $2.50 postage ($5 overseas). 1991.

**ERIC Digest**. Center for Applied Linguistics, 1118 22nd St., NW, Washington, DC 20037. A free leaflet on opportunities for TEFL teachers.

**How to Get a Job and Teach in Japan**. Bonnie Kuroaka, 3595 S.E. First St., Gresham, OR 97030. $9 (postpaid). 1991. Provides useful information on living and working in Japan. Complete with contact information.

**The ISS Directory of Overseas Schools**. International Schools Service, P.O. Box 5910, Princeton, NJ 08543, Tel. 609/452-0990, $29.95 plus $3.00 shipping. Also available through Peterson's and Impact Publications. Organized by country, this guide provides detailed information on overseas schools attended by American and international students in expatriate communities in 133 countries.

**Jobs in Japan**. John Wharton. Global Press, 697 College Parkway, Rockville, MD 20850, Tel. 202/466-1663. $16.95 (postpaid). This periodically revised book only focuses on teaching jobs in Japan. Includes names and addresses of schools as well as information on living and working in Japan.

**Schools Abroad of Interest to Americans**. Porter Sargent Publishers, 11 Beacon St., Suite 1400, Boston, MA 02108, $35 plus $1.98 postage. Includes 800 elementary and secondary schools in 130 countries with American and English-speaking students.

**Teach Abroad**. 1993. The Central Bureau, Seymour Mews House, Seymour Mews, London, W1H 9PE. $18.95 plus $3.50 postage. Also available in the United States through Seven Hill Book Distributors (49 Central Ave., Cincinnati, OH 45202, Tel. 800/545-2005). Includes volunteer and paid teaching opportunities.

**Teaching EFL Outside the U.S.**. TESOL, 1600 Cameron St., Suite 300, Alexandria, VA 22314-2751, Tel. 703/836-0774. $22 plus $2.50 postage. Outlines both public and private teaching opportunities and employment conditions. Includes a listing of institutions offering TEFL courses.

**Teaching English Abroad**. Transitions Abroad, 18 Hulst Rd., P.O. Box 1300, Amherst, MA 01004-1300. $9.95 postpaid. Newly revised booklet describes country-by-country teaching opportunities for both experienced and inexperienced English language teachers. Includes job directories, training centers, agencies and organizations, and resource books.

**Teaching English Abroad**. Susan Griffith, Vacation Work, 9 Park End St., Oxford OX1 1HJ, England. $15.95 (from Peterson's or Impact Publications). This classic annual directory includes thousands of short- and long-term teaching positions for both certified and uncertified teachers. Organized by country. Includes useful information on training and job search.

**Teaching English in Eastern Europe**. Citizens Democracy Corps, 2021 K St., NW, Suite 215, Washington, DC 20006, Tel. 800/394-1945. Free upon request. Lists organizations placing volunteer teachers in Eastern Europe, the Baltics, and Russia.

**Teaching Opportunities in the Middle East and North Africa**. 1987. AMIDEAST, 1100 17th St., NW, Suite 30, Washington, DC 20036. $18. Includes contact and application information on over 140 schools in the region.

**Teaching Overseas: The Caribbean and Latin American Area**. Carton H. Bowyer. 1989. Inter-Regional Center for Curriculum and Materials Development, Foundations of Education, College of Education, Memphis State University, Memphis, TN 38152. Provides information on teaching opportunities in 30 U.S.-sponsored schools in the Caribbean and Latin America.

The U.S. government publishes useful information on teaching opportunities with the Department of Defense Dependents Schools, State Department schools, and the Fulbright Exchange Program:

**Opportunities Abroad for Educators:** U.S. Information Agency, Office of Academic Programs, Fulbright Teacher Exchange Branch, 301 4th St., SW, Washington, DC 20547. Free. Provides information and application form for K-12 educators who are interested in classroom exchanges in 34 countries.

**Overseas Employment Opportunities for Teachers:** Office of Overseas Schools, U.S. Department of State, Rm. 245, SA-29, Washington, DC 20522-2902, Tel. 703/235-9600. Free. Includes over 100 international schools.

**Overseas Employment Opportunities for Educators:** Department of Defense Dependent Schools, Teacher Recruitment Section, 2461 Eisenhower Ave., Alexandria, VA 22331, Tel. 703/325-0885 or 703/746-7864. Free. Includes information on employment opportunities in the more than 200 military base schools administered by the U.S. Department of Defense.

# 11

# INTERNSHIPS, VOLUNTEER PROGRAMS & STUDY ABROAD

*O*ne of the best ways to break into the international employment arena is to acquire an international internship in the United States or abroad. With an internship you may gain valuable international work experience as well as develop important contacts for gaining full-time international employment. Many internships also provide unique opportunities to study and travel while working abroad. Sponsoring internship organizations normally arrange all the details for placement, travel, and accommodations. Upon completing the internship, participants can expect the sponsoring organization to arrange for letters of recommendation from the interns' employers.

International internships come in several forms. Ideally, most people would like to find paid internships with organizations overseas that might lead to being hired on a full-time basis. Some internships come in this form, especially those for business, engineering, and science majors sponsored by the International Association of Students in Economics and Business Management (AIESEC) and the International Association for the Exchange of Students of Technical Experience (IAESTE). These are the two premier international internship organizations that offer paid internships with major international companies.

Most internships, however, tend to be nonpaid, volunteer positions sponsored by colleges and universities or nonprofit organizations. Many of these internships require enrollment, tuition, or program fees to participate in the program. Some of these internship experiences are basically study abroad programs which include a short work experience. Most such programs are designed for students in linguistics, social sciences, and the humanities. If sponsored by a college or university, students can usually earn academic credits while participating in the internship program. A three to twelve-month internship program may cost participants between $3,000 and $6,000, including international transportation, insurance, visas, and room and board. Like many volunteer positions, these internships may involve basic living and working conditions, such as participating in homestays and workcamps.

Other international internships are based in the United States with nonprofit public interest, education, and research organizations. While these groups give interns an opportunity to work with important international organizations and issues, they involve little or no international travel. Many of these internships will involve basic research, copyediting, and clerical tasks, but they also offer opportunities to attend seminars, conferences, and make important international contacts.

Many internships are for two to three-month periods while others run for six to twelve-months or coincide with regular or summer college semester programs. Others may be flexible, depending on the individual interns interests and skills. Many internships can lead to full-time employment with the sponsoring organization.

Most international internship programs tend to be centered in Washington, DC, the center for hundreds of government, nonprofit, and consulting organizations involved in international affairs.

Most internship programs have application deadlines and several charge fees for processing applications. Some require an application package consisting of a resume, transcript, writing sample, recommendations, and a letter of availability and interest. Be sure to call, fax, or write the organization for current application details.

If you are interested in an internship or volunteer position with an organization involved in the international arena, do not restrict your search efforts only to the organizations included in this chapter. You should be creative, aggressive, and persistent. Many of the organizations and employers listed in previous chapters, especially nonprofit organizations and consultants, are open to enterprising individuals who approach them with a proposal for an internship. In other words, you can create your own internship by directly approaching an organization with a detailed proposal. Do your homework on the organization. Identify what knowledge and skills you can bring to such a position as well as the experience you hope to acquire from such an experience. You'll be surprised how many employers will be interested in your proposal. In the process you will gain invaluable international work experience specifically tailored to your needs and long-term international career goals.

# MAJOR INTERNSHIP ORGANIZATIONS AND PROGRAMS

The following businesses, government agencies, nonprofit organizations, and educational institutions offer a variety of internship experiences throughout the world. Many of the internships are based in the United States while others involve working overseas.

### ACCESS: A Security Information Service
1730 M Street, NW, 605
Washington, DC 20046
Tel. 202/785-6630

A computerized database clearinghouse that assists educators, researchers, journalists, and other interested groups in acquiring information on international affairs. Has three internship positions which pay $50 per week: inquiry/speakers referral intern; outreach intern; and publications intern. Positions require good communication, research, marketing, and coordination skills and a strong background in international affairs. Contact the Internship Coordinator.

---

### ACCION International
130 Prospect Street
Cambridge, MA 02139
(no phone calls please)

A nonprofit group operating in Central and Latin America for the purpose or reducing poverty and improving the employability of the poor. Offers two types of internships: Latin American operations intern and resource development intern. These are unpaid, volunteer internships open to college undergraduates, graduates, graduate students, and those with work experience. Positions require good organization and communication skills. Contact the Communications Specialist.

## AIESEC-United States, Inc.

841 Broadway
Suite 608
New York, NY 10003
Tel. 212/757-3774

One of the premier international internship organizations managed by students for students majoring in economics and business. Operates with local chapters on 73 member campuses throughout the U.S. Focuses on international management. Approximately 300 internships available each year with such companies as AT&T, IBM, and Unisysm. These are paid internships ($200-$400 a week). Most internships are for 2-18 month periods. Applicants must apply through campus chapters. Most applicants are college juniors or seniors who have completed at least two years of basic business and language courses.

## American Institute for Foreign Study, College Division

102 Greenwich Avenue
Greenwich, CT 06830
Tel. 800/727-AIFS, Ext. 6097
Fax 203/869-9615

This organization arranges the international exchange of high school and college students and adults. Its field of operations encompasses 14 campuses in Mexico, Europe, Asia, and Australia. It offers about 40 internships each year for a duration of 12 to 15 weeks each. Participants combine academic classes with work experience. These are unpaid, voluntary internships for college juniors, seniors, and graduate students. Requires a $35 applicant processing fee.

## The American-Scandinavian Foundation

725 Park Avenue
New York, NY 10021
Tel. 212-879-9779
Fax 212/249-3444

This nonprofit organization promotes educational and cultural exchanges between the United States and Denmark, Finland, Norway, and Sweden. Designed for college juniors and seniors, this program offers 50-100 summer internships for engineers, computer specialists, agriculturalists, and horticulturalists. These are paid internships in which participants receive a stipend. Participants are expected to pay from $120 and $385 each month for housing. Application deadline is December 15. Requires a $50 applicant processing fee and a resume.

## American Slavic Student Internship
1841 Broadway, Suite 607
New York, NY 10023
Tel. 212/262-3862

This nonprofit organization arranges internships in Russia in the fields of education, business, publishing, media, tourism, and sports. Participants receive a monthly stipend. Duration of internships is from one month to two years. Requires program fees ranging from $1,500 to $4,500, depending on the destination, duration of program, and type of accommodations provided.

## Africa News Service
Internship Program
Box 3851
Durham, NC 27702
Tel. 919/286-0747

Offers 10 internships for students of journalism and African affairs. Work involves research, writing, and clerical duties. These are unpaid internships, but the Africa News Agency will assist in finding inexpensive living accommodations in Durham, NC. Applicants must summit an approach letter, letters of recommendations, transcripts, and a writing sample.

## Amnesty International USA, Washington Office
304 Pennsylvania Avenue, SE
Washington, DC 20003
Tel. 202/544-0200
Fax 202/546-7142

This global nonprofit organization focuses on the release of prisoners of conscience. It lobbies international organizations and governments as well as focuses media attention on the release of political prisoners and the end of torture and executions. It offers 10 unpaid internships each year for a minimum of 10 weeks each. Applicants must be high school graduates.

## The Arms Control Association
11 Dupont Circle, Suite 250
Washington, DC 20036
Tel. 202/797-4626
Fax 202/797-4611

This nonprofit research organization focusing on educating the public about arms control and related issues. Offers 12 unpaid internships each year involving research, writing, proofreading, editing, layout, and general clerical work. Open to college sophomores, juniors, seniors, college graduates, and graduate students.

Application deadline is May 15. Contact the Intern Coordinator for information and application details.

## ASHOKA: Innovators for the Public
1700 North Moore St.
Suite 1920
Arlington, VA 22209
Tel. 703/527-8300
Fax 703/527-8300

This nonprofit organization awards fellowships for innovation ideas related to social change in Africa, Asia, and Latin America. Offers 15 unpaid internships each year related to publications, press relations, publicity, fundraising, and fellowship relations. Duration of internships varies. Contact the Intern Coordinator for information and application procedures.

## Association to Unite the Democracies
1506 Pennsylvania Avenue, SE
Washington, DC 20003
Tel. 202/544-5150
Fax 202/544-3742

This association promotes world order and democracy through educational programs, publications, and conferences. It offers paid internships ($250 per month) for periods of 4-6 months each. Candidates should have an interest in international relations, demonstrate a good command of English, and have good computer and foreign language skills. Applicants must submit a resume, writing sample, transcript, recommendation, and a letter explaining their interest in working for AUD. Application deadline is January 1 for spring, May 1 for summer, and August 1 for fall.

## The Atlantic Council of the United States
1616 H Street, NW
Washington, DC 20006
Tel. 202/347-9353
Fax 202/737-5163

This nonprofit, nonpartisan organization formulations policy recommendations for the developed democracies of the European and Asian communities. Offers several 8-12 week nonpaid internships. Most internships involve program development, policy research and recommendations, special projects, fundraising, and publication support. Open to college juniors, seniors, graduates, and graduate students. Contact the Internship Coordinator for further information.

## Beaver College Center for Education Abroad
Beaver College
Glenside, PA 19038
Tel. 800/767-0029

Beaver College arranges junior-senior year study abroad programs for numerous colleges and universities. It offers 60 unpaid internships each year. Internships run for one semester. Candidates must be currently enrolled in an accredited American college or university with a GPA of 3.0 and at least a 3.3 in three courses in the internship discipline. Interns receive academic credit for courses taken during the internship period. Open to college juniors and seniors. Requires a $35 application fee. Application deadlines are October 15 for spring and April 20 for fall. Contact the Program Coordinator for further information.

## Brethren Volunteer Service
1451 Dundee Avenue
Elgin, IL 60120
Tel. 708/742-6103
Fax 708/742-6103

Sponsored by the Church of the Brethren, this organization promotes peace, justice, and human and environmental welfare through numerous programs in 20 countries. Offers over 100 domestic and overseas internships. Domestic internships run for 1 year. Overseas internships require a 2-year minimum commitment and involve working in one of 34 projects in such countries as China, El Salvador, France, Germany, Israel, the Netherlands, Nicaragua, Nigeria, Northern Ireland, and Poland. Internships pay $45-$65 per month and include free room and board. Candidates for overseas internships should be college graduates, Christians, at least 21 years of age, and in good health. Candidates for domestic internships should be high school graduates, Christians, and at least 18 years of age. Application deadlines are July 1 for fall, January 1 for spring, and May 1 for summer. Contact the Recruiter for further information.

## CDS International, Inc.
330 7th Avenue
New York, NY 10001
Tel. 212/760-1400
Fax 212/268-1288

CDS combines language training and work experience for Americans interested in Germany and Germans interested in the U.S. Offers different types of 3, 6, 12, and 18 month paid internships. Requires an in-person interview. Open to college juniors, seniors, and graduates. Favors individuals with majors in a business, technical, or agricultural field. Application deadline is five months prior to starting the internship. Contact the Program Officer for detailed information on different internship programs.

## Center for the Study of Conflict
5842 Bellona Avenue
Baltimore, MD 21212
Tel. 301/323-7656

This is a research and education organization dedicated to the study and application of conflict resolution methods. Offers two unpaid internships each year. Length of internship is flexible. Interns perform research, copyediting, and general office work. Open to high school seniors, high school graduates, college students, college graduates, graduate students, and others. Contact the Director.

## Committee for National Security
1601 Connecticut Avenue
Washington, DC 20009
Tel. 202/745-2450
Fax 202/387-6298

This nonprofit educational research group focuses on the study of arms control, defense budgets, and chemical and biological weaponry. It offers three unpaid research and legislative tracking internships lasting 3-4 months each. Each semester one internship is awarded to an minority student who also receives a $500 stipend. Open to college sophomores, juniors, seniors, and graduate students. Apply to the Program Coordinator with a letter, resume, transcripts, and recommendations. Final selection requires an in-person interview. Application deadlines are May 1 for summer, August 1 for fall, and December 1 for spring.

## Delegation of the Commission of the European Communities
2100 M Street, NW, Suite 707
Washington, DC 20037
Tel. 202/862-9544; Fax 202/429-1766

This organization promotes better communication and understanding between the United States and the European Community. It offers 10-12 internships in academic affairs, public inquiries, speakers' bureau, and the Europe Magazine. Individuals perform research, information dissemination, and clerical duties. Each internship is unpaid and lasts five months. Open to college juniors, seniors, graduates, and graduate students. Contact the Assistant for Academic Affairs for more information.

## Educational Programs Abroad
540 Giordano Drive
Yorktown Heights, NY 10598
Tel. 914/245-6882

This nonprofit organization provides 80-100 internships in Europe (Bonn, Cologne, London, Madrid, Paris, and Strasbourg) for a variety of fields—advertising, business, law, education, health care, politics, social science, theater, and urban planning. During the academic year internships run for one semester; summer internships last 10 weeks. These are unpaid internships in which participants are expected to pay a program fee ranging from $1,780 to $6,300 which includes room and board. Open to college juniors, seniors, and graduate students. Foreign language competence a necessity for interns in Bonn, Paris, and Madrid. Requires an application fee of $25. Applicants should send a transcript, two letters of recommendation, and an essay on their career goals.

## Export-Import Bank of the United States (Eximbank)
811 Vermont Avenue, NW
Washington, DC 20571
Tel. 202/566-8834

This independent government agency promotes the export financing of U.S. goods and services. It sponsors 15-20 summer and semester interns each year in the areas of accounting, economics, financial analysis, and computer work. Open to undergraduate and graduate students. Favors majors in business administration, computer science, economics, finance, and marketing. Applicants must summit an SF 171 and college transcripts. Application deadline is March 31.

## General Electric Company
Recruiting and University Development
1285 Boston Avenue, Building 23CE
Bridgeport, CT 06601
Tel. 203/382-2000

General Electric Company hires numerous undergraduate and graduate interns for offices around the world: aerospace, aircraft engines, National Broadcasting Company (NBC), electrical distribution and control communications and services, motors, financial services, industrial and power systems, lighting, transportation systems, appliance, medical systems, and plastics. These are paid internships. Applicants should send a resume and cover letter indicating their desired position.

## Independent University
3001 Veazey Terrace, NW
Washington, DC 20008
Tel. 202/362-7855
Fax 202/364-0200

Promoting better relations between the United States and the Commonwealth of Independent States, this organization primarily holds conferences, seminars, and education programs for students and leaders in business, politics, and academia in these countries. It offers two unpaid program coordinator internships for a period of 4 months. Applicants should be proficient in WordPerfect and dBase software. Open to college juniors, seniors, graduates, and graduate students. Contact the President for more information.

## INET For Women
P.O. Box 6178
McLean, VA 22106
Tel. 703/873-8541
Fax 703/241-0090

This international trade and business organization promotes more effective strategies for cross-border transitions. It offers several unpaid internships lasting from 1½-6 months in information systems, public relations, advertising, marketing, membership administration, and events planning. Open to college juniors, seniors, graduates, and individuals re-entering the work force. Requires a $10 registration and processing fee. Contact the President for more information.

## Institute for Central American Studies (ICAS)
Apartado 300
1002 San Jose, Costa Rica

ICAS promotes the peace, justice, and well-being of people in Central America through research and information dissemination. It offers 12-18 internships each year for journalism and area studies majors. Internships last six months and can commence at any time. Applicants pay a $200 administrative fee. Open to recent college graduates as well as some undergraduate and graduate students. Must have a working knowledge of Spanish.

## The International Center
731 8th Street, SE
Washington, DC 20003
Tel. 202/547-3800
Fax 202/546-4783

The International Center focuses on U.S. foreign policy in Asia and Russia for the purpose of promoting democratic movements and the resolution of regional conflicts. It offers 10 internships. The internships involve research, writing, and general clerical duties centering on projects relating to Asia and Russia as well as the New Forests Project (promotes reforestations and economic development in developing countries). These are unpaid internships lasting for a period of 10 weeks. Open to college juniors, seniors, graduates, and graduate students. Application deadlines are June 30 for the fall, November 30 for the spring, and March 31 for the summer.

## International Visitors Information Service (IVIS)
1623 Belmont Street, NW
Washington, DC 20009
Tel. 202/939-5566
Fax 202/232-9783

Affiliated with the Meridian International Center, IVIS sponsors programs and provides services to international visitors in Washington, DC. Offers one paid ($5.85 per hour) internship involving general office work. Duration of internship is one semester. Candidates should have foreign language skills. Contact the Executive Director for more information.

## Legacy International
128 North Fayette Street
Alexandria, VA 22314
(no phone calls please)

Primarily focusing on Russia, this organization sponsors research, programs, and projects for promoting environmentally sound development, resolution of ethnic and religious conflicts, education, and experiential leadership training. Offers unpaid internships involving research, administration, and clerical support. Preferred candidates should have a background in international politics, Russian area studies, environmental studies, and intercultural education. Open to college graduates. Requires an in-person interview. Contact the Administrator.

## Marymount Study Abroad Program
Marymount College
Terrytown, NY 10591-3796
Tel. 914/332-8222
Fax 914/631-8586

This unique study abroad program is designed for undergraduates who attend universities and polytechnics in central London. The program provides unpaid internships in a variety of fields, such as fashion design, merchandising, public relations, publishing, museums, journalism, communications, hotel management, and international business. Open to college juniors and seniors. Contact the Director, Study Abroad Program for more information.

## The Ohio International Agricultural Intern Program
Ohio State University
2120 Fyffe Road
Columbus, OH 43210-1099
(no phone calls please)

This program provides both American and foreign agricultural students with opportunities to learn about agricultural/horticulture and veterinary medicine in different national and cultural settings. About 50 American internships are available each year for 3 month periods. These are paid ($4.25-$8.00 an hour) internships. Applicants should have backgrounds in agriculture/horticulture, veterinary, or medicine and the ability to speak a foreign language. Open to 19-26 year old college students and college graduates. Requires a $120 fee for administration and visas. Contact the program manager for more information.

## People to People International
501 East Armour Boulevard
Kansas City, MO 64109-2200
Tel. 816/531-4701
Fax 816/561-7502

This nonprofit educational and cultural exchange organization administers exchange programs for high school, college, and adult/professional groups in over 30 countries. Offers unpaid internships for 2-3 month periods. Interns are responsible for matching individuals to the various exchange programs. Candidates should have overseas experience. Open to college seniors, graduates, and graduate students, and career changers. Contact the Vice President for Programs. Application deadline is April 15 for summer; some fall and spring placements.

## Radio Free Europe/Radio Liberty Fund, Inc.
Training Department Personnel Division
Box 86 Oettingenstrasse 67, D-8000
Munich 22 Germany

This independent news and broadcasting corporation promotes better communication with the peoples of Eastern Europe and the Commonwealth of Independent States. It hires more than 10 research and electrical engineering interns for 8-12 week periods. Interns are paid $48 a day. Research interns travel to Munich and should be fluent in a language of Eastern Europe or the Commonwealth of Independent States. Electrical engineering interns should be fluent in German, Portuguese, or Spanish. Open to highly qualified undergraduates and graduate students. Application deadline in mid-February. For more information, including an application, contact: Summer Internship Program, RFE/FL, Inc., 1201 Connecticut Avenue, NW, Washington, DC 20036.

## Robert Bosch Foundation Fellowship
## Program, CDS International, Inc.
330 Seventh Avenue
New York, NY 10001
Tel. 212/760-1400

This program takes place in Germany and is for Americans with degrees in business, economics, journalism, law, mass communications, political science, and public affairs. It provides 15 paid ($2200-$2500 per month) executive level internships in the German government and private sector for 9 month periods (September to May). Open to graduate students and individuals with graduate or law degrees. Application deadline is October 15. Contact the program officer for more information.

## Sister Cities International

1210 South Payne Street
Alexandria, VA 22314-2939
(no phone calls please)
Fax 703/836-4815

This nonprofit association assists U.S. communities in developing formal linkages with other cities throughout the world for the purposes of increasing international understanding and promoting exchanges. Offers one unpaid internship for a minimum of 6 weeks. Candidates should have some international and community service background and be computer literate. Open to college juniors, seniors, graduates, graduate students, and career changers. For more information, contact the Personnel Office.

## United Nations Association of the USA

485 Fifth Avenue
New York, NY 10017
Tel. 212/697-3232

The purpose of this nonprofit organization is to strengthen the United Nations system and promote U.S. participation in the organization. It offers several unpaid internships of variable duration. Most internships involve research, proofreading, writing, and general office responsibilities. Open to college juniors, seniors, graduates, graduate students, and career changers. Application deadlines are April 1 for summer, August 19 for fall, and January 15 for spring. Contact the Intern Coordinator for more information.

## The U.S. Chamber of Commerce

Personnel Department, Internship Coordinator
1615 H Street, NW
Washington, DC 20062
Tel. 202/659-6000

This organization promotes business, trade, and professional associations. Hiring 85 interns each year, it offers unpaid semester-long international internships for college juniors and seniors. Interns conduct research, write articles, attend congressional hearings, and follow legislation.

## U.S. and Foreign Commercial Service (U.S.&FCS)
Work-Study Internship Program
Office of Foreign Service Personnel
P.O. Box 688
Ben Franklin Station
Washington, DC 20044-0688

This U.S. Department of Commerce organization promotes U.S. exports and business. It sponsors a summer work-study intern program for 10 to 12 week periods. Open to college juniors, seniors, and graduate students. It offers several unpaid internships involving research, writing, and marketing/promotion. Interns work abroad and are responsible for financing all of their travel, living, and other expenses. Applicants must submit an SF 171, transcripts, two letters of reference, and a 500 to 700-word essay on their career goals. Deadlines for applications are November 1.

## Visions in Action
3637 Fulton Street, NW
Washington, DC 20007
Tel. 202/625-7402
Fax 202/625-2553

This nonprofit organization offers 10-15 unpaid internships each year in urban areas of Kenya, South Africa, Uganda, and Zimbabwe. Visions in Action focuses on urban development and includes such issues as refugee relief, famine relief, women, agriculture, family planning, appropriate technology, and youth work. Interns work on urban development, public relations, administrative support, and fundraising. Open to college students, graduates, graduate students, and career changers. For more information, contact the U.S. Director.

## World Federalists
418 7th Street, SE
Washington, DC 20003
Tel. 202/546-3950
Fax 202/546-3749

This organization promotes the work of the United Nations in the areas of environmentalism, human rights, and conflict resolution. It offers four paid ($100) internships for one semester each. Interns get experience in conducting policy research, coordinating conferences, writing, editing, public relations, and lobbying. Open to college students, graduates, and graduate students. Applicants should submit a resume and cover letter to the Director of Student Programs.

## WorldTeach

Harvard Institute for International Development
One Eliot Street
Cambridge, MA 02138
Tel. 617/495-5527; Fax 617/495-1239

Each year WorldTeach places nearly 200 teaching interns in Africa, Asia, Latin America, and Europe. Most interns teach English as a foreign language but some also teach science and mathematics. Individuals must pay a fee of $3,000 to participate in the program, a fee which covers their insurance, training, and international transportation. The program provides housing and a small monthly stipend. It also offers 8 unpaid summer teaching positions in China and an unpaid sports coaching position in Black South African townships for 6 month periods. Candidates for teaching English should have an undergraduate degree from any accredited college or university as well as 25 credit hours of TEFL (Teaching English as a Foreign Language). Contact the Internship Coordinator for more information.

## Youth for Understanding
## International Exchange

3501 Newark Street, NW
Washington, DC 20016-3167
Tel. 202/966-6808
Fax 202/895-1104

This nonprofit, educational organization seeks to promote greater world peace and understanding through exchange programs for high school students. It offers several unpaid internships in consumer services, public relations, finance, school relations, sales and marketing, sports, and promotion. Open to college students, graduates, graduate students, and career changers. For more information, contact the Assistant Director Volunteer Services.

# OTHER INTERNSHIP OPPORTUNITIES

Numerous other organizations—from government agencies to private companies and nonprofit firms—offer internship opportunities. You may want to contact some of the following:

**Africare**
Director of International Development
440 R Street, NW
Washington, DC 20001
Tel. 202/462-3614

**Agency for International Development**
ATTN: Student Programs Coordinator
Office of Human Resources Development
    and Management
2401 E Street, NW
Washington, DC 20523-0105

**The Aires Group, Ltd.**
Vice President, Projects
1745 Jefferson Davis Highway, Suite 404
Arlington, VA 22202
Tel. 703/802-9123

**American Association of Overseas Studies**
Summer Internship Coordinator
158 West 81st Street, Suite 112
New York, NY 10024
Tel. 800/338-2748

**American Bar Association**
International Legal Exchange Program
Executive Director
1700 Pennsylvania Ave., NW, Suite 620
Washington, DC 20006
Tel. 202/393-7122

**American Friends Service Committee**
Personnel Department
1501 Cherry Street
Philadelphia, PA 19102
Tel. 215/241-7295

**American Jewish Congress**
Office of the Washington Representative
Internship Coordinator
2027 Massachusetts Ave., NW
Washington, DC 20036
Tel. 202/332-4001

**American Society of Travel Agents**
Education Department
1101 King Street
Alexandria, VA 22314
Tel. 703/739-2782, Ext. 608

**American Security Council (ASC)**
Executive Director
916 Pennsylvania Avenue, SE
Washington, DC 20003
Tel. 202/484-1676

**Americas Society**
Director of Personnel and Administration
680 Park Avenue
New York, NY 10021
Tel. 202/628-3200

**Amigos De Las Americas**
Recruiting
5618 Star Lane
Houston, TX 77057
Tel. 800/231-77796

**Army JAGC Professional Recruiting Office**
(Summer Intern)
Building 1834, Franklin Road
Fort Belvoir, VA 22060-5818
Tel. 800/336-3315
in Virginia 703/355-3323 collect

**The Asia Foundation**
Personnel Officer
P.O. Box 193223
San Francisco, CA 94119-3223
Tel. 415/982-4640
Fax 415/392-8863

**The Atlantic Council of the United States**
Internship Coordinator
1616 H Street, NW
Washington, DC 20076

**Beijing-Washington, Inc.**
4340 East West Highway
Suite 200
Bethesda, MD 20814
Tel. 301/656-4801

**The Brookings Institution**
Governmental Studies Program
1775 Massachusetts Avenue, NW
Washington, DC 20036
Tel. 202/797-6052

**CARE**
660 First Avenue
New York, NY 10016
Tel. 212/686-3110

**Carnegie Endowment for International Peace**
Intern Coordinator
2400 N Street, NW
Washington, DC 20037
Tel. 202/862-7900

**Caribbean Conservation Corp.**
RA/Internship Program
P.O. Box 2866
Gainesville, FL 32602

**The Catholic University of America**
Parliamentary Internship Program
Department of Politics
Washington, DC 20064
Tel. 202/635-5000

**Center for Strategic and International Studies (CSIS)**
CSIS Intern Coordinator
1800 K Street, NW
Washington, DC 20006
Tel. 202/887-0200

**Central Intelligence Agency**
Student Programs Office
P.O. Box 1255
Department IEH
Pittsburgh, PA 15230

**Commission on Security and Cooperation in Europe (CSCE)**
237 Ford House Office Building
Washington, DC 23515
Tel. 202/225-1901

**Council on Hemispheric Affairs**
Secretary of Internships
724 9th Street, NW
Suite 401
Washington, DC 20009
Tel. 202/393-3322
Fax 202/393-3424

**Council for Inter-American Security (CIS)**
Director of Research
122 C Street NW
Suite 710
Washington, DC 20001
Tel. 202/393-6622

**Department of State, PER/CSP**
Intern Coordinator
P.O. Box 18657
Washington, DC 20036

**The Ford Foundation**
Manager Employment & Training
320 East 43rd Street
New York, NY 10017
Tel. 212/573-4794

**Freedom House, Inc.**
Intern Coordinator
120 Wall Street, 26th Floor
New York, NY 10005
Tel. 212/514-8040

**Georgetown University**
Center for Immigration Policy and Refugee Assistance
Director of Internship Programs
P.O. Box 2298
Washington, DC 20057-1011
Tel. 202/298-0229 or 202/298-0214

**Global Exchange**
2141 Mission Street Room 202
San Francisco, CA 94110
Tel. 415/255-7298
Fax 415/255-7498

**Grassroots International**
P.O. Box 312
Cambridge, MA 02139
Tel. 617/497-9180
Fax 617/497-4397

**Habitat for Humanity International**
ATTN: Personnel Department
Habitat and Church Streets
Americus, GA 31709-3498
Tel. 912/924-6935

**Human Rights Watch/Everett Public
Service Internships**
Intern Coordinator
486 Fifth Avenue
New York, NY 10017

**Institute of International Education**
Educational Counseling Center
P.O. Box 3087
Laredo, TX 78044
Tel. 525/211-0042, ext. 3500

**International Atomic Energy Agency**
Personnel Office (Internships)
Wagramerstrasse 5, P.O. Box 100
A-1400 Vienna
Austria

**International Finance Corporation**
Summer Employment Program
1818 H Street, NW, Room I-2001
Washington, DC 20433

**International Labor Office**
Personnel Office (Internships)
1828 L Street, NW, Suite 801
Washington, DC 20036

**International Monetary Fund**
Summer Internship Program
Recruitment Division
Room 6-525
700 19th Street, NW
Washington, DC 20431

**Interns for Peace**
270 West 89th St.
New York, NY 10024
Tel. 212/580-0540
Fax 212/580-0693

**Joint Baltic American National Committee**
Director of Public Relations
400 Hurley Avenue
P.O. Box 4578
Rockville, MD 20849
Tel. 301/340-1954

**MAP International**
RDIF Coordinator
2200 Glynco Parkway
P.O. Box 50
Brunswick, GA 31521

**Meridian International Center**
Director of Personnel
1630 Crescent Place, NW
Washington, DC 20009
Tel. 202/667-6800

**The Middle East Institute**
Internship Coordinator
1761 N Street, NW
Washington, DC 20036
Tel. 202/785-1141

**Minnesota Studies in International Development (MSID)**
Program Associate
106 Nicholson Hall
University of Minnesota
Minneapolis, MN 55455
Tel. 612/625-3379

**National Resources Defense Council (NRDC)**
Intern Coordinator
1350 New York Avenue, NW
Suite 300
Washington, DC 20005
Tel. 202/783-7800

**Organization of American States**
OAS Internship Coordinator
1889 F St., NW, Seventh Floor
Washington, DC 20006
Tel. 202/458-3519

**Overseas Private Investment Corporation**
Intern Program Coordinator
1615 M Street, NW
Washington, DC 20527
Tel. 202/457-7094

**Overseas Schools Assistance Corporation**
International Schools Internship Program
445 R West Center Street, P.O. Box 103
West Bridgewater, MA 02379
Tel. 508/588-0477

**Pan American Development Foundation**
ATTN: Internship Coordinator, Personnel
1889 F St., NW
Washington, DC 20006
Tel. 202/458-3969
Fax 202/458-6316

**The Partnership for Service-Learning**
Director
815 Second Avenue
Suite 315
New York, NY 10017
Tel. 212/986-0989

**Population Institute**
Director of Future Leaders Program
107 2nd Street, NE
Washington, DC 20002
Tel. 202/544-3300

**Society for International Development**
Executive Director
1401 New York Avenue, NW
Suite 1100
Washington, DC 20005
Tel. 202/347-1800

**TransAfrica**
Administrative Director
545 Eighth Street, SE
Washington, DC 20003
Tel. 202/547-2550

**UNICEF**
The Internship Coordinator
Three United Nations Plaza
New York, NY 10017

**The United National Ad Hoc Internship Program**
Internship Coordinator, United Nations
Recruitment Programs Section, Room 2475
Office of Personnel Services
New York, NY 10017

**United Nations**
Recruitment Programmes Section
Room 2500
Office of Personnel Services
New York, NY 10017

**United Nations**
Coordinator of the DPI Graduate
Student Intern Programme
Room S-1037G
Department of Public Information
New York, NY 10017

**United Nations Development Program
(UNDP) Summer Internship Program**
Chief, Recruitment Section
Summer Internship Program
Division of Personnel
UNDP, One United Nations Plaza
New York, NY 10017

**United Nations Fund for Population Activities**
Chief, Recruitment Section (Internships)
One United Nations Plaza
New York, NY 10017

**The United Nations Headquarters Internship Program**
Coordinator, Internship Program
Room S-2500E, United Nations
New York, NY 10017
Tel. 212/963-1223

**United Nations Industrial Development Organization (UNIDO)**
Personnel Services Division
UNIDO, Room E0554
Vienna International Centre
P.O. Box 300
A-1400 Vienna, Austria
Tel. 43-1-211 31

**United Nations Institute for Training and
Research (UNITAR) Internship Program**
Executive Director of UNITAR
801 United Nations Plaza
New York, NY 10017

**United Nations Office at Geneva**
Information Service
Palais des Nations
CH-122 Geneva 10
Switzerland

**U.S. Department of State**
Intern Coordinator
P.O. Box 9317
Arlington, VA 22219

**Voice of America**
VOA Internship Program
Room 3521, HHS-N
330 Independence Avenue, SW
Washington, DC 20547

**The Washington Center for Internships and Academic Seminars**
514 Tenth Street, NW
Suite 600
Washington, DC 20004
Tel. 202/624-8000

**The Washington International Studies Center**
214 Massachusetts Avenue, NE, Suite 450
Washington, DC 20002
Tel. 202/547-3275

**Washington Office of Africa (WOA)**
Executive Assistant
110 Washington Avenue, NE
Suite 112
Washington, DC 20002
Tel. 202/546-1545

**Washington Office on Latin America (WOLA)**
Intern Coordinator
110 Maryland Office, NE
Washington, DC 20002-5695
Tel. 202/544-8045
Fax 202/546-5288

**The Wilson Center**
Smithsonian Institution Building
Washington, DC 20560
Tel. 202/357-2567

**Women's International League for
Peace and Freedom (WILPF)**
1213 Race Street
Philadelphia, PA 19107-1691
Tel. 215/563-7110

**The World Bank**
Summer Employment Program
Room O-5079
1818 H St., NW
Washington, DC 20433
Tel. 202/477-1234

**YMCA of Metropolitan Washington**
Intern Abroad Program
Director
1711 Rhode Island Avenue, NW
Washington, DC 20036
Tel. 202/862-9622

**Zero Population Growth (ZPG)**
Internship Program
1400 16th Street, NW
Suite 320
Washington, DC 20036
Tel. 202/332-2200

# ADDITIONAL RESOURCES

The organizations listed above for internship opportunities are only a few of many offering such opportunities. For more information on these and other international internship programs, please consult the following books and directories:

**Development Opportunities Catalog: A Guide to Internships, Research, and Employment With Development Organizations** (San Francisco: Overseas Development Network, 1990).

**Directory of International Internships: A World of Opportunities**, Thomas D. Luten, Charles A. Gliozzo, and Timothy J. Aldinger eds. (East Lansing, MI: Michigan State University, Career Development and Placement Services, 1990).

**The Imaginative Soul's Guide to Foreign Internships**, Laura Hitchcock (Greenville, NY: Ivy House, 1992).

**International Directory of Youth Internships**, Cynthia Morehouse (Croton-on-Hudson, NY: Apex Press, 1993).

**International Internships and Volunteer Programs**, Will Cantrell and Francine Modderno (Oakton, VA: WorldWise Books, 1992).

**International Schools Internship Program** (West Bridgewater, MA: Overseas Schools Assistance Corporation).

**Internships: 1994** (Princeton, NJ: Peterson's, 1994).

**Internships and Careers in International Affairs**, James Muldoon, Jr., ed. (New York: United National Association of the U.S., 1989).

**Internships in Foreign and Defense Policy: A Complete Guide for Women (and Men)**, Women in International Security (Arlington, VA: Seven Locks Press, 1990).

If you are interested in volunteer or study abroad programs, we recommend consulting the following directories:

**Academic Year Abroad**, Sarah J. Steen, ed. (New York: Institute of International Education, 1993-1994).

**Alternatives to the Peace Corps: A Directory of Third World and U.S. Volunteer Opportunities** (San Francisco: Food First Books, 1993).

**Fellowships, Scholarships, and Related Opportunities in International Education**, James Gehihar, ed. (Knoxville, TN: University of Tennessee, 1994).

**Going Places: The High School Student's Guide to Study, Travel, and Adventure Abroad** (New York: St. Martin's Press, 1994).

**Guide to International Education in the United States**, David S. Hoopes and Kathleen R. Hoopes (Detroit, MI: Gale Research, 1990).

**International Directory of Volunteer Work**, David Woodworth, ed. (Oxford, England: Vacation Work, 1993).

**International Scholarship Book**, Daniel J. Cassidy, ed. (Hawthorne, NJ: Career Press, 1993).

**International Workcamp Directory** (Belmont, VT: Volunteers for Peace, 1993).

**Kibbutz Volunteer**, John Bedford (Oxford, England: Vacation Work, 1993).

**Smart Vacations: The Traveler's Guide to Learning Adventures Abroad**, Priscilla Tovey, ed. (New York: St. Martin's Press, 1993).

**Study Abroad** (Princeton, NJ: Peterson's, 1994).

**Study Abroad, 1992-1994** (New York: UNESCO, 1991).

**Study Abroad: The Astute Student's Guide**, David Judkins (Charlotte, VT: Williamson Publishing, 1989).

**Time Out: Taking a Break from School to Travel, Work, and Study in the U.S. and Abroad**, Robert Gilpin with Caroline Fitzgibbons (New York: Simon and Schuster, 1992).

**Vacation Study Abroad**, Sarah J. Steen, ed. (New York: Institute of International Education, 1993-94).

**Volunteer-Sending Organizations for Eastern Europe** (Washington, DC: Citizens Democracy Corps, 1993).

**Volunteer Vacations**, Bill McMillon (Chicago: Chicago Review Press, 1993).

**Volunteer Work** (London: Central Bureau, 1993).

**Work, Study, Travel Abroad: The Whole World Handbook**, CIEE (New York: St. Martin's Press, 1994).

**The World of Learning** (Bristol, PA: International Publications Service, 1994).

For arranging your own short-term paid work abroad, review these useful resources:

**The Au Pair and Nanny's Guide to Working Abroad**, Susan Griffith and Sharon Legg (Oxford, England: Vacation Work, 1993).

**Directory of Overseas Summer Jobs**, David Woodworth, ed. (Oxford, England: Vacation Work, 1993).

**Summer Jobs Britain**, Emily Hatchwell, ed., 1993 (Oxford, England: Vacation Work, 1993).

**Work Your Way Around the World**, Susan Griffith, ed. (Oxford, England: Vacation Work, 1993).

**Working Holidays 1993** (London: Central Bureau, 1993).

**Working in Ski Resorts—Europe**, Victoria Pybus and Charles James, ed. (Oxford, England: Vacation Work, 1993).

# 12

# MAKING KEY JOB CONTACTS

*T*here are many ways to find an international job. Your best job finding strategy involves doing your own investigative work on organizations hiring in the international arena. The previous chapters in this book identify many such organizations which you may want to pursue according to the job finding advice we outline in *The Complete Guide to International Jobs and Careers.* You should research these international employers, network for information, advice, and referrals, and persist until you uncover the right job for you.

## STRATEGIES

If you have few international skills as well as little international experience, your chances of getting an international job should be better by pursuing opportunities with nonprofit organizations and the travel industry rather than with government, international organizations, and business firms. International positions with government and international organizations are designed for individuals with strong international qualifications. Businesses tend to promote individuals from within the organization to what are considered to be senior international positions rather than hire international specialists directly for such positions. The first and foremost consideration for a business is that the employee know their business. Becoming internationally competent—foreign language ability, knowledge of countries, cross-cultural adjustments, living abroad—is something experienced employees can learn once they are overseas in their assignments.

At the same time, you may want to monitor international job vacancy announcements that appear in several reliable publications. In this chapter, as well as in Chapter 13, we identify several such publications which we believe are useful to survey as part of your job search. In Chapter 13 we provide information on how to subscribe to each. However, we caution you to not become preoccupied in surveying these listing nor responding to the announcements with resumes, letters, telephone calls, and faxes. Job listings and vacancy announcements only represent a small percentage of international job opportunities available at any particular time.

Except in the case of some reputable teacher placement services, you need not—indeed should not—pay someone else to find you an international job. If you become drawn to so-called international employment firms that promise to find you an international job for up-front fees, you may quickly discover unscrupulous firms that take advantage of individuals who are highly motivated to work abroad but who are basically "job dumb". These firms are notorious for extracting fees— ranging from $300 to $5000—from individuals who mistakenly believe these firms have an inside track to the international job market. Our basic rule of thumb for weeding out the good from the bad is this: If a firm requires up-front fees without written performance guarantees, even for conducting preliminary employment testing, avoid them. This is often a sign that you are about to be taken down the familiar road so many other disappointed international job seekers have traveled—to your bank account only! You will be left with dashed expectations and less cash after such a firm finishes with you. This experience will once again confirm the often heard lament of many unsuccessful job seekers—"it's really tough to find an international job; there are no international jobs available these days; I don't have the necessary international work skills."

At the same time, there are many reputable firms that are involved in the international employment business. A few are job search and placement firms, but most are "executive recruiters" or "headhunters" who are paid by employers to find qualified employees for particular positions. Rather than recruit employees directly, many international employers prefer hiring such firms to do the necessary recruitment and preliminary screening of candidates. Remember, these firms are paid by the employer—either on a retainer or contingency fee basis—and not by the job seeker. Any firm that tells you they have been retained by employers to find them employees, but then requires you to pay them, is probably ripping you off with an up-front fee requirement. Reputable firms get paid by employers on the basis of their performance which is measured by recruiting the necessary skills and experience required by the employer.

In this chapter we identify some of the more reputable firms that are involved in the international job finding business. However, your single best source of information on such firms is an annual directory published by Kennedy Publications: *The Directory of Executive Recruiters*. This book is available through Impact Publications. Even though these firms work for employers, you may want to contact some of them with information on your international experience, qualifications, and interests. But keep in mind that these firms primarily work with individuals who have a great deal of work experience, have a specific hard-to-find technical skill, or possess some exotic combination of international skills. Some recruit for positions that pay $50,000 a year or more, but most focus on the $80,000 to $100,000+ a year positions. Many of these firms are based in major U.S. cities as well as maintain offices abroad. Some recruit in many different skill and industry areas, but most tend to specialize in one or two major areas. These firms are not in the business of recruiting individuals with little experience or who have few demonstrated international work skills for entry-level positions.

## JOB LISTINGS

Several publications and services specialize in international job vacancy announcements. A disproportionate number of nonprofit organizations are included in these publications because nonprofits are more likely to conduct national and international searches for candidates. Vacancies in government and international organizations are primarily announced through agency personnel offices and posted on bulletin boards although some are included in the major job listing publications identified in this section. However, few businesses advertise international vacancies in such publications. They are more likely to work through executive search firms which, in turn, place ads in major trade journals and national and international publications such as the *New York Times, National Business Employment Weekly, Washington Post*, and the *Los Angeles Times*. These are the publications of choice for many high level business and technical people looking for international positions.

The following publications include numerous international job vacancy announcements. We include addresses and order information on each publication in Chapter 13 ("Job Listings, Databases, and Subscriptions" on pages 302-305). Again, keep in mind that these publications by no means represent the universe of international job vacancies. Most of the listings in these publications will be oriented toward nonprofit organizations, PVOs, educational institutions, and contracting firms doing international development work—the subjects of Chapters 6, 7, 8, and 9:

**Career Network:** A monthly job listing bulletin for international health care professionals. Includes nearly 60 vacancies per issue.

**Community Jobs:** This monthly newspaper primarily focuses on vacancies with nonprofit organizations in the U.S. but also includes several international nonprofit positions in each issue.

**Federal Career Opportunities:** A biweekly listing of vacancies throughout the Federal government. Includes over 3,000 positions in each issue, some of which are with the international-related agencies identified in Chapter 2.

**Federal Jobs Digest:** Another biweekly listing of Federal government job vacancies. Includes several international listings outside government.

**International Career Employment Opportunities:** This biweekly newsletter includes over 500 international job openings in the U.S. and abroad. Includes both professional and nonprofessional positions.

**International Employment Gazette:** One of the most comprehensive biweekly publications listing more than 400 vacancies in each issue. Represents a wide range of nonprofessional and professional international jobs, from construction to business, education, and nonprofit groups.

**International Employment Hotline:** A monthly listing of job vacancies available worldwide in government, consulting firms, nonprofit organizations, educational institutions, and business. Includes informative articles on the problems, pitfalls, and promises of finding an international job, including useful job search tips.

**International Jobs Bulletin:** A biweekly publication listing information on hundreds of organizations (government, education, PVOs) offering job vacancies overseas.

**International Affairs Career Bulletin:** A monthly newsletter that provides information on international job vacancies, especially those with government, consulting firms, and PVOs.

**Monday Developments:** This biweekly newsletter includes several vacancy announcements with nonprofit organizations that are members of InterAction, a major network of PVOs.

**Options:** This bimonthly newsletter includes volunteer positions for health care professionals in the U.S., East Asia, the Pacific, Latin America, and Africa.

If you are a **Returned Peace Corps Volunteer**, you will want to use the job services available through the Returned Volunteer Services office: Peace Corps, 1990 K Street, NW, Room 7664, Washington, DC 20526, Tel. 202/606-3126. Please do not contact this office unless you are a returned volunteer. This already over-worked office can only provide information and services to its former volunteers and staff members— both formerly or recently separated. If you left Peace Corps 30 years ago, you can still use this service. The Peace Corps has an excellent library of international resources (5th Floor, Tel. 202/606-3307) as well as numerous job listings relevant to its volunteers. It also publishes a biweekly job listing bulletin called *Hotline: A Bulletin of Opportunities for Returned Peace Corps Volunteers*. It may well be worth your time and effort to visit this center. After all, Washington, DC is located in the heart of hundreds of organizations offering international job opportunities for those interested in pursuing jobs and careers with nonprofit organizations as well as with consulting firms and educational organizations relevant to the Peace Corps experience. Better still, many of these organizations are staffed by individuals who are part of the growing "old boy/girl network" of ex-Peace Corps volunteers who look favorably toward individuals with Peace Corps experience. Many nonprofit organizations, consulting firms, and educational organizations automatically contact this office when they have impending vacancies.

# ELECTRONIC BULLETIN BOARDS AND DATABASES

During the past two years several electronic bulletin boards and databases have developed to assist job seekers in general and international job seeks in particular. The electronic bulletin boards primarily include job listings, although many job seekers report luck in locating potential employers by leaving messages on the bulletin boards. The most popular such electronic bulletin boards are operated by America OnLine, CompuServe, and Prodigy. They are also found in the Internet system which can be accessed through these other online telecommunication services.

The electronic databases are primarily designed to link employers with candidates via an "electronic resume" which is "read" through the use of sophisticated search and retrieval software. Individuals need to be members of the databases which usually require an annual membership fee, typically ranging from $30 to $100. Some memberships are free for students and alumni of particular colleges and universities or the fees are discounted for members of certain associations.

For detailed information on these new job search services, see the two new books written by Joyce Lain Kennedy and Thomas J. Morrow, *Electronic Job Search Revolution* and *Electronic Resume Revolution* (New York: Wiley & Sons, 1994) and Peter D. Weddle's new *Electronic Resumes for the New Job Market: Resumes That Work for You 24 Hours a Day* (Manassas Park, VA: Impact Publications, 1994). All three books are available through Impact Publications.

The largest electronic bulletin boards and databases primarily include domestic job listings, although you may find a few listings for international positions. Those specializing only in international jobs include:

**International Career Databank:** Includes overseas job vacancies, internships, and fellowships. Updated monthly.

**International Placement Network:** This service matches individuals' backgrounds with appropriate job vacancies.

**Talent Bank:** Specializes in maintaining a resume bank for short-term consulting opportunities in international development.

Other electronic bulletin boards and databases which may include some international job listings and employers seeking individuals with international expertise include:

- **Career Placement Registry**
- **Connexion®**
- **Internet**
- **Job Bank USA**
- **kiNexus**

Access and subscription information on these electronic bulletin boards and databases also is included in Chapter 13 (pages 306-307).

## EXECUTIVE RECRUITERS

Thousands of executive recruiters or "headhunters" are found throughout
the United States and abroad. Many are involved in recruiting qualified
individuals for international firms, especially construction, oil, and trading
firms with major operations abroad. Most of these firms have offices in
major U.S. cities.

However, inclusion of these firms here in no way should indicate our
endorsement or recommendation. You must investigate each and approach
them with caution as you normally would do with any type of new
business transaction. Also, many of these firms are very small and
frequently change addresses. Some of the better known such firms
include:

**Adams & Associates International**
978 Hampton Park
Barrington, IL 60010

**Agra Placements, Ltd.**
4949 Pleasant St., Suite 1
West 50th Place III
W. Des Moines, IA 50265

**American Executive Management**
30 Federal St.
Salem, MA 01970

**Anderson Bradshaw Associates**
1225 N. Loop West, Suite 820
Houston, TX 77008

**Peter Barrett Associates**
302 N. El Camino Real, #200
San Clemente, CA 92672

**BDO Seidman**
1430 Broadway, 6th Fl.
New York, NY 10023

**Battalia & Associates**
275 Madison Ave., Suite 2315
New York, NY 10016

**Boardroom Planning &**
**Consulting Group**
175A East 2nd St.
Huntington Station, NY 11646

**Bowden & Co., Inc.**
5000 Rockside Rd., Suite 550
Cleveland, OH 44131

**Boyden International**
260 Madison Ave.
New York, NY 10016

**D. Brown and Associates**
610 SW Alder, Suite 1111
Portland, OR 97205

**CanMed Consultants**
62 Queen St. S.
Mississauga, Ontario
Canada L5H 1K4

**Century Personnel**
3737 N. Meridian St., Suite 500
Indianapolis, IN 46208

**Cherbonnier Group, Inc.**
471 N. Post Oak Lane
Houston, TX 77024

**Compass Group, Ltd.**
401 Woodward, Suite 460
Birmingham, MI 48009

**Conex, Inc.**
919 Third Ave., 18th Fl.
New York, NY 10022

**Walter V. Connor**
**International, Inc.**
2 E. Read St., Suite 100
Baltimore, MD 21202-2470

**DHR International**
10 S. Riverside Plaza, Suite 1650
Chicago, IL 60606

**DRC Associates**
452 Hudson Plaza
Englewood Cliffs, NJ 07632

**Dougan & McKinley**
The Phoenix Tower
3200 SW Freeway, 33rd Fl.
Houston, TX 77027-5726

**Dunhill Employment Agency**
230 N. Michigan Avenue
Chicago, IL 60603

**Elliott Co., Inc.**
400 W. Cummings Park
Suite 2750
Woburn, MA 01801

**FGI**
1595 Spring Hill Rd., Suite 350
Vienna, VA 22182

**Fairfaxx Management Associates**
100B East Ave.
Norwalk, CT 06851

**Leon A. Farley Assoc.**
468 Jackson St.
San Francisco, CA 94111

**Finnegan Associates**
P.O. Box 1183
Palos Verdes Estates, CA 90274

**Global Job Search Local**
1605 Ridgelake Drive
Metaire, LA 70001

**Glou International, Inc.**
687 Highland Ave.
Needham, MA 02194-2232

**Group Fischer**
18552 MacArthur Blvd., Suite 375
Irvine, CA 92715

**Hamilton Personnel**
3655 NW 87th Avenue
Miami, FL 33137

**GHK Technical Placements**
P.O. Box 131
Trumbull, CT 06611

**Haskell & Stern Associates**
529 Fifth Avenue
New York, NY 10017

**Heidrick & Struggles**
20 N. Wacker Drive, Suite 2850
Chicago, IL 60606-4590

**Hyman, Mackenzie &**
**Partners, Inc.**
3650 Victoria Park Ave., #203
Willowdale, Ontario
Canada M2H 3P7

**Johnson Smith & Knisely**
475 Fifth Ave., 14th Fl.
New York, NY 10017

**International Business Associates**
Frick Building
Pittsburgh, PA 15220

**International Career Network**
1645 Tullie Circle, NE
Atlanta, GA

**International Placement**
**and Recruiting**
207 W. Greenfield Ave.
Miami, FL 33137

**International Staffing Consultants**
19762 MacArthur Blvd.
Irvine, CA 92715

**K/N International**
P.O. Box 073
Wilton, CT 06897-0073

**Karam Group International**
1675 Larimer St., Suite 310
Denver, CO 80202

**Kearney Executive Search**
222 W. Adams
Chicago, IL 60606

**Kling Personnel Assoc.**
180 Broadway, Suite 501
New York, NY 10038

**Korn/Ferry International**
237 Park Ave.
New York, NY 10017

**Kors Montgomery International**
1980 Post Oak Blvd., Suite 2280
Houston, TX 77056

**J. Krauss Associates**
29 Polly Drive
Huntington, NY 11743

**Kunzer Associates, Ltd.**
2001 Spring Road
Oak Brook, IL 60521

**LCW Group**
6750 France Ave. S., Suite 144
Edina, MN 55435

**Tom Mahon and Associates**
#1 Starbuck Lane
P.O. Box 1208
Saratoga Springs, NY 12866

**Maiorino & Weston
Associates, Inc.**
90 Grove St., Suite 205
The Executive Pavilion
Ridgefield, CT 06877

**Management Search International**
15375 Barranca Pkwy., Suite B-205
Irvine, CA 92718

**Mark Stanley & Co.**
Two Alhambra Plaza, Suite 1106
Coral Gables, FL 33134

**Marlar International**
100 E. Pratt St., Suite 2530
Baltimore, MD 21202

**Bruce Massey and Partners, Inc.**
330 Bay St., Suite 1104
Toronto, Ontario
Canada M5H 2S8

**McCartan Associates**
722 Chews Landing Rd.
Lindenwold, NJ 08021

**Merlin International**
185 Arch St.,
P.O. Box 313
Ramsey, NJ 07446

**The Neil Michael Group, Inc.**
305 Madison Ave., Suite 902
New York, NY 10165

**Pacific Rim Human
Resources Services**
690 Market St., Suite 625
San Francisco, CA 94105

**Poirier, Hoevel & Co.**
12400 Wilshire Blvd., Suite 1250
Los Angeles, CA 90025

**Preng & Associates**
2925 Briarpark, Suite 1111
Houston, TX 77042

**Preston Robert & Associates**
570 Taxter Road, Suite 565
Elmsford, NY 10523-2399

**Professional Search Personnel**
4900 Leesburg Pike, Suite 402
Alexandria, VA 22302

**Professions, Inc.**
4665 Cornell Rd., Suite 160
Cincinnati, OH 45241

**QVS International**
1640-21 Powers Ferry Rd.
Atlanta, GA 30067

**Raines International, Inc.**
1180 Ave. of the Americas
Suite 1830
New York, NY 10036

**Paul R. Ray & Co., Inc.**
301 Commerce St., #2300
Ft. Worth, TX 76102

**Russell Reynolds Assoc.**
200 Park Ave.
New York, NY 10166

**E. J. Rhodes Associates**
2 W. 25th St.
New York, NY 10036

**Robert Half Employment Agency**
3600 Wilshire Blvd.
Los Angeles, CA 90010

**Robert Half Employment Agency**
409 Camino Del Rio S., Suite 305
San Diego, CA 92111

**J. D. Ross International**
375 Park Ave., Suite 3101
New York, NY 10152

**Sage/Walters Ltd.**
666 Fifth Ave.
New York, NY 10103

**Schuyler & Frye
International, Inc.**
5600 Glenridge Dr., NE, #225
Glenridge Centre E.
Atlanta, GA 30342

**The Search Center**
595 Market St., Suite 1400
San Francisco, CA 94105

**Spencer Stuart & Associates**
55 E. 52nd St.
New York, NY 10055

**Splaine & Associates**
15951 Los Gatos Blvd. Suite 13
Los Gatos, CA 95032

**St. Lawrence International, Inc.**
219 Lamson St.
Syracuse, NY 13206

**Stevenson Group/SES**
836 Farmington Ave., Suite 223
West Hartford, CT 06119

**TASA, Inc.**
750 Lexington Ave., Suite 1800
New York, NY 10022

**TRS-Total Recruiting Service**
3333 Michelson Dr., A1-30
Irvine, CA 92730

**VanReypen Enterprises**
3100 Monroe Ave.
Rochester, NY 14618

**Vision Tech**
2927 W. Liberty Ave., Suite 196
Pittsburgh, PA 15216

**Vista Resource Group**
620 Newport Center Dr.
Newport Beach, CA 92660

**WDI, International**
1000 Abernathy Rd.
Suite 1240
Atlanta, GA 30328

**Ward Howell International**
99 Park Ave., 20th Fl.
New York, NY 10016

**C. Weiss Associates**
60 W. 57th Street
New York, NY 10019

**Winguth & Co.**
2180 Sand Hill Rd.
Suite 170
Menlo Park, CA 94025

**Wytmar & Co., Inc.**
400 E. Randolph Dr.
Suite 6B
Chicago, IL 60601

Before contacting any of these firms, be sure you understand exactly what they do. Many specialize in recruiting individuals in a particular skill or industrial area, such as engineering, banking, health care, accounting, energy, or manufacturing. You will waste both your time and their time if you just randomly send them your resume and cover letter or make telephone calls. We strongly recommend getting a copy of the latest edition of Kennedy Publication's *The Directory of Executive Recruiters* to research these firms *prior to* contacting them. If you are interested in European executive search firms, you should also review a copy of Kennedy Publication's *Key European Search Firms and Their U.S. Links*. Both books are available through Impact Publications.

# 13

# KEY JOB
# SEARCH
# RESOURCES

*N*umerous resources are available to help you find an international job. While we mentioned several key directories, books, job listings, and placement services relevant to subjects of previous chapters, many other resources are available to assist you with your job search.

In this chapter we outline the major directories, books, subscriptions, audio programs, computer software, job search databases, and CD-ROM programs which should prove helpful in locating the right international job. Some of these resources may be available in local bookstores and public and university libraries, but most will be hard to find. You may be disappointed in discovering that few if any of these resources are readily available near where you live. Consequently, you may have to request your library to acquire specific ones through its Inter-Library Loan Program. For your convenience, most of these resources are available directly from Impact Publications. The publisher has assembled one of the largest collections of international career resources for individuals and institutions interested in locating key resources in this career area. You will find an order form at the end of this book which includes many of the resources annotated in this chapter.

As you will quickly discover, libraries are excellent sources for conducting an effective international job search. They subscribe to many of the key directories you will want to consult for contact information on prospective international employers. Some also are equipped with CD-ROM and online services that will save you a great deal of time searching for names and addresses of relevant international employers.

Whatever you do, make sure you visit your library *before* you invest a great deal of time and effort in trying to find an international employer. These library resources may well become your ticket to job search success!

## MAJOR DIRECTORIES

Several excellent directories provide key contact information for international job seekers. You should carefully examine these directories for information on employers: type of activity, staff size, annual income, addresses, and telephone and fax numbers. We have found the following directories to be some of the most useful for international job seekers:

**The Directory of American Firms Operating in Foreign Countries** (New York: World Trade Academy Press, 1994, $195). This invaluable three-volume, 2,500+ page directory provides contact information on more the 3,200 U.S. companies operating in more than 120 countries. Provides information on the products/service lines of each company as well as identifies the counties in which they operate. Includes employment statistics and contact information. Available in major libraries or can be purchased directly from the publisher: World Trade Academy Press, 50 E. 42nd St., Suite 509, New York, NY 10017.

**Directory of Executive Recruiters** (Fitzwilliam, NH: Kennedy Publications, 1994, $39.95). This annual directory of executive recruiters includes numerous firms operating in the international arena. Includes nearly 4,000 offices of 2000 firms in the U.S., Canada, and Mexico. These firms work for employers in recruiting individuals with the right mix of skills and experience for specific positions. Complete with names, addresses, and telephone numbers for contacting key firms with employment contacts.

**Encyclopedia of Associations**, Carol A. Schwartz, ed. (Detroit, MI: Gale Research, 1994, $910.00). This annually revised three-volume set describes over 22,400 associations. Provides a wealth of information on each organization: names, address, phone and fax number, name of primary official, founding date, staff size, number of members, activities, budget, official publications, regional, state, and local groups.

**Encyclopedia of Associations: International Organizations**, Jackie Barrett, ed. (Detroit, MI: Gale Research, 1994, $455.00). Lists nearly 13,000 international organizations, including over 5,000 national organizations headquartered outside the U.S. Provides detailed information on trade and professional associations, social and welfare and public affairs organizations, and religious, sports and hobby groups with voluntary members, binational organizations, and national organizations in more than 180 countries.

**Encyclopedia of Women's Associations Worldwide**, Lesley Ripley Greenfield, ed. (Detroit, MI: Gale Research, 1993, $84.95). Identifies over 6,000 organizations throughout the world concerning women and women's issues. Includes groups focusing on such diverse topics as breast cancer, divorce, right-to-life and reproductive rights, rape, domestic violence, and family, parent, and infant issues. Includes contact information.

**Government Directory of Addresses and Telephone Numbers** (Detroit, MI: Omnigraphics, 1994, $129.95). The newest edition of this comprehensive directory includes addresses and telephone numbers of federal, state, county, and local government offices throughout the U.S.

**Hoover's Handbook of World Business**, Gary Hoover, Alta Campbell, Patrick J. Spain, and Alan Chai, eds. (Austin, TX: Ready Reference Press, 1994, $34.95). Surveys the major movers and shakers in the international business community. Includes facts, statistics, corporate histories, and profiles, along with contact information. Rates company strengths and identifies today's top world companies.

**InterAction Member Profiles** (Washington, DC: InterAction, 1993, $37.50). Profiles nearly 150 private humanitarian agencies that are members of the American Council for Voluntary International Action, one of the largest and most active groups of nonprofit organizations involved in all forms of development assistance, from health care and refugee aid to child care, environment management, human rights, disaster relief, and community development. Gives complete contact information on each organization, including names of key officers, as well as summarizes activities, identifies countries of operation, and financial details of each organization. Arranged alphabetically but also includes program and geographic indexes. This 356-page directory is an essential reference for anyone interested in working with U.S.-based international nonprofit organizations. This may be a hard-to-find publication. You can order it directly from the publisher: InterAction, 1717 Massachusetts Avenue NW, 8th Fl., Washington, DC 20036, Tel. 202/667-8227.

**The International Affairs Directory of Organizations: The ACCESS Resource Guide**, Bruce Seymore II, ed. (Santa Barbara, CA: AFC-CLIO,

Inc., 1992, $75.00). Profiles 865 organizations, specialists, and resources in 81 countries. Includes information on each organization's goals, strengths, resources, and specialists as well as an extensive bibliography.

**Internet Profiles, 1989-1990** (Chapel Hill, NC: Network for International Technical Assistance, 1989, $500). One of the most useful resources available for locating all types of organizations involved in development assistance, from engineering and construction firms operating in the Middle East and Asia to consulting firms, nonprofit organizations, and PVOs involved in delivering technical assistance in the areas of health care, population planning, and rural development in Africa and Latin America. Provides detailed information on all development-oriented organizations. Not widely available in public libraries. Now out of print and with no plans to publish an updated edition. Contact the publisher for information on where to find this directory: Network for International Technical Assistance, P.O. Box 3245, Chapel Hill, NC 27515, Tel. 919/968-8324.

**Key European Search Firms and Their U.S. Links** (Fitzwilliam, NH: Kennedy Publications, 1991, $39.95). This 200-page report, heavily cross-indexed, identifies European and U.S. search firms connected to each other by ownership, formal network, or affiliation. Profiles 100 international networks and identifies linkages of more than 500 search offices in the U.S. and 23 European countries. Includes names, addresses, and telephone and fax numbers.

**National Directory of Addresses and Telephone Numbers**, Darren L. Smith, ed. (Detroit, MI: Omnigraphics, 1994, $99.95). One of the best resources for contacting thousands of key organizations and employers. Provides current names, addresses, and telephone and fax numbers for businesses and services throughout the U.S. Includes over 140,000 listings organized alphabetically (white pages) and by business type (classified yellow pages). Includes over 110,000 fax numbers and over 14,500 toll-free numbers. Listings include top U.S. businesses, colleges and universities, travel and transportation services, government agencies, embassies and consulates, state and city chambers of commerce, U.S. Senators and Representatives, and business associations.

**National Fax Directory** (Detroit, MI: Gale Research, 1993, $85.00). This 2,200-page directory provides access to over 120,000 fax numbers for U.S. companies, organizations, government agencies, and libraries. Entries include complete addresses, fax numbers, and voice phone numbers.

**Personnel Executives Contactbook**, Cindy Spomer, ed. (Detroit, MI: Gale Research, 1993, $149.00). Offers complete contact information for key personnel officers in 30,000 companies across the U.S. Arranged alphabetically by company name, listings contain information most frequently requested by job hunters: company name, address, and phone number; SIC code; number of employees; annual revenues; name of the key personnel executives; and names of other human resource staff.

**Principal International Businesses 1992: The World Marketing Directory** (New York: Dun and Bradstreet International, 1991). Selective profiles of 50,000 firms in 143 countries. Includes information on sales volume, business activities, management, number of employees, and import/export rations.

**Russia 1994: Political and Economic Analysis and Business Directory**, Jonathan Schmidt, ed. (Bonn, New York, Taipei: Chamber World Network, 1994, $84.95). This new post-*perestroika* guide offers a comprehensive perspective on the historical, political, economic, and administrative context for doing business in Russia. Lists hundreds of Russian companies, arranged by industry. Includes Russian politics, economic reform programs, foreign assistance, foreign trade, foreign investment, labor, transportation, customs, and tips for getting set up in Russia. Identifies major international companies now operating in Russia.

**Ward's Business Directory of U.S. Public and Private Companies**, Information Access Company, ed. (Detroit, MI: Gale Research, 1993, $1,210.00). The most sought-after company directory on the market today. This monumental 5-volume set contains verified data on more than 135,00 U.S. businesses—over 90% of which are privately held. Includes names, addresses, phone and fax numbers; financial information and employee figures; number of employees; import/export information. Lists up to five company officers. The special Volume 4 includes the top 1,000 privately held and top 1,000 publicly held companies ranked by sales volume; top 1,000 U.S. employers ranked by number of employees; top 1,000 companies by revenue per employee.

**World Guide to Environmental Issues and Organizations**, Peter Prackley, ed. (Detroit, MI: Gale Research, 1991, $125.00). Provides comprehensive, international coverage of almost 250 key environmental issues and organizations including government organizations, public and private research projects, and regulatory and campaign organizations.

# EDUCATION, TRAVEL, AND STUDY ABROAD

If you have little or no international experience, you can quickly get experience by enrolling in an undergraduate or graduate international education program or participating in the many study and travel abroad programs sponsored by colleges, universities, and other educational organizations. Such programs help focus your international interests, clarify your career goals, and develop important contacts for future international employment. Some of the best sources of information on these programs include the following books and directories:

**Going Places: The High-School Student's Guide to Study, Travel, and Adventure Abroad**, Council on International Education Exchange (New

York: St. Martin's Press, 1994, $14.95). The ultimate guide for high school students desiring to study and travel abroad—from canoeing in Lithuania to studying French in Paris. Includes more than 200 programs for ages 12 to 18: study abroad, language institutes, creative arts, organized tours, outdoor activities, volunteer service, and homestays.

**Guide to International Education in the U.S.,** David and Kathleen Hoopes (Detroit, MI: Gale Research, 1991, $110.00). Includes nearly 3,800 descriptive entries arranged in three parts. A comprehensive guide to various programs, organizations, and publications concerned with international studies in the U.S. Topics in International, Intercultural, and Global Education; Area Studies by Region; and Area Studies by Country.

**International Scholarship Directory**, Daniel J. Cassidy (Hawthorne, NJ: Career Press, 1993, $24.95). Provides a comprehensive listing of scholarships and government- and armed forces-sponsored programs. Highlights special corporate programs that offer excellent "earn as you learn" training. Includes "exceptional" training opportunities for veterans, minorities, and disabled workers.

**Smart Vacations: The Traveler's Guide to Learning Adventures Abroad**, Council on International Education Exchange (New York: St. Martin's Press, 1994, $14.95). Features more than 200 one- to six-week learning vacations throughout the world: study tours, outdoor adventures, voluntary service, field research/archaeological digs, environmental and professional projects, fine arts, and more. Complete with practical details on programs and tips on selecting programs.

**Study Abroad, 1994.** (Princeton, NJ: Peterson's, 1994, $18.95). A comprehensive guide to semester and year abroad academic programs for both undergraduate and graduate students. Profiles over 1,300 programs offered by 350 accredited U.S. and international colleges and universities located in nearly 80 countries. Includes courses taught, credits, faculty, facilities, costs, financial aid, living arrangements, extracurricular activities, internship opportunities, and much more.

**Time Out: Taking a Break from School to Travel, Work, and Study in the U.S. and Abroad**, Robert Gilpin with Caroline Fitzgibbons (New York: Simon and Schuster, 1992). Profiles over 350 programs in the United States and abroad offering travel, work, and study opportunities for high school and college students.

**Work, Study, Travel Abroad: The Whole World Handbook**, Council on International Education Exchange (New York: St. Martin's Press, 1994, $13.95). One of the most useful guides to international living for students. Includes information on grants, exchange programs, teaching, travel, and work.

# JOB SEARCH BOOKS

Finding an international job involves much more than identifying the names, addresses, and telephone and fax numbers of major international employers. Indeed, one of the major weaknesses of many international job seekers is their over-reliance on contact information. Many fail to do their initial homework which involves acquiring the necessary job search skills in order to function effectively in the international job market. These job search skills are outlined in several major books which we identify in this section.

**Change Your Job, Change Your Life**, Ronald L. Krannich (Manassas Park, VA: Impact Publications, 1994, $14.95). One of the most highly acclaimed career books, this new edition outlines the key job and career issues facing millions of Americans today. Eleven how-to chapters on job search, relocation, entrepreneurship, and implementation specify how to organize and implement an effective job search, relocate to a new community, and start a business. Includes separate chapters on skills assessment, goal setting, research, resume and letter writing, networking, job interviews, and salary negotiations.

**The Complete Job Finder's Guide to the 90's**, Scott A. McDonald (Manassas Park, VA: Impact Publications, 1993, $13.95). Offers a strategy for quickly finding jobs and changing careers. Includes everything from setting goals, doing research, writing resumes and letters, and networking to conducting interviews, negotiating salaries, and relocating to new communities. Complete with numerous examples of effective resumes and cover letters.

**Electronic Job Search Revolution**, Joyce Lain Kennedy and Thomas J. Morrow (New York: Wiley and Sons, 1994, $12.95). The first book to outline the quiet revolution taking place in today's job market—electronic job hunting. Shows job seekers how computer resume databases work, how much they cost, and where they're located. Outlines the ins and outs of new applicant tracking software, electronic recruitment ads, computer-assisted interviewing, and more. Profiles several major companies in the forefront of this new revolution.

**Knock 'Em Dead**, John Yate (Holbrook, MA: Bob Adams, 1994, $19.95). This popular job search book covers the entire job search. Includes where the jobs are, finances, safety networking, electronic bulletin boards, corporate resume databases, the job interview, and salary negotiations.

**Rites of Passage at $100,000+**, John Lucht (New York: Viceroy Press, 1993, $29.95). One of the most comprehensive and insightful job search guides for executives and professionals. Includes tips on letters, resumes, interviewing, negotiating, contracts, and much more. Especially designed for high income earners.

**Through the Brick Wall**, Kate Wendleton (New York: Villard Books, 1992, $13.00). This complete job search guide gives practical advice on identifying skills, targeting jobs, writing resumes and letters, interviewing, networking, and negotiating salaries. One of the better general job search books.

**What Color is Your Parachute?**, Richard N. Bolles (Berkeley, CA: Ten Speed Press, 1994, $14.95). Newest annual revised edition of this classic career planning book provides a basic orientation to the job search process. Strong on self-assessment. The most popular career book ever published.

# RESUMES AND COVER LETTERS

Whether you like it or not, you will have to write a resume and write several letters if you plan to seek an international job. But how do you write resumes and letters that clearly communicate your qualifications to international employers? How long should your resume be and how does it different from a CV (curriculum vita) requested by many international employers? What exactly are electronic resumes and how do they differ from traditional resumes? How can you best distribute your resume so it gets into the hands of those who have the power to hire? When and how should you follow-up? These and many other questions relating to the form, content, distribution, and follow-up of your written job search communication are answered in several of the following books.

**200 Letters for Job Hunters**, William S. Frank (Berkeley, CA: Ten Speed Press, 1993, $17.95). Includes over 200 different letters designed to help job-hunters in many different situations.

**Dynamite Cover Letters**, Ron and Caryl Krannich (Manassas Park, VA: Impact Publications, 1994, $10.95). Outlines the major principles for writing outstanding letters relevant to conducting an effective job search: resume, application, approach, thank you, rejection, and acceptance. Includes numerous examples of outstanding letters.

**Dynamite Resumes**, Ron and Caryl Krannich (Manassas Park, VA: Impact Publications, 1994, $10.95). Outlines key resume principles, from writing each section to producing, distributing, and following-up. Includes numerous examples and evaluation instruments for transforming an average resume into a more powerful resume that will enhance the chances of being called for a job interview.

**Electronic Resume Revolution**, Joyce Lain Kennedy and Thomas J. Morrow (New York: Wiley and Sons, 1994, $12.95). Reveals how to get your resume in the fast evolving electronic job market. Shows how to write a resume that stands out when computers read it, from key woods to graphics.

**Electronic Resumes for the New Job Market: Resumes That Work for You 24 Hours a Day**, Peter D. Weddle (Manassas Park, VA: Impact Publications, 1992, $11.95). Prepares job seekers for one of the most important resources for finding jobs in the 1990s—electronic databases used by computerized job banks. Shows how to write a powerful resume that best fits into electronic databases. Explains how to use electronic job banks; design resumes; incorporate the right language to get your resume "read" frequently; and distribute your resume to electronic job banks. Includes numerous examples of effective electronic resumes.

**High Impact Resumes and Letters**, Ron Krannich and William Banis (Manassas Park, VA: Impact Publications, 1992, $12.95). Four times excerpted in the *National Business Employment Weekly* of *The Wall Street Journal* and widely adopted on college campuses nationwide, this bestselling book gives the latest advice on how to write a winning resume. Covers everything from self-assessment to resume production, distribution, and follow-up.

**Job Search Letters That Get Results: 201 Great Examples**, Ron and Caryl Krannich (Manassas Park, VA: Impact Publications, 1992, $12.95). Includes 201 examples of the six most important types of letters every job seeker needs to write. Based on key job search and letter writing principles.

**The Perfect Resume**, Tom Jackson (New York: Doubleday, 1990, $12.00). Revised and updated for the 1990s, this bestselling resume guide takes the reader through each step in the process of constructing an outstanding resume. Includes some examples but primarily stresses the resume development process.

**The Resume Catalog: 200 Damn Good Examples**, Yana Parker (Berkeley, CA: Ten Speed Press, 1999, $15.95). Includes a wide variety of resume examples, completely indexed and cross referenced, as well as tips on strengthening resume content. One of the best resume books that primarily presents examples.

**Resumes for Employment in the U.S. and Overseas** (New York; World Trade Academy Press, Inc., 1990, $16.95). The only resume book available which focuses only on international resumes. Includes resume writing tips, examples, and work permit requirements.

# NETWORKING

The most effective international job seekers know how to network for job information, advice, and referrals. Indeed, the best way to find an international job is by networking. But few people know how to network their way to job and career success. Here are the key books on networking. They outline practical strategies anyone can use in order to expand

and build their network of contacts for business, career, and social success.

**Dynamite Tele-Search**, Ron and Caryl Krannich (Manassas Park, VA: Impact Publications, 1994, $10.95). Addresses one of the most important activities in finding a job—using the telephone for uncovering job leads, getting interviews, and following-up resumes, letters, referrals, informational interviews, and job interviews. Outlines major principles for effective telephone communication and presents numerous sample dialogues and handy checklists for organizing and conducting a powerful telephone job search.

**Great Connections**, Anne Baber and Lynne Waymon (Manassas Park, VA: Impact Publications, 1992, $11.95). Shows how to develop small talk and networking skills in all types of business, social, and career situations. Filled with numerous examples and tips on how to make small talk work.

**How to Work a Room**, Susan RoAne (New York: Warner Books, 1989, $10.95). Shows how to successfully mingle at meetings, parties, and conventions. Presents numerous tips on how to develop new relationships and network.

**The *New* Network Your Way to Job and Career Success**, Ron and Caryl Krannich (Manassas Park, VA: Impact Publications, 1993, $12.95). Provides practical guidance on how to organize effective networks for job success. Shows how to prospect for new job leads, write effective networking letters, conduct informational interviews, and more. Includes examples of networking dialogues.

**Power Networking**, Donna and Sandy Vilas (Denver, CO: Bard Productions, 1992, $12.95). Packed with 55 proven networking methods for achieving success. Shows how to identify, organize, and expand networks; create visibility; make positive impressions; and more. Includes a self-assessment quiz.

**The Secrets of Savvy Networking**, Susan RoAne (New York: Warner Books, 1993, $11.99). Offers advice on the whys, hows, whens, and wheres of power networking. Shows how to know who's who, be heard and remembered, give and receive referrals, "work" the phone, tune into the grapevine, interpret different styles of men and women, and more.

# DRESS, APPEARANCE, IMAGE, ETIQUETTE

**Letitia Baldrige's Complete Guide to the New Manners for the '90s** (New York: Rawson Associates/Macmillan, 1990, $25.95). This up-to-date etiquette guide addresses numerous questions important to business and social situations in the 90s, from proper manners at home to dress, tipping, eating, relationships, and telephone manners.

**Lions Don't Need to Roar**, D. A. Benton (New York: Warner Books, 1993, $10.99). Reveals the techniques anyone can use to develop a powerful new corporate image. Covers the empowering pause, shaking hands, physical contact, posture, gestures, and more.

**Red Socks Don't Work: Messages From the Real World About Men's Clothing**, Kenneth J. Karpinski (Manassas Park, VA: Impact Publications, 1994). Presents everything men need to know about dress, appearance, and style, from avoiding 74 common fashion errors to selecting suits, jackets, ties, shirts, and trousers. Includes tailoring tips.

**The Winning Image**, James Gray, Jr. (New York: AMACOM, 1993, $17.95). Shows how to present oneself with confidence and style for career success. Includes wardrobe, body type, colors; speaking voice; interviews; meetings; and conversations.

# INTERVIEWING AND NEGOTIATING SALARIES

The job interview is the single most important step in getting a job. Employers want to see you in person where they can determine if they will "feel good" in hiring you. How well you do in the interview—from dress and appearance to answering and asking specific questions—will determine if you will be offered the job. The following books represent some of the best advice on how to conduct effective job interviews.

**Dynamite Answers to Interview Questions**, Caryl and Ron Krannich (Manassas Park, VA: Impact Publications, 1994, $10.95). Shows how to turn possible negative responses into positive answers for getting the job. Includes numerous examples of key questions interviewees need to both answer and ask.

**Dynamite Salary Negotiations**, Ron and Caryl Krannich (Manassas Park, VA: Impact Publications, 1994, $13.95). Outlines the major issues involved in determining salaries. Dispels numerous myths. Reveals how to value positions; acquire salary information; calculate your worth; respond to ads and applications requesting salary history; handle tough interview questions; negotiate salary and terms of employment; and finalize the job offer.

**Interview for Success**, Caryl and Ron Krannich (Manassas Park, VA: Impact Publications, 1993, $11.95). Fourth edition of this highly praised book prepares job seekers for different interviews, handle stress, observe etiquette, dress appropriately, listen, negotiate salary, and more. Includes informational interviewing along with job interviews and salary negotiations.

**Sweaty Palms**, H. Anthony Medley (Berkeley, CA: Ten Speed Press, 1991, $9.95). This popular interview guide describes common interview situations, explains the process, and suggests ways to turn any interview into a successful encounter. Filled with useful advice.

# INTERNATIONAL JOB STRATEGIES, EMPLOYERS, AND CONTACTS

A growing number of books provide important information on how to find an international job as well as lists of major international employers. While each one takes a different approach to the subject matter, they tend to cover similar territory—the job finding process and employers. We cover regional and country-specific guides in the next section. The following international job and career guides are some of the best available today.

**Almanac of International Jobs and Careers**, Ron and Caryl Krannich (Manassas Park, VA: Impact Publications, 1994, $19.95). Outlines the major international employers: government, international organizations, businesses, private voluntary organizations, nonprofit organizations, consulting firms, and education. Includes special chapters on internships, teaching abroad, and international job search resources.

**The Canadian Guide to Working and Living Overseas**, Jean-Marc Hachey (Ottawa: Intercultural Systems, 1992, $37.00). A comprehensive guide to major Canadian employers operating overseas, from government agencies to businesses and NGOs. Also includes the United Nations and a few U.S.-based consulting firms and NGOs. Briefly profiles each employer. Includes job search tips and an extensive annotated bibliography. One of the best international career books available. Relevant to non-Canadians. Difficult to find in the U.S. Order directly from the publisher: Intercultural Systems, P.O. Box 588, Station B, Ottawa, Ontario, Canada K1P 5P7; Tel. 613/238-6169 or Fax 713/238-5274.

**Careers in International Affairs**, Maria Pinto Carland and Daniel H. Spatz, Jr., eds. (Washington, DC: School of Foreign Service, Georgetown University, 1991, $15.00). Profiles major international employers: U.S. government, commercial banking, law, consulting, trade and professional associations, research organizations, and nonprofit organizations. Includes contact information. A hard-to-find book which is best acquired directly from Georgetown University's School of Foreign Service.

**The Complete Guide to International Jobs and Careers**, Ron and Caryl Krannich (Manassas Park, VA: Impact Publications, 1992, $13.95). Helps job seekers better understand the what, where, and how of the international job market. Provides frank answers to the most important questions about international jobs. Exposes myths and provides a realistic view of today's competitive international job market. Outlines the most effective job search strategies for finding an international job. The companion volume to the authors' *Almanac of International Jobs and Careers.*

**The Directory of Jobs and Careers Abroad**, Andre De Vries (Oxford, England: Vacation Work, 1993, $16.95). A guide to permanent career opportunities abroad for people of educational and professional achievement. Lists the top trades and professions in Europe, Australia, and New Zealand as well as details on qualifications.

**Guide to Careers in World Affairs**, Foreign Policy Association, eds. (Manassas Park, VA: Impact Publications, 1993, $14.95). One of the finest international job and career books available. This new addition profiles hundreds of major international employers in the fields of business, consulting, finance, banking, journalism, law, translation, government, health, research, education, and development assistance and includes special essays on each field. Includes names, addresses, telephone numbers, staff information, qualifications, and application procedures.

**International Careers: An Insider's Guide**, David Win (Charlotte, VT: Williamson Publishing, 1987, $10.95). Presents an entire international career-building process. Surveys public and private sector organizations. Includes tips on how to market expertise internationally.

**International Jobs**, Eric Kocher (Reading, MA: Addison-Wesley, 1993, $14.95). Fourth edition of this guide discusses over 500 international career opportunities. Discusses educational opportunities as well as profiles major employers along with contact information.

**Making It Abroad**, Howard Schuman (New York: Wiley and Sons, 1988, $12.95). Examines how to find an international job with various types of public and private organizations. Includes the job search process along with a useful resource section.

**Passport to Overseas Employment**, Dale Chambers (New York: Prentice-Hall, 1990, $14.95). Provides basic information on employment abroad which is readily available in other published sources. Includes country-by-country work permit requirements, and employment opportunities with the United Nations, U.S. government, airlines, cruise lines, and tourist organizations.

## MAJOR REGIONS AND COUNTRIES

If your employment interests center on specific regions or countries, you may want to consult some of the following international job books which are organized by region or country rather than ones which are organized by employer or industry.

**Getting Your Job in the Middle East**, David Lay (Tampa, FL: DCL Publications, 1992, $19.95). Reveals numerous employment opportunities in the Middle East. Takes readers step-by-step through the process of landing an overseas job. Includes tax advantages, labor conditions, jobs

available, and addresses and phone numbers for contacting potential
employers.

**How to ....  Series** (Plymouth, United Kingdom: How to Books, 1991-
1994, $17.95 each; available in the U.S. through Impact Publications).
Most books in this series address job opportunities in major countries in
Europe as well as in Saudi Arabia, Japan, Hong Kong, Australia, New
Zealand, and Canada. Each book addresses entry requirements, work
permits, employment, doing business, getting around, health, education,
lifestyles, and much more.

- **How to Get a Job Abroad**
- **How to Get a Teaching Job**
- **How to Live and Work in Australia**
- **How to Live and Work in Belgium**
- **How to Live and Work in Canada**
- **How to Live and Work in France**
- **How to Live and Work in Germany**
- **How to Live and Work in Hong Kong**
- **How to Live and Work in Italy**
- **How to Live and Work in Japan**
- **How to Live and Work in New Zealand**
- **How to Live and Work in Portugal**
- **How to Live and Work in Saudi Arabia**
- **How to Live and Work in Spain**

**How to Get a Job in Europe**, Robert Sanborn (Chicago, IL: Surrey
Books, 1993, $17.95). This practical, how-to guide shows how to get a job
in Western Europe. Explains exactly where to look, how to conduct a
European job search, coping with regulations and paperwork, and landing
the job you want in 12 countries.

**How to Get a Job in the Pacific Rim**, Robert Sanborn (Chicago, IL:
Surrey Books, 1992, $17.95). Provides names, addresses, and phone
numbers for American and foreign companies hiring Americans. Discusses
career trends, salaries, required paperwork, programs, options, and much
more on employment in each Pacific Rim country.

**The Job Hunter's Guide to Japan**, Terra Brockman (New York:
Kodansha America, Inc., 1990, $12.95). An intelligent and practical
manual for job search success in Japan. Examines several different
occupational fields appropriate for foreigners in Japan.

**Jobs in Russia and the Newly Independent States**, Moira Forbes
(Manassas Park, VA: Impact Publications, 1994, $15.95). This unique
book identifies numerous opportunities in Russia and the Newly Independent States, from business and government jobs to volunteer opportunities.
Summarizes recent developments in each country, describes opportunities,
includes names and addresses of employers, and much more.

**Working in the Persian Gulf**, Blythe Camenson (Coral Springs, FL: Desert Diamond Books, 1991, $16.95). Addresses numerous questions about working in the Persian Gulf. Includes information on job hunting, pre-arrival, and settling-in produces. Discusses where the jobs are, salaries, benefits, resumes, social life, culture shock, rules to follow, and job contacts.

# GOVERNMENT

The federal government offers numerous international job opportunities. While most people think the Department of State is the major employer of international specialists, it is only one of many. International positions are found throughout the federal government, from the State Department to the Agency for International Development, Peace Corps, Department of Commerce, Department of Education, Department of Defense, and committees on Capitol Hill. Sorting out which agencies do international work and then mastering the art of getting a federal job are extremely time consuming tasks. The following books help simplify this process for you.

**Almanac of American Jobs and Careers**, Ron and Caryl Krannich (Manassas Park, VA: Impact Publications, 1991, $14.95). The companion volume to the authors' *Find a Federal Job Fast*. Profiles federal government agencies and provides critical contact information for finding jobs with the agencies.

**Find a Federal Job Fast**, Ron and Caryl Krannich (Manassas Park, VA: Impact Publications, 1994, $14.95). A basic primer on how to find a federal job in today's highly competitive job market. Dispels myths, outlines hiring procedures, provides tips on the all-important SF 171, and includes contact information.

**How to Find an Overseas Job With the U.S. Government**, Will Cantrell and Francine Modderno (Oakton, VA: WorldWise Books, 1992, $28.95). The first book to focus solely on international job opportunities throughout the federal government. Profiles the major agencies offering international job opportunities. Describes agencies, qualifications required, and application procedures.

**The Right SF 171 Writer**, Russ Smith (Manassas Park, VA: Impact Publications, 1994, $19.95). The definitive guide to completing the all-important Standard Form 171. Dispels myths, outlines what federal employers look for on the SF 171, specifies major writing principles, summaries the best language to use, shows how to customize the form, and provides critical information for completing the form. Includes examples of completed SF 171s.

# INTERNSHIPS AND VOLUNTEER EXPERIENCES

Internships are readily available with international organizations located in the U.S. and abroad. As noted in the previous chapter on internships and volunteer experiences, many of these internships are unpaid and primarily designed for undergraduate and graduate students who combine study, travel, and work experiences.

**Directory of International Internships: A World of Opportunities**, Thomas D. Luten, Charles A. Gliozzo, and Timothy J. Aldinger, eds. (East Lansing, MI: Michigan State University, Career Development and Placement Services, 1990, $20.00). Identifies hundreds of paid and unpaid internships with organizations located abroad.

**International Directory of Voluntary Work**, David Woodworth (Oxford, England: Vacation Work, 1993, $15.95). Newest edition of this popular guide describes over 600 organizations that need short- and long-term volunteers with varied skills, from working on an agricultural project in Africa to helping in a Romanian orphanage.

**International Internships and Volunteer Programs**, Will Cantrell and Francine Modderno (Oakton, VA: WorldWise Books, 1992, $18.95). One of the most comprehensive guides on internships and volunteer programs for Americans. Includes internships with government, international organizations, academic programs, and nonprofit organizations. Gives contact information and profiles.

**Internships: 1994** (Princeton, NJ: Peterson's, 1994, $29.95). This annual directory includes a section on international internships. Profiles employers, including contact information, duration of internships, compensation, and application process and deadlines.

**Volunteer! The Comprehensive Guide to Voluntary Service in the U.S. and Abroad**, Adrienne Dorney, ed. (New York: Council on International Education Exchange, 1992, $8.95). Describes over 200 voluntary service organizations offering short- and long-term volunteer opportunities in the U.S. and abroad.

**Volunteer Vacations**, Bill McMillon (Chicago: Chicago Review Press, 1993, $11.95). Profiles more than 240 groups which sponsor volunteer projects in the U.S. and abroad.

# TRAVEL AND HOSPITALITY INDUSTRY

Many individuals interested in international jobs and careers are really most interested in travel. They believe an international job is synonymous with travel. While this is true in some cases, it is not true in other cases.

Indeed, some international jobs may restrict travel, especially if they are in countries with strict work permit, tax, and travel requirements. Consequently, many so-called international job seekers might be better off pursuing their real passion—a job in the travel and hospitality industry. These are some of the most exciting and satisfying jobs available today. We expect they will increase dramatically in number during the second half of the 1990s as more and more people travel in the booming economy of the late 1990s. The following books and directories outline major opportunities in this industry.

**Flying High in Travel**, Karen Rubin (New York: Wiley and Sons, 1992, $16.95). Surveys the travel industry and profiles different job options, including hundreds of jobs people outside the industry never hear about. Includes useful resource section with addresses.

**Guide to College Programs in Hospitality and Tourism**, Council on Hotel, Restaurant, and Institutional Education (New York: Wiley and Sons, 1993, $19.95). This directory includes a complete, up-to-date listing of the colleges and universities offering courses in the hospitality and tourism field. Examines career opportunities in the industry and explains how to go about choosing a curriculum. Covers programs in culinary arts, hotel/motel management, restaurant and food services, and travel and tourism.

**How to Get a Job With a Cruise Line**, Mary Fallon Miller (Tampa, FL: Ticket to Adventure, 1991, $12.95). Provides insider's information on what one needs to do to get a job with a cruise line. Includes skills required, who's hiring whom, types of jobs, job contacts, where to write, and more.

**The Insider's Guide to Air Courier Bargains: How to Travel Worldwide for Next to Nothing**, Kelly Monagham (New York: The Intrepid Traveler, 1994, $14.95). Reveals the best kept secret in budget travel—how to become an air courier and travel free or at a fraction of the lowest available fare. Identifies the what, why, and how of air couriers. Includes contact information.

**Jobs for People Who Love Travel**, Ron and Caryl Krannich (Manassas Park, VA: Impact Publications, 1993, $12.95). Identifies numerous jobs and careers that enable individuals to travel both at home and abroad. Surveys hundreds of jobs in business and government, including summer jobs abroad, international careers, jobs in the travel industry, import/export opportunities, and sales and training positions. Includes tips on how to get the right job as well as names, addresses, and telephone numbers for contacting potential employers.

**Travel and Hospitality Career Directory**, Bradley J. Morgan, ed. (Detroit, MI: Visible Ink Press, 1992, $17.95). Examines career opportunities in airlines, cruise lines, hotels, resorts, meeting planning, and travel agencies. Includes a directory of nearly 250 companies offering entry-level positions or internships, publications, professional associations, and job listings.

# SHORT-TERM JOBS ABROAD

You may be surprised to discover how many short-term job opportunities are available abroad. Many are most appropriate for young, single college students who want to work briefly abroad but who do not expect to make a great deal of money. Many of these jobs are part-time, low paying, and relatively unskilled positions. Au pair and nanny's, for example, are in great demand in England and France; several placement firms can arrange for Americans to find such childcare positions in the United Kingdom and Europe. Other jobs can be found in ski resorts, hotels, and restaurants as well as on farms, in factories, and on yachts.

The following set of books and directories identify exactly where you can find such jobs. Most are organized by countries and include critical contact information for landing a short-term job. While all of these directories are published in the United Kingdom, several of them are widely distributed in the United States.

**The Au Pair and Nanny's Guide to Working Abroad**, Susan Griffith and Sharon Legg (Oxford, England: Vacation Work, 1993, $14.95). Shows how to prepare for and acquire a childcare job abroad. Includes a listing of placement agencies.

**Directory of Overseas Summer Jobs**, David Woodworth, ed. (Oxford, England: Vacation Work, 1994; $14.95; available in the U.S. through Peterson's). Reveals more than 50,000 jobs worldwide. Includes whom to contact, length of employment, number of openings, pay rates, how/when to apply, and visa and work permit requirements.

**The Hitchhiker's Guide to the Oceans: Crewing Around the World**, Alison Bennet and Clair Davis (Seven Seas Press, 1990, $10.95). Shows how world travelers and enterprising job seekers can find yacht jobs throughout the world.

**Jobs in Paradise**, Jeffrey Maltzman, ed. (New York: HarperCollins, 1992, $12.95). A guide to cruise ship, resort, and 200,000+ other dream jobs in the U.S., Canada, South Pacific, and Caribbean. Includes everything from mountain climbing, skiing, and white water rafting to lake resorts, amusement parks, and cruise ships. Includes contact information.

**Summer Jobs Britain 1994**, Emily Hatchwell, ed. (Oxford, England: Vacation Work, 1994, $15.95; available in the U.S. through Peterson's).

Identifies 30,000 jobs in Scotland, Wales, and England for hotel/resort workers, office help, farm laborers, chambermaids, lorry drivers—plus tips on applications, visas, and work permits.

**Work Your Way Around the World**, Susan Griffith (Oxford, England: Vacation Work, 1994, $17.95; available in the U.S. through Peterson's). Provides detailed information and inside tips on working in Europe, North America, Australia, Africa, Asia, and the Caribbean. Includes names and addresses for jobs in agriculture, tourism, teaching, domestic work, business, and industry. Most jobs listed in this directory are low paying positions appropriate for budget travelers interested in "experiencing" the world by picking up short-term work to pay their expenses as they wander the globe. Not for serious career-minded international types.

**Working in Ski Resorts—Europe**, Victoria Pybus and Charles James (Oxford, England: Vacation Work, 1994, $13.95). Outlines the various types of jobs available in European ski resorts. Identifies the major employers and employment conditions and includes contact information.

# BUSINESS, ENTREPRENEURSHIP, CONSULTING

The 1990s appear to be a banner decade for businesses, entrepreneurs, and consultants who know how to market their products and services to others in the international arena.

**Building an Import/Export Business**, Kenneth D. Weiss (New York: Wiley & Sons, 1991, $14.95). A complete guide to entering the import/export business. Includes everything from product selection to handling the details of the business.

**Doing Business in Mexico**, Jay and Maggie Jessup (Rocklin, CA: Prima Publications, 1993, $21.95). This how-to guide to exporting, importing, investing, and manufacturing in Mexico includes information on franchising opportunities, tourism, environmental products, emerging industries, trade shows, and consultants.

**How to Be an Importer and Pay For Your World Travel**, Mary Green and Stanley Gillmar (Berkeley, CA: Ten Speed Press, 1993, $8.95). New edition of this classic guide shows how to make a career out of your favorite pastime—travel. Filled with useful tips for success.

**The International Businesswoman of the 1990s: A Guide to Success in the Global Marketplace**, Marlene L. Rossman (New York: Praeger, 1990, $19.95). Explores important trends today's businesswomen traveling abroad should address. Includes travel, customs, and even dress.

**The International Consultant**, H. Peter B. Guttman (New York: Wiley and Sons, 1988, $22.95). Outlines how to become an international consultant. Includes tips on making this a rewarding career and lifestyle.

# RELOCATION AND LIVING ABROAD

Deciding on where you want to work involves knowing something about a country and process of relocating and living abroad. Several directories and books will assist you in acquiring this specialized knowledge.

**An American's Guide to Living Abroad**, Louis M. Guido, ed. (Princeton, NJ: Living Abroad Publishing, Inc., 1992, $29.95). Presents practical information on living abroad. Produced in five separate editions: Western Europe, Eastern Europe, the Middle East, Japan, and Asia/Pacific. Since these publications are not widely available, it's best to order from the publisher: Living Abroad Publishing, Inc., 199 Nassau St., Princeton, NJ 08540.

**Craighead's International Business, Travel, and Relocation Guide to 81 Countries, 1994-1995**, Craighead Publications, Inc. (Detroit: Gale Research, 1993, $425). The most comprehensive resource available on business practices, economies, customs, communications, tours, attractions, and other highlights of 81 countries. These two big volumes (2,680 pages) include country profiles as well as details on restrictions, currency, culture, transportation, health, and more. Includes sections on visas, passports, transportation, and shopping, financial planning, legal matters, insurance, education, housing, and other family concerns.

**The *New* Relocating Spouse's Guide to Employment**, Fran Bastress (Manassas Park, VA: Impact Publications, 1993, $14.95). Addresses critical employment issues facing millions of mobile families in corporations, the military, the foreign service, academia, the ministry, and other work settings. Shows how to approach the job search under adverse circumstances. Includes everything from identifying skills to writing resumes, networking, and interviewing.

**Women's Guide to Overseas Living**, Nancy J. Piet-Pelon and Barbara Hornby (Yarmouth, ME: Intercultural Press, 1992, $14.95). One of the best overseas living guides. Discusses culture shock, handling stress and loneliness, staying healthy, handling children, finding employment, and re-entry.

# JOB LISTINGS, DATABASES, AND SUBSCRIPTIONS

Several companies publish international job listings on a biweekly, monthly, or quarterly basis. A few companies now operate electronic databases with regularly updated international job listings and resume banks. We include in this section some of the major such publications, databases, and job banks for international jobs, federal government jobs, nonprofit organizations, and international teaching positions, We also identify two publications which include informative articles on work, study, living, and travel abroad.

**Bulletin of Overseas Teaching Opportunities** (72 Franklin Avenue, Ocean Grove, NJ 07756; also available through Impact Publications; 1 year subscription is $38). This monthly bulletin lists numerous job openings for teachers worldwide. Includes positions in all subject areas, including TESOL, at both the elementary and secondary levels. Most positions require little or no teaching experience, and the only language requirement is English.

**Career Network** (National Council for International Health, 1701 K Street, NW, Suite 600, Washington, DC 20036, Tel. 202/833-0070 or 202/833-5900; 1 year subscription is $60 for members and $120 for nonmembers). This monthly job listing bulletin includes nearly 60 vacancies per issue. Includes jobs for international health care professionals only.

**Community Jobs**. (ACCESS: Networking in the Public Interest, 50 Beacon St., Boston, MA 02108, Tel. 617/720-5627; also available through Impact Publications; $39 for 6 months; $69 for 1 year). A monthly 40+ page newspaper which lists jobs with the nonprofit sector. Includes informative articles, book reviews, resource lists, profiles of nonprofits, and over 200 listings with nonprofit organizations in the U.S. and abroad. Includes internships—from entry-level to executive director.

**Federal Career Opportunities** (Federal Research Service, P.O. Box 1059, Vienna, VA 22183-1059, Tel. 800/822-5627 or 703/281-0200; also available through Impact Publications; $39 for 6 issues or $175.00 for 26 issues). Published biweekly, this 64-90 page directory is the most comprehensive listing of current federal job vacancies. Includes 3,400 positions from grades GS5 thru SES.

**Federal Jobs Digest** (Breakthrough Publications, P.O. Box 594, Millwood, NY 10546, Tel. 800/824-5000 or 914/762-5111; also available through Impact Publications; $29 for 6 issues or $110 for 25 issues). Largest source of current job openings, listing over 15,000 immediate civil service vacancies in the U.S. and overseas in each issue. Published biweekly. Includes informative articles.

**International Affairs Bulletin** (Jeffries & Associates, 17200 Hughes Rd., Poolesville, MD 20837, Tel. 301/972-8034; $95 for 12 issues). Published monthly, this job bulletin includes vacancy information on positions with government agencies, consulting firms, educational institutions, and PVOs.

**International Career Databank** (Jeffries & Associates, 17200 Hughes Rd., Poolesville, MD 20837, Tel. 301/972-8034; $275 plus $5 shipping for first year and $125 for subsequent annual renewal). Updated monthly, this database includes overseas job vacancies, internships, and fellowships with the U.S. federal government and United Nations as well as vacancies with businesses and nonprofit organizations. Requires IBM or compatible computer with Microsoft Windows.

**International Career Employment Opportunities** (Route 2, Box 305, Stanardville, VA 22973, Tel. 804/985-6444; also available through Impact Publications; $195.00 for 26 biweekly issues). Each biweekly 44-page newsletter includes over 500 current job openings in the U.S. (40%) and abroad (60%), in foreign affairs, trade and finance, development and assistance, foreign languages, program administration, and education and exchange programs. Includes government, business, nonprofits, international institutions, and internships.

**International Educator** (P.O. Box  513, Cummaquid, MA 02637, Tel. 508/362-1414; also available through Impact Publications; one year subscription is $29.00). Published four times a year. Each 50+ page issue includes numerous job vacancies along with informative articles on international educators. Subscribers receive a free 16-page booklet, *"TIE's Complete Guide to Finding a Job in an International School,"* which outlines job opportunities with 800 elementary and secondary schools that hire American teachers and administrators.

**International Employment Gazette** (1525 Wade Hampton Blvd,. Greenville, SC 29609, Tel. 800/882-9188; also available through Impact Publications; $36 for 6 issues; $55 for 12 issues or $95 for 24 issues). Published every two weeks, each issue includes over 400 international job vacancies representing a wide range of international skills. Especially good for locating overseas vacancies.

**International Employment Hotline** (P.O. Box 3030, Oakton, VA 22124, Tel. 703/620-1972; also available through Impact Publications; 1 year subscription is $39.00). Monthly report on "who's hiring now" for overseas jobs with the government, private sector, and nonprofit organizations. Includes informative articles on trends and strategies.

**International Jobs Bulletin** (International Employment Service, University Placement Center, Carbondale, IL 62901-4703, Tel. 618/453-2391; $20 for 12 issues). This biweekly publication includes job listings with government, education, and volunteer organizations. Send a stamped, self-addressed envelope for a free sample copy.

**International Living** (Agora Publishing, 824 E. Baltimore St., Baltimore, MD, 21202, Tel. 800/433-1528; 12 issues for $29 or 24 issues for $48). This monthly newsletter includes informative articles on living, working, and investing abroad.

**International Placement Network** (Global Resources Organization, 1525 Wade Hampton Blvd,. Greenville, SC 29609, Tel. 800/882-9188, $45). This service attempts to match an individual's occupational interests, geographic preferences, skills, and experience with available job openings. After completing and submitting an application/registration form, this service generates a 15 to 40 page printout, consisting of four jobs per page, which meet the individual's requirements.

**Monday Developments** (InterAction, 1717 Massachusetts Ave., NW, 8th Floor, Washington, DC 20036, Tel. 202/667-8227; $65 for 1 year). This biweekly newsletter includes several vacancy announcements for positions with nonprofit organizations that are members of InterAction, the major association of international PVOs.

**Options** (Project Concern, 3550 Afton Road, San Diego, CA 92123, Tel. 619/279-9690; $25 a year). This bimonthly publication includes volunteer positions for health care professionals in the U.S., East Asia, the Pacific, Latin America, and Africa. Includes nearly 250 listings per issue.

**Talent Bank** (TransCentury Corporation, 1901 N. Fort Meyer Drive, Suite 1017, Arlington, VA 22209, Tel. 703/351-5500). Specializing in short-term consulting opportunities in international development, this service compiles resumes for referral to companies seeking relevant international talent. In order to get into the resume bank, you need to request and complete a "Professional Skills Registration Form." Send it, along with your resume, to TransCentury Corporation.

**Transitions Abroad** (Transitions Abroad, Box 3000, Denville, NJ 07834; $19.95 per year). This bimonthly magazine includes informative articles and essential information on travel, work, living, and study. Be sure to get the special July/August issue entitled *"Educational Travel Resource Guide"* which is one of the most extensive and up-to-date directories of key resources and organizations on travel, work, living, and study abroad. This special issue can be purchased for $5.00.

# AUDIO/WORKBOOK PROGRAM

The following audiocassette program is the only one of its kind for international job seekers.

**How to Get a Job Overseas** (Denver, CO: Slater Associates, 1992, $79.95; available through Impact Publications). This complete audio/workbook program includes over 5 hours of intensive instruction. Includes everything from the structure of the job market to writing resumes, interviewing, negotiating salaries, and approaching numerous types of international employers.

# COMPUTER SOFTWARE

**INSTANT™ Job Winning Letters** (Englewood, CO: CareerLab, 1993, $39.95). Easy-to-use software (IBM) based on Bill Frank's book, *200*

*Letters for Job Hunters.* Includes more than 200 letters. Use to answer want ads, impress recruiters, break into new companies, make cold calls, arrange interviews, negotiate salary, and much more. IBM and compatibles only.

**Quick and Easy 171s** (Harrisonburg, PA: DataTech, 1994, $49.95 for single user program; $59.95 for 2-user program; $129.95 for 8-user program; $399.95 for unlimited user program). Produces outstanding SF 171's for federal government employment. Provides direct support for over 50 dot matrix printers, the DeskJet 500, and laser printers that are compatible with the Hewlett Parkard LaserJet II. Prints the form. Approved by OPM. For IBM/compatible systems only. Available for both DOS and Windows.

**The Ultimate Job Finder**, Daniel Lauber (Orem, UT: InfoBusiness, 1993, $59.95). This unique, inexpensive, and easy-to-use software program gives instant access to over 4,500 sources of job vacancies, including job hotlines, trade press, and job-matching services. Includes several government and international sources. IBM or compatible. Requires 2.5 Mb on hard drive.

# ELECTRONIC RESUME DATABASES

Several companies operate electronic databases which link employers to job seekers. Participation in these databases involves a yearly membership and a resume. The companies use sophisticated search and retrieval software that literally "reads" your resume in reference to qualifications specified by employers. Membership in these databases does not guarantee you will be contacted by employers. It means your resume is in the database and it may lead to making contact with employers who seek your qualifications. Some employers who seek candidates for international positions use these databases. If you decide to use these databases, be sure you prepare your resume according to principles outlined in two new books on this subject (see section above on Resumes and Cover Letters): *Electronic Resumes for the New Job Market* and *Electronic Resume Revolution.*

**Career Placement Registry** (Career Placement Registry, Inc., 302 Swann Ave., Alexandria, VA 22301, Tel. 800/368-3093 or 703/683-1085. Includes over 110,000 employers in its database. Individuals can register for a six-month period for a variety of fees, depending on desired salary level. For example, students can register for $15; individuals seeking a job up to $20,000 register for $25; those with salary expectations in the $20,001-$40,000 range register for $35; those expecting a salary of $40,000+ register for $45. Recruiters can access the Career Placement Registry on DIALOG.

**Connexion®** (Peterson's Connexion® Services, 202 Carnegie Center, P.O. Box 2123, Princeton, NJ 08543-2123, Tel. 800/338-3282, Ext. 561 or Fax 609-243-9150). Advertised as "the innovative recruitment network that links you with thousands of employers and graduate schools who may be seeking candidates with your specific experience or training." Unlike other electronic networks, Connexion® includes graduate schools in its recruitment base. Membership is free for currently enrolled full-time students. Others can enroll for an annual fee of $40. Those who do not want their resumes sent to employers, but who want access to other Connexion® privileges and communiques, can join as Associate Members for an annual fee of $24.95. Network can be accessed on CompuServe.

**Internet** (Online Career Center, Online Resume Service, 1713 Hemlock Lane, Plainfield, IN 46168). This nonprofit organization, sponsored by 40 major corporations, allows job seekers to review hundreds of vacancy announcements posted in its computer database. It also accepts resumes so that companies can search for talented employees. For a fee of only $6.00, job seekers can have their resume entered into the computer database for a 90-day period. Computer users can browse through hundreds of vacancy announcements and resumes by accessing Internet, a worldwide group of 25,000 corporate, education, and research computer networks used by over 20 million people. Approximately 3,000 companies use Internet for recruiting purposes. You need access to Internet in order to access the Online Career Center. If you have access, you should send the following electronic mail message: occmsen.com. Then type "info" on the subject line. You will receive instructions on what to do next. You can get access to Internet by contacting the following companies: American Online (800/827-6364); CompuServe (800/848-8199); Delphi (800/491-3393); IDS (401/884-7856); or Worldline (800/NET-2-YOU). Finally, if you do not have a computer and modem, send a copy of your resume along with $6.00 to: Online Resume service, 1713 Hemlock Lane, Plainfield, IN 46168. If your resume runs more than three pages, add $1.50 for each additional page.

**Job Bank USA** (1420 Spring Hill Road, Suite 480, McLean, VA 22102, Tel. 800/296-1USA or Fax 703/847-1494). Advertised as the "nation's premier database company," Job Bank USA is an all purpose employment resource for both employers and job seekers. Individuals can enroll in the Job Bank USA database for a basic annual fee of $48.50. Other levels of enrollment cost $78.00 and $129.00. Members receive several services in addition to entry of their resume into the database. Job Bank USA also offers testing/assessment and resume writing services.

**kiNexus** (Information Kinetics, Inc., 640 N. LaSalle St., Suite 560, Chicago, IL 60610, Tel. 800/229-6499 or Fax 312/642-0616). Advertises itself as "the nation's first and largest computerized database of experienced executives, college and university students and alumni seeking part-time and full-time employment." Its current database includes over 150,000 active job seekers. Designed primarily for graduating college students and companies interested in communicating directly with career and placement centers in advertising job vacancies and identifying and interviewing candidates, this on-campus electronic job listing and advertising system operates "Career Network" on over 100 college and university campuses. Students and alumni at nearly 800 colleges and universities can register with kiNexus through their Career Center at no charge. If you have any questions on your free eligibility or wish to enroll directly, contact kiNexus for information on their services: Tel. 800-229-6499.

# CD-ROM

CD-ROM programs designed for job seekers should increasingly become available in the coming months as more and more CD-ROM players come into use with personal computers. One of the first such programs, which includes eleven of our career planning and job search books, along with a comprehensive job search video program and key reference book, has just been released as this book goes to press.

**Job Power Source: Job Finding Skills for the 90s** (Orem, UT: InfoBusiness, 1994, $49.95 for Individual Version; $149.95 for Institutional Version). This unique multimedia CD-ROM takes users through the process of identifying their skills and matching those skills with a specific job/career. Includes occupational outlooks on over 200 career areas with in-depth descriptions of salaries, educational and training requirements, working conditions, prospects for future career growth, and more. Enables users to write effective resumes and letters. Teaches the principles of networking, interviewing, and negotiating salaries. Program includes eleven career and job search books written by Ron and Caryl Krannich and two hours of job search videos by award winning communications specialist/trainer Pat Sladey. Institutional Version ($149.95) includes the *Dictionary of Occupational Titles* which is absent from the less expensive Individual Version ($49.95).

# INDEX

---

## SUBJECTS

---

# ORGANIZATIONS AND EMPLOYERS

# M

M.W. Kellogg Company, 128
Management Sciences for Health, 195-196
Management Systems International, Inc., 130
Manufacturers Hanover, 88
MAP International, 169, 264
Marine Midland Bank, 88
Maritz Travel, 97
Marriott Corp., 96
Marymount Study Abroad Program, 255
Massachusetts Institute of Technology, 217
Mathtech, Inc., 131
Matsushita, 97
McKinsey and Co., 90
Medical Care Development, Inc., 196
Medical Service Corporation International, 131
Meharry Medical College, 218
Mellon Bank Corporation, 89
Mennonite Central Committee, 169
Mercer Consulting Group, 90
Mercy Corps International, 169
Meridian House International, 74
Meridian International Center, 265
Meridien Hotels, 96
Merrill Lynch & Co., Inc., 89
Meta Systems, Inc., 131
Metcalf & Eddy International, Inc., 131-132
Michelin, 97
Michigan State University, 218
MidAmerican International Agricultural Consortium, 196
Middle East Institute, 265
Minnesota Mining and Manufacturing (3M), 85
Minnesota Studies in International Development, 265
Mississippi State University, 219
Mitsubishi International Corporation, 89
MMM Design Group, 132
Monsanto Chemical Co., 85
Montana State University, 219
Montgomery Watson, Inc., 132
Morehouse School of Medicine, 219
Morgan Guaranty Trust Company of New York, 89
Morgan Stanley, 89
Morgan State University, 220
Morris Travel—Ask Mr. Foster, 95
Morrison-Knudsen Corporation, 132-133
Morrison-Maierle/CSSA, Inc., 133
Motorola, Inc., 85
Mudge, Rose, Guthrie, Alexander, and Feldon, 91
Murray State University, 220

# N

National Aeronautics and Space Administration, 30

## O

# ANNOTATED INTERNATIONAL RESOURCES

# CAREER
# RESOURCES

Contact Impact Publications to receive a free copy of their latest comprehensive and annotated catalog of over 1,000 career resources (books, subscriptions, training programs, videos, audiocassettes, computer software, and CD-ROM).

The following career resources, many of which are mentioned in previous chapters, are available directly from Impact Publications. Complete the following form or list the titles, include postage (see formula at the end), enclose payment, and send your order to:

**IMPACT PUBLICATIONS**
9104-N Manassas Drive
Manassas Park, VA 22111-5211
Tel. 703/361-7300 or fax 703/335-9486

Orders from individuals must be prepaid by check, moneyorder, Visa or MasterCard number. We accept telephone and fax orders with a Visa or MasterCard number.

| Qty. | TITLES | Price | TOTAL |
|------|--------|-------|-------|

**INTERNATIONAL JOBS**

| | | | |
|------|--------|-------|-------|
| ___ | Almanac of International Jobs and Careers | $19.95 | _____ |
| ___ | Complete Guide to International Jobs & Careers | $13.95 | _____ |
| ___ | Directory of Jobs and Careers Abroad | $16.95 | _____ |

___ Guide to Careers in World Affairs     $14.95 ___
___ International Careers     $10.95 ___
___ International Jobs     $14.95 ___
___ Making It Abroad     $12.95 ___
___ Passport to Overseas Employment     $14.95 ___

## MAJOR REGIONS AND COUNTRIES

___ Getting Your Job in the Middle East     $19.95 ___
___ How to Get a Job in Europe     $17.95 ___
___ How to Get a Job in the Pacific Rim     $17.95 ___
___ How to Live and Work in Australia     $17.95 ___
___ How to Live and Work in Belgium     $17.95 ___
___ How to Live and Work in Canada     $17.95 ___
___ How to Live and Work in France     $17.95 ___
___ How to Live and Work in Germany     $17.95 ___
___ How to Live and Work in Hong Kong     $17.95 ___
___ How to Live and Work in Italy     $17.95 ___
___ How to Live and Work in Japan     $17.95 ___
___ How to Live and Work in New Zealand     $17.95 ___
___ How to Live and Work in Portugal     $17.95 ___
___ How to Live and Work in Saudi Arabia     $17.95 ___
___ How to Live and Work in Spain     $17.95 ___
___ Job Hunter's Guide to Japan     $12.95 ___
___ Jobs in Russia and the Newly Independent States     $15.95 ___
___ Working in the Persian Gulf     $16.95 ___

## KEY DIRECTORIES AND REFERENCE WORKS

___ American Salaries and Wages Survey     $94.95 ___
___ Career Training Sourcebook     $24.95 ___
___ Careers Encyclopedia     $39.95 ___
___ Complete Guide for Occupational Exploration     $29.95 ___
___ Consultants and Consulting Organizations Directory     $835.00 ___
___ Dictionary of Occupational Titles     $39.95 ___
___ Directory of Executive Recruiters (annual)     $39.95 ___
___ Encyclopedia of Associations (3 volumes)     $910.00 ___
___ Encyclopedia of Associations: International Organizations     $455.00 ___
___ Encyclopedia of Careers and Vocational Guidance     $129.95 ___
___ Encyclopedia of Women's Associations Worldwide     $84.95 ___
___ Enhanced Guide for Occupational Exploration     $29.95 ___
___ Government Directory of Addresses and
Telephone Numbers     $129.95 ___
___ Hoover's Handbook of World Business     $34.95 ___
___ Key European Search Firms and Their U .S. Links     $39.95 ___
___ Job Bank Guide to Employment Services (annual)     $149.95 ___
___ Job Hunter's Sourcebook     $59.95 ___
___ Job Seeker's Guide to Private and Public Companies     $379.95 ___
___ National Directory of Addresses & Telephone Numbers     $99.95 ___
___ National Fax Directory     $85.00 ___
___ National Job Bank (annual)     $249.95 ___
___ National Trade and Professional Associations     $79.95 ___

| | | |
|---|---|---|
| ___ Occupational Outlook Handbook | $22.95 | _____ |
| ___ Personnel Executives Contactbook | $149.00 | _____ |
| ___ Professional Careers Sourcebook | $85.95 | _____ |
| ___ Russia 1994 | $84.95 | _____ |
| ___ Ward's Business Directory of U.S. Public and Private Companies | $1,210.00 | _____ |

## INTERNSHIPS AND VOLUNTEER EXPERIENCES

| | | |
|---|---|---|
| ___ International Directory of Voluntary Work | $15.95 | _____ |
| ___ International Internships and Volunteer Programs | $18.95 | _____ |
| ___ Internships: 1994 | $29.95 | _____ |
| ___ Invest Yourself | $8.95 | _____ |

## TEACHING ABROAD

| | | |
|---|---|---|
| ___ The ISS Directory of Overseas Schools | $29.95 | _____ |
| ___ Teaching English Abroad | $15.95 | _____ |

## SHORT-TERM JOBS ABROAD

| | | |
|---|---|---|
| ___ Directory of Overseas Summer Jobs | $14.95 | _____ |
| ___ Jobs in Paradise | $12.95 | _____ |
| ___ Summer Jobs Britain 1994 | $15.95 | _____ |
| ___ Work Your Way Around the World | $17.95 | _____ |

## EDUCATION, TRAVEL, AND STUDY ABROAD

| | | |
|---|---|---|
| ___ Going Places: A High School Student's Guide to Study, Travel, and Adventure Abroad | $13.95 | _____ |
| ___ Guide to International Education in the U.S. | $110.00 | _____ |
| ___ International Scholarship Book | $24.95 | _____ |
| ___ Study Abroad | $18.95 | _____ |
| ___ Smart Vacations: The Traveler's Guide to Learning Adventures Abroad | $14.95 | _____ |
| ___ Work, Study, Travel Abroad | $13.95 | _____ |

## TRAVEL AND HOSPITALITY INDUSTRY

| | | |
|---|---|---|
| ___ Flying High in Travel | $16.95 | _____ |
| ___ Guide to College Programs in Hospitality and Tourism | $19.95 | _____ |
| ___ How to Get a Job With a Cruise Line | $12.95 | _____ |
| ___ The Insider's Guide to Air Courier Bargains | $14.95 | _____ |
| ___ Jobs for People Who Love Travel | $12.95 | _____ |
| ___ Travel and Hospitality Career Directory | $17.95 | _____ |

## BUSINESS, ENTREPRENEURSHIP, CONSULTING

| | | |
|---|---|---|
| ___ Building an Import/Export Business | $14.95 | _____ |
| ___ Canada Company Handbook | $54.95 | _____ |
| ___ Doing Business in Mexico | $21.95 | _____ |

___ Doing Business in Latin America & the Caribbean          $29.95   _____
___ Entrepreneur's Guide to Starting a Successful Business   $16.95   _____
___ Exporting From the United States                         $14.95   _____
___ Have You Got What It Takes?                              $12.95   _____
___ How to Be an Importer and Pay For Your World Travel       $8.95   _____
___ How to Start, Run, and Stay in Business                  $12.95   _____
___ Importing Into the United States                         $14.95   _____
___ The International Business Woman of the 1990s            $19.95   _____
___ The International Consultant                             $22.95   _____
___ Vietnam: The No BS Guide                                 $28.95   _____

## JOB LISTINGS AND SUBSCRIPTIONS

___ Bulletin of Overseas Teaching Positions (1 year)          $38.00   _____
___ Community (Nonprofit) Jobs (1 year)                       $69.00   _____
___ Federal Career Opportunities (6 biweekly issues)          $39.00   _____
___ Federal Jobs Digest (6 biweekly issues)                   $29.00   _____
___ International Career Employment Opportunities (1 year)    $195.00   _____
___ International Employment Gazette (6 biweekly issues)       $35.00   _____
___ International Employment Hotline (1 year)                  $39.00   _____
___ International Educator (1 year)                            $29.00   _____
___ The (Executive) Search Bulletin (6 issues)                $97.00   _____

## MILITARY TO CIVILIAN TRANSITION

___ Beyond the Uniform                                        $12.95   _____
___ Civilian Career Guide                                     $12.95   _____
___ Does Your Resume Wear Combat Boots?                        $9.95   _____
___ From Army Green to Corporate Gray                         $15.95   _____
___ Job Search: Marketing Your Military Experience            $14.95   _____
___ Re-Entry                                                  $13.95   _____
___ Retiring From the Military                                $22.95   _____

## RELOCATION

___ Complete Relocation Kit                                   $17.95   _____
___ Craighead's International Business, Travel,
    and Relocation Guide to 81 Countries                     $425.00   _____
___ Moving and Relocation Directory                          $149.00   _____
___ Places Rated Almanac                                      $21.95   _____

## JOB SEARCH STRATEGIES AND TACTICS

___ 40+ Job Hunting Guide                                     $23.95   _____
___ 110 Biggest Mistakes Job Hunters Make                    $14.95   _____
___ Change Your Job, Change Your Life                        $14.95   _____
___ Complete Job Finder's Guide to the 90s                   $13.95   _____
___ Complete Job Search Handbook                             $12.95   _____
___ Electronic Job Search Revolution                         $12.95   _____
___ Five Secrets to Finding a Job                            $12.95   _____
___ Go Hire Yourself an Employer                              $9.95   _____
___ How to Get Interviews from Classified Job Ads            $14.95   _____

___ Job Hunting After 50 $12.95 _____
___ Joyce Lain Kennedy's Career Book $29.95 _____
___ Knock 'Em Dead $19.95 _____
___ Professional's Job Finder $18.95 _____
___ Right Place at the Right Time $11.95 _____
___ Rites of Passage at $100,000+ $29.95 _____
___ Super Job Search $22.95 _____
___ Through the Brick Wall $13.00 _____
___ What Color is Your Parachute? $14.95 _____

## BEST JOBS AND EMPLOYERS FOR THE 90s

___ 100 Best Companies to Work for in America $27.95 _____
___ 100 Best Jobs for the 1990s and Beyond $19.95 _____
___ 101 Careers $12.95 _____
___ American Almanac of Jobs and Salaries $17.00 _____
___ America's 50 Fastest Growing Jobs $9.95 _____
___ America's Fastest Growing Employers $14.95 _____
___ Best Jobs for the 1990s and Into the 21st Century $12.95 _____
___ Job Seeker's Guide to 1000 Top Employers $22.95 _____
___ Jobs! What They Are, Where They Are, What They Pay $13.95 _____
___ Jobs 1994 $15.95 _____
___ Jobs Rated Almanac $15.95 _____
___ New Emerging Careers $14.95 _____
___ Top Professions $10.95 _____

## ALTERNATIVE JOBS AND CAREERS

___ Adventure Careers $9.95 _____
___ Business and Finance Career Directory $17.95 _____
___ Career Opportunities in TV, Cable, and Video $27.95 _____
___ Careers for Foreign Language Speakers $12.95 _____
___ Careers for Travel Buffs $12.95 _____
___ Careers in Health Care $16.95 _____
___ Careers in High Tech $16.95 _____
___ Environmental Career Guide $14.95 _____
___ Environmental Jobs for Scientists and Engineers $14.95 _____
___ Health Care Job Explosion $14.95 _____
___ Marketing and Sales Career Directory $17.95 _____
___ Nurses and Physicians Career Directory $17.95 _____
___ Opportunities in Computer Science $13.95 _____
___ Opportunities in Environmental Careers $13.95 _____
___ Opportunities in Health & Medical Careers $13.95 _____
___ Opportunities in Television & Video $13.95 _____
___ Radio and Television Career Directory $17.95 _____
___ You Can't Play the Game If You Don't Know
the Rules: Career Opportunities in Sports Management $14.95 _____

## GOVERNMENT AND NONPROFIT CAREERS

___ Almanac of American Government Jobs and Careers $14.95 _____
___ Complete Guide to Public Employment $19.95 _____

| | |
|---|---|
| ___ Federal Jobs in Law Enforcement | $15.95 ___ |
| ___ Find a Federal Job Fast! | $14.95 ___ |
| ___ How to Find an Overseas Job With the U.S. Government | $28.95 ___ |
| ___ Government Job Finder | $14.95 ___ |
| ___ Jobs and Careers With Nonprofit Organizations | $15.95 ___ |
| ___ Jobs in Washington, DC | $11.95 ___ |
| ___ Non-Profit's Job Finder | $16.95 ___ |
| ___ The Right SF 171 Writer | $19.95 ___ |

## SKILLS, TESTING, SELF-ASSESSMENT, EMPOWERMENT

| | |
|---|---|
| ___ 7 Habits of Highly Effective People | $11.00 ___ |
| ___ Discover the Best Jobs for You | $11.95 ___ |
| ___ Do What You Are | $14.95 ___ |
| ___ Do What You Love, the Money Will Follow | $10.95 ___ |

## RESUMES AND COVER LETTERS

| | |
|---|---|
| ___ 200 Letters for Job Hunters | $17.95 ___ |
| ___ Best Resumes for $70,000+ Executive Jobs | $14.95 ___ |
| ___ Dynamite Cover Letters | $10.95 ___ |
| ___ Dynamite Resumes | $10.95 ___ |
| ___ Electronic Resume Revolution | $12.95 ___ |
| ___ Electronic Resumes for the New Job Market | $11.95 ___ |
| ___ High Impact Resumes and Letters | $12.95 ___ |
| ___ Job Search Letters That Get Results | $12.95 ___ |
| ___ The Perfect Resume | $12.00 ___ |
| ___ The Resume Catalog | $15.95 ___ |
| ___ Resumes for Re-Entry: A Woman's Handbook | $10.95 ___ |

## NETWORKING

| | |
|---|---|
| ___ Dynamite Tele-Search | $10.95 ___ |
| ___ Great Connections | $11.95 ___ |
| ___ How to Work a Room | $10.95 ___ |
| ___ *New* Network Your Way to Job and Career Success | $12.95 ___ |
| ___ Power Networking | $12.95 ___ |
| ___ The Secrets of Savvy Networking | $11.99 ___ |

## DRESS, APPEARANCE, IMAGE, ETIQUETTE

| | |
|---|---|
| ___ John Molloy's New Dress for Success | $10.95 ___ |
| ___ Letitia Baldridge's Complete Guide to the New Manners for the 90s | $25.95 ___ |
| ___ Lions Don't Need to Roar | $10.99 ___ |
| ___ Red Socks Don't Work! | $14.95 ___ |
| ___ The Winning Image | $17.95 ___ |

## INTERVIEWS & NEGOTIATING SKILLS

| | |
|---|---|
| ___ 60 Seconds and You're Hired! | $9.95 ___ |
| ___ Dynamite Answers to Interview Questions | $10.95 ___ |